The Clatter of
Forks and Spoons

The Clatter of Forks and Spoons

Richard Corrigan
with Sheila Keating

Photographs by Kristin Perers

FOURTH ESTATE · *London*

First published in Great Britain in 2008
Fourth Estate
A division of HarperCollinsPublishers
77–85 Fulham Palace Road
London W6 8JB
www.4thestate.co.uk

1 3 5 7 9 8 6 4 2

A catalogue record for this book is available from the British Library

ISBN 978-0-00-724890-2

Designed by Joby Barnard
Typeset in Garamond and Neuzeit by GS Typesetting
Printed and bound in Italy by L.E.G.O. SpA - Vicenza

Mixed Sources
Product group from well-managed
forests and other controlled sources
www.fsc.org Cert no. SW-COC-1806
© 1996 Forest Stewardship Council

FSC is a non-profit international organisation established to promote the
responsible management of the world's forests. Products carrying the FSC
label are independently certified to assure consumers that they come
from forests that are managed to meet the social, economic and
ecological needs of present and future generations

Find out more about Harper Collins and the environment at
www.harpercollins.co.uk/green

For my incredible wife, Maria, and my amazing children, Richard, Jessica and Robbie … and of course all my loyal customers.

Without you it's pointless.

Richard Corrigan is one of Britain's most respected and outspoken chefs. He has been a key pioneer in the rehabilitation of British and Irish food, a champion of small producers, and is dedicated to rediscovering and reinterpreting the traditional and often wild foodstuffs of these islands.

Richard was born to a farming family in County Meath, Ireland. After spending four years cooking in the Netherlands, he was head chef of Mulligan's in Mayfair, and won his first Michelin star at Stephen Bull's Fulham Road, before opening the acclaimed Michelin-starred Lindsay House in 1997.

He now runs the famous Bentley's Seafood Bar & Grill in London and has recently opened an Irish Bentley's based in Dublin. Richard hosts the Irish primetime television series *Corrigan Knows Food* and has also been a presenter on the popular BBC2's *Full on Food*. His natural earthiness, deftness in the kitchen and instinctive passion about real food without fripperies, marks him out as an important voice in British and Irish food.

Contents

Notes

Temperatures given are for a conventional oven.

I haven't mentioned salt and pepper in every ingredients list; only when you need a certain quantity or there is something to say about either of them. For normal seasoning we use sea salt and freshly ground black pepper.

Choose free-range eggs, large ones.

Butter is unsalted.

Sugar used in the Puddings chapter is specified, but we tend to use caster sugar for everything, unless otherwise suggested.

We use full fat milk.

I like the native, strongly flavoured curly variety of parsley unless it is for a Mediterranean-style recipe.

Recipes are really just for ideas and I hardly ever cook the same thing the same way twice, but I've mostly included sauces and accompaniments where they really work well, instead of having you turn to a separate chapter all the time. Of course, most of them can be used however and whenever you like. The most adaptable ones are listed opposite.

Dressings and Sauces

Honey, Mustard and Dill Dressing (page 42)
Japanese-style Dressing (page 44)
Gremolata (page 49)
Salad Cream (page 54)
Butter Sauce (page 71)
Hollandaise Sauce (page 85)
Tartare Sauce (page 88)
Aioli (page 90)
Honey and Black Pepper Dressing (page 126)
Mayonnaise (page 138)
House Dressing (page 139)
Salsa Verde (page 188)
Harissa (page 205)
Garlic Béarnaise (page 214)
Bread Sauce (page 238)
Romesco Sauce (page 286)

Accompaniments

Russian Salad (page 53)
German-style Potato Salad (page 68)
Coriander Mash (page 75)
Seaweed Tapenade (page 85)
Mushy Peas (page 88)
Nettle and Potato Mash (page 170)
Cabbage (page 170)
Red Cabbage (page 190)
Champ (page 203)
Tabbouleh (page 205)
Colcannon (page 270)
Celery Slaw (page 287)
Celeriac and Apple Mash (page 289)
Rosemary Roast Potatoes (page 374)

For Puddings

Custard (page 334)
Vanilla Ice Cream (page 347)
Almond Biscuits (page 348)
Chocolate Shortbread (page 362)

The Farmer
in Me

People often say to you: 'What was your road to Damascus experience?' Well, mine was being brought up on a farm. It was a small farm, 25 acres, and a cottage, and my father had to drive a truck part-time to keep his family of seven children going, but the farming mentality teaches you lots of things. It makes you very unpretentious about good food for a start, and it instils respect, because you know the hard graft that goes into producing it. We had two vegetable gardens, one for the lettuces and the spring onions and the rhubarb, and a bigger one, more like a field, for the likes of potatoes and carrots. And one of my many jobs was to do the weeding. When you're out thinning the leek beds and weeding every night, I'm telling you, you appreciate what you grow. Where our farm was, right in the middle of the bog land in County Meath, the soil was so rich and peaty that the weeds popped up like an Amazon rainforest overnight. The midges would be eating your head off as you were working, then Mum would call you in for a cold supper. Lunch was the main meal of the day, but in the evening there would be cold hams and salads, boiled eggs and fresh ripe tomatoes from the glasshouse in summer. Everything produced on the farm.

When I say to people I was brought up in a bog in the 1960s, like some Beverly hillbilly, they say, 'Ah come on, are you dreaming it up?' Even my wife Maria says to me sometimes, 'Were you born in the 1920s?' But we were the last gasp of a rural era that in most places in Ireland had disappeared twenty to thirty years before. My father was a handsome young charmer, a socialist with a farmer's heart who dashed around on a Sunbeam motorbike. My mother's family, the McDonaghs, came to County Meath from Connemara, on a government scheme to bring native Irish speakers to English-speaking Meath. Like so many people in the 1950s who took a mail boat to America, and the last they saw of Ireland was the harbour at Cobh or Dun Laoghaire, she went off to Boston to work in domestic service. But when she had enough dollars saved, she came home for a holiday and met my father at a dance.

There was music and a cadence in the way she spoke Irish; and she was a brilliant *sean nos* singer. Sean nos is the purest kind of Irish traditional song. No accompaniment, all of the music is in the voice. It's raw, eerie sometimes, a link to the distant past. When I was small I used to be embarrassed when she sang. Maybe because it was old-fashioned, or too raw and emotional. But now, what wouldn't I give to hear her sing again.

We kids walked everywhere, five miles a day to school and back, or if you were lucky you'd get a lift. In the winter you'd need torchlight going to school; it was pitch black until the clocks changed to European time.

There's a mysticism in the Irish land. No question. It could be a spooky place in the country sometimes, when the mist was rising over those fields. If you were out late at night, you'd swear the trees really did talk to you. There were stories about a woman called Maggie the Knitter who lived in the woods (we called her Maggie the Nutter), that she would take away children, and my mother used to talk about banshees (the fairies that wail to warn of death), and if she heard the wailing then sure enough next morning something would be dead: but then that was often the nature of living on a farm, and you just accepted it.

We were outside all the time, especially in summer. There was always something to do. As well as the garden to be weeded, there were cows to be brought in, the pig to be fed. As the light faded in winter, you'd get home from school at four and you had to get the ducks and chickens in by five, for fear of the foxes.

We planted an extraordinary amount of trees: fruit trees in the orchard and chestnut trees. Over the years there would always be some blown down, others cut for burning wood, and replenishing what you took was a part of our farming psyche.

Then there'd be stick cutting and trellis making and log splitting, and of course the turf cutting in August. We needed the turf so we had fuel for cooking and to keep the house warm in winter. Everything was about working and preparing for the next season. The turf-cutting process took weeks. First you had to prepare the high bank of turf, cleaning off any growth. The first cut would be spurge, which made good kindling. Then you'd go down until you got to the black stuff and sometimes you'd cut through six layers. My dad would throw up the lumps of wet sod, and we'd take turns catching them and putting them out to dry, then you'd turn them and heap them up in castles to harden more, before stacking them up in the turf sheds. It was backbreaking work.

At the same time we kids were free spirits, not a care in the world. We played out in the woods, hide and seek. We had a hut in the middle of the bog, hiding in the ferns, and we built a magical tree house in two tiers like a ship. One of the local lads, Wattie Leach, had engineer's hands, and we'd make go-carts, real racing buggies, out of bits of prams. We'd put string on the front and fly down the road. Where we were, there was a great sense of isolation, but there was camaraderie between us and our neighbours.

The kids in school called me Bog Man. Two and a half miles down the road they had electricity and were eating Angel Delight for tea, but we and our neighbouring smallholding families didn't have the cash for electricity, until around 1973; I remember we got it on the day the bishop came for Confirmation. Up until then we had oil lamps and then moved on to gas lamps; no television, but sport and music on the radio; and people were always dropping in. We were a small community and people cared for each other. We weren't caught up in consumerism and triple mortgages. No one went short of anything, because there was always an exchange going on. If you had a glut of homemade butter or birchwood you'd be offering it out; if you needed grain someone would help you; and everyone came around to give of their days when it came to the sileage-making or the pig-killing.

In our house and in the other houses around, the rosary was said every evening at half past eight, down on your knees. God was an important factor in our lives. He was in charge, because people needed rules to live by and be guided by; there was no 'let's make a lot of money and to hell with everyone else'. There was a discipline to Irish country life; it wasn't idyllic, it was hard, but it was great to be self-sufficient. Living off the land you knew your place, where you were in the scheme of things, and there was an orderliness. Everything had to be put back in the sheds the way you found it: all the forks had to be cleaned and hung up in the right places, as set out by my dad's uncles, Richard and Tommy, who had the land before him, but as they had died childless, the farm passed to my father.

We were cash poor, but we lived really well, and there was a lot of happiness involved in cooking and eating. As a family we enjoyed the ritual of sitting around the table. Ask any of my brothers and sisters: to this day you would never see a TV dinner in a Corrigan household.

So as a kid I never got hung up on things like class, because I always felt like I was the lord of the manor. We would have a pig that was killed in the autumn and kept us in pork and ham and bacon. We made our own black pudding. We never thought of game as anything special because you'd go out to the outhouses and there were always pheasants and wild ducks hanging behind the door. You might shoot a rabbit, or poach a salmon, but always for the pot. We treated the animals that gave us our meat with respect; they were well looked after. If we saw a hare or a rabbit we would shoot it, but never snare it, which would cause it pain.

We had beehives, but my father always preferred wild honey. If we heard there was a nest of bees, my dad would stop everything and we had to head into the fields, looking to raid it. He'd put the honeycombs in a colander by the fire and the honey would melt and run down, and filter into a bowl. We'd eat the combs too; they were crunchy and gorgeous. There's something quite mad about wild honey.

Mum would churn the butter and make the bread. My mother's repertoire wasn't large, maybe not more than ten or fifteen recipes, but what she did was very, very good. We weren't educated about food, but we knew a hell of a lot. That whole country cycle of farming, shooting, fishing, cooking, eating is what teaches you. The art of country cooking was much finer than you would ever imagine, people were quite regal in what they liked and didn't, what was correct cooking and what wasn't … and the taste! I think there's an appreciation about food and flavour that's formed in your childhood. It's about a collection of stories: the boiled hams, the potatoes and the apple crumbles, the rhubarb tarts cooling on the windowsill under a cloth; those are my food stories and the flavours have never gone out of my head.

Growing up on a farm also teaches you respect for the cycles and seasonality of food. I grew up with the simple idea that the sun comes up and goes down, and with each movement of the calendar, nature has something else to give us.

The farmer in me also makes it hard for me to throw things away. Everything on our farm was used; my mother would always have one eye on the next meal. If you had a chicken, the carcass would be boiled up for soup. When the pig was killed the fat would be rendered down and kept in jars for frying. If something gives up flavour, I find it very wasteful to throw it away. I'm always looking in the bins in my restaurant kitchens. Not because I'm mean, but when people throw things away, they're not thinking properly, not using their brains. Why would you throw away fish trimmings and bones when you could use them in a stock? Like I said, knowing the time and work that goes into producing good food makes you hate to waste any of it.

Shortage of money only caused problems for my mum and dad when their young family started to grow up and enter into a more moneyed, competitive, heart-attack society. Ireland had gone into Europe and was discovering materialism. The smallholding lifestyle was becoming redundant, people were leaving the land, and bungalow blight was taking over old farmsteads. We weren't little kids running around on the farm any more; we needed things. By 1979 my parents realised we had to catch up with the rest of Ireland, that the bog land was too poor to carry on making a living out of, and so they sold up and built a bungalow a few miles down the road.

We were proud people and sad to leave, but my parents were realists. We didn't properly understand at the time, but not only did they have us to support, they also had to get a life: imagine my mother with seven children, hand-washing clothes in the bath, churning butter, making the bread. Suddenly, though, we were out in a different social order we didn't recognise. It was Ireland that had *really* moved on, rather than us; we were in a world where you needed cash and you had bills to pay and we had the shock of our lives. We felt completely out of place.

As kids we came home from school to a bungalow with a garden, like all the others. We planted an avenue of chestnut trees as we had always done, and we had a glasshouse at the side of the house with tomatoes, but they never tasted the same. The ancient kind of energy you feel when you are connected to the land had gone. But I was born with the farming DNA and it's that that keeps my feet on the ground and keeps me driving on. I'm really proud of where I come from, because it made me what I am today. Having your own restaurant is like having your own farm, and all good farmers are driven. The energy I put into keeping my restaurants alive is born out of the energy we used to put into our land. If you don't tend something constantly it will die.

Farmers always covet the field next door; you can never have enough land. I should be happy with whatever I've got in life. I was brought up with very little money in the house and I'm always glad to have a few pounds in my pocket, but still, I always have one eye on the field next door. There is one Richard Corrigan thinking, 'Do I really need to open another restaurant?' but the other Richard Corrigan, the farmer, is saying, 'Go for it.'

As a chef I know I look back and tend to romanticise having grown up in a family where we understood the land and the food it gave us, and where everything we ate was produced simply without chemicals and tasted of what it should. But my mum and dad had it hard; their life was relentless and that ages you. They died when they were only in their late sixties, and no matter how successful I am, I'll never be able to send a cheque to them to say thank you.

Just Food
You Want
to Eat

What is good food about? Really? A couple of combinations that make you say, 'God, that's good.' That English thing of cake and tea: Victoria sponge, freshly made, with a cup of tea is one of the best things in the world. You want to gorge the whole thing, not just one slice. A darne of fresh, wild salmon for breakfast; a bowl of mashed spuds and cabbage with a fat slice of bacon on top; fish in perfect crunchy batter with chips; ripe melon with Parma ham ... I'm sorry if that sounds like a lot of clichés. The thing is – don't ask me why – but your palate goes into some culinary heaven. Food that makes you feel like that is fantastic. I've got a million ideas in my head, rolling off each other, but I'm not afraid to serve anything that simply makes me say, 'I just want to eat that.' A freshly cooked, dressed crab with nothing but some brown bread, butter and mayonnaise. Heaven, heaven, heaven. New season's rhubarb ... I've come into the kitchen and the boys are telling me, 'We're looking for a recipe.' Why? What recipe do you need? New season's rhubarb, maybe a little bit of stem ginger, some vanilla ice cream – put it on the menu, please.

I've experimented in my career, of course I have – chefs and their techniques and their toys. For too many years when I was younger I was trying to be too innovative for my own good; wanting to be different for difference's sake – and you can get carried away with ego and the pretension of it all. When I hear chefs talking about their philosophy – and those are words I might have muttered myself in the past – it gets a bit embarrassing. Philosophy of life, politics, religion maybe – but cooking? It's just people trying to sound more meaningful than they really are. Now I just want to row the boat backwards as fast as I can, and be confident about doing it.

What you learn along the way in your cooking career, the ideas and influences, all play a part in the way you think and cook, of course they do, but really, what is good cooking all about? Knowing your ingredients, and understanding what goes with what.

I hardly ever make the same recipe the same way twice, which can drive some people crazy, but I like cooking on the hoof, being totally ingredients led: what's good? What's here? What can we put it with? I've always encouraged that.

We frequently have to babysit young chefs who arrive from other Michelin-starred kitchens and might have learned the skills, but they are cooking by numbers, not by instinct. They are looking for purée of this, purée of that, out-of-season asparagus for garnish. They are completely lost at first. 'Is there a picture?' 'Is there a recipe written down in a book in the kitchen?' No. You've got a great piece of fish, think about it, what do you want to do with it? You've got chickpeas, you've got chorizo, you've got lobster shells and crab shells to make a bisque; you want some harissa? Make some. Shoot from the hip. Go for it. Whereas, you could give the boys who have worked with me over time a basket of any ingredients and they would knock out great dishes just like that.

The older I get, the more puritan I become about food, the more I want to leave it alone. I don't feel I have to impress people any more. I'm deeply comfortable with what I am doing. What interests me isn't cheffy talk: you do this, then that, then take it out, then do something else … What is wrong with opening the fridge, taking out a great piece of meat, letting it come to room temperature, putting a pan on the stove and cooking it? What interests me is giving respect to the farmers and producers of good food by not messing around with it too much. People want to tweak and tease and shape and carve and you end up with over-refined food with no character. Maybe that's why molecular gastronomy doesn't interest me. Why are we worshipping these false gods? I don't want to make magic, I'm not over-inspired by jellies and foams, I just want to serve great produce from great people and enhance it slightly – but not too much. Yes, be a bit clever. But not too clever. It's not about ego, it's just about food you want to eat.

Extreme
Artisans

I like stubborn, cranky people producing food for me. I'm a cranky chef myself, and I shake the tree a lot. I get very angry sometimes when I see waste or carelessness in my kitchen, but most of all when produce arrives that doesn't come up to scratch. So I shake the tree, and when I shake the tree the branches fall off. I'll chop the tree down if I have to, because I want what I want, from the raw materials that come in at the kitchen door to the food that goes on the plate.

And what I want is for the people who supply my fish and meat and fruit and vegetables and cheese to care as much as I do. I don't want to buy from wishy-washy individuals, because I know that their food will be wishy-washy when I'm not watching them. As chefs we crave consistency of quality, and for ingredients to be great time and time again a producer needs to be on top of everyone and everything, just as I have to be when I run my restaurants.

To be honest, I never came across a baker or a gardener or cheese maker who didn't give a damn but got lucky enough to produce something wonderful to eat. Behind the perfect smoked fish, the unpasteurised cheese or the traditionally cured bacon, there is always a passionate individual. And I've always tried to hunt out and support the committed small producer. Back in the early 1990s, when I started Mulligan's, Frances Smith was growing some of the best salad leaves I've ever tasted down on her farm in Appledore in Kent. When I asked her would she supply us, she said, 'You haven't seen my farm.' So I drove down and I saw and I tasted. I've never experienced rocket like hers before or since. I ended up taking the guinea fowl her husband raised, too, because they were astonishing. They tasted wild. Since she gave up the business, I haven't found guinea fowl that comes even close. The point is, Frances was absolutely right to say no unless I came to see her. Otherwise how do you know, understand and appreciate the process and commitment that's gone into the stuff that arrives in your kitchen?

Randolph Hodgson of Neal's Yard is another really committed individual, and a huge champion of artisan producers. At Lindsay House we have been one of his biggest clients for a long time, and if it wasn't for him, a lot of small, farmhouse cheese makers would be out of business.

At this stage of my life, though, I've accelerated to the point where I'm almost fanatical about simplicity and about the provenance of ingredients, and I want to turn almost my entire kitchen over to the small producer. I'm really pushing very hard for it. Not just talking about it, or making a big deal about writing 'meat from so-and-so's farm', or 'fish from such-and-such a loch' everywhere on my menu. But really putting it into action; finding the little guys and spending time with them. I like the direct line of communication to driven individuals and I'm happiest when my money is falling into the lap of someone who truly deserves it, not some middle guy who is really nothing more than the delivery man.

Coming from a farming background myself, I have huge respect for the small pig farmers and beef farmers, the cheese and butter makers, who often can't live well on the money they earn. It's a vocation, no question. You have to be absolutely devoted to what you do. That's why we have to support these people, because over the years I've heard so many farmers saying that none of their children want to go into the business.

Now, though, things are changing, in Britain and in Ireland. When I leave behind the London stressheads and go off into the Irish countryside, I'm meeting more people who are rediscovering what attracted them to farming in the first place and realising that they can be special at what they do. There's a whole new attitude of care and attention and sheer bloody determination to fight uphill battles that's a million miles from factory production, and when you see what fabulous stuff is being produced, it is so humbling that it gives you a real energy to keep going yourself. What is so happy and inspiring about the situation in Ireland is that it isn't only the native Irish but also immigrants who have settled there and brought their skills and ethos of quality who are laying down the DNA for a new generation of food producers. Sometimes it takes a new eye to see the richness and potential in a country. And it isn't just about people bringing skills with them, but about learning new ones. In Britain as well as Ireland, it's extraordinary how many businessmen, stockbrokers and city high flyers are swapping their stressed-out lifestyles for raising rare breed pigs, hand-making chocolates, making cheese or baking artisan bread. What a change from making million-dollar deals to putting sourdough into a paper bag at the farmers' market down in Schull in West Cork on a Sunday morning. These are the guys whose children will want to take over, and in some cases they will be even more extreme than their parents and drive things even further forward.

I don't want to get into yet another rant about the onward march of supermarkets and the religious-like zeal of these massive companies taking over our high streets, but all those cellophane alleys with so much wrapped food, no smells, no excitement, have really screwed things up and corrupted the way we think about food. We're all governed by shelf life and use by and sell by dates, which, let's be honest, means that you are often buying old food, pushed to the end of its life span with preservatives and technological packaging, which is why, once you open up your bags and packets, your salad leaves will wither or your meat go off so quickly. I've done it at home, bought a supermarket chicken, opened it up and three days later it's turned. That's wrong. Fresh food doesn't do that.

I strongly sympathise with the Slow Food Movement and the idea of supporting local artisan produce – forget the politics and the elitism that can sometimes get in the way; we need the leaders and the preachers, and hopefully the followers will come. And I think there really is a sense now of people saying, 'I don't want to spend £200 in the supermarket each week. Maybe I'll leave the trolley outside and go in with just a basket. I'll spend £100 and use the rest to buy meat from a good butcher, or vegetables from the farmers' market; and maybe instead of buying chicken breasts wrapped in plastic, I'll buy a whole free-range organic chicken and make two or three meals from it.'

I'm not talking about an idealistic world, I'm just saying that you can save yourself a lot of money and eat better by doing things properly in the old-fashioned way. Seek out good ingredients and learn to cook simply again. Really, that's it.

Recipe
For a
Good Dinner

I'm at home one Sunday, cooking for twelve people. I have roast beef on the go, vegetables, a little salad of peas, a rosemary, garlic and mustard dressing, and I'm cooking shellfish because I've decided to make a big fruits de mer for starters. I'm looking at the time, which is ebbing away, and the panic button is about to go off. Then I realise I haven't enough oil to make mayonnaise for my fruits de mer. So I have to ring up one of the guests and ask them to bring some.

I've been in the restaurant business for thirty years and still, when I'm cooking at home, where I don't have the luxury of pots of stocks and sauces and everything chopped up, ready to go, I feel the pressure of making Sunday lunch for twelve friends.

My answer is to have plenty of nice ice-cold drinks ready for everyone when they come in, then not to show any stress, keep everything relaxed, and say, 'Would you like to just do that for me?' You end up with your friends helping out, drink in hand, enjoying themselves. On that particular day, lunch went happily on into the evening, when we wound up eating strawberries and cream and shortcake.

It's that old question of why do you invite people to your home? Is it so you can impress them with whatever is topping the fashionable dessert list? Do you want to show off how nicely you've decorated your dining room? Or do you just want your friends to come and gather around your table, eat the kind of food you like to cook, get some great conversation going and enjoy themselves?

Personally, I'd say don't invite people that you don't really like round for dinner. Life is too short. Stick with friends who take you and your food the way you are. My recipe for a good dinner party is to invite a couple of lefties, a couple of Tories and, in my case, a good sprinkling of independently minded Irish people, to stop everyone agreeing about everything. And because you don't want to miss out on any of the fun, keep it simple in the kitchen. What's the point of having friends around and then spending all the time at the stove?

Choose your ingredients well and don't try too hard. If you're confident enough to cook spontaneously on the hoof, great: a person after my own heart. But if you're not, wait until a dish has become an old friend before you cook it for guests, or, if you really want to try something new, read the recipe over a few times and visualise it before you start, so that you have a clear picture in your head of what you are going to do and how long it will take you.

The recipes in this book have all been written from the point of view of cooking at home, with only a few that need a bit of time in the preparation. A great big fish pie in the middle of the table with a bowl of salad, a good bottle of wine and some fresh fruit and cheese to follow. Why not? That's gastronomy, it really is.

The Beacon of Ballymaloe

Myrtle Allen, at Ballymaloe House down in Shanagarry in County Cork, has been shouting about everything I'm saying about simplicity and provenance of ingredients for the last forty-four years at the restaurant she opened back in 1964. She's a lovely wise woman, Myrtle, and she's inspired and encouraged a whole movement of people like me who care about great food. I remember when I started cooking at Mulligan's she gave me a copy of her wonderful little *Ballymaloe Cookbook*, which has never been out of print, and it just summed up her country attitude to good food.

It's incredible to think she is over eighty now. A few years back I showed up and gatecrashed her eightieth birthday party. I remember we had a simple roast duck with stuffing, and it was divine. I woke up the next morning and had some local bacon, with a poached egg, and thought, 'I'm in Heaven.' And there's Myrtle running around at half eight in the morning, after her eightieth birthday party. That said it all to me. So much energy and such a sense of fulfilment. To have a place like Ballymaloe is the pinnacle; she must be the happiest person in the world. And the joyousness is infectious. I've never seen so many serving staff with smiles on their faces in my life.

Whenever I'm travelling in Ireland I try to stop off there. There is a feeling that time has stopped. No ringing phones or TV, but a lot of laughter and fun, and the comforting idea that the great table in the Irish country household – the fat brown goose and the big hams and spiced beef, the beautiful floury potatoes wrapped in a white napkin and the huge pudding in its big dish that James Joyce talked about amid the happy clatter of forks and spoons in his book *The Dead* – still prevails in this corner of Cork. It's the kind of place where you can relax and get a bit happy-drunk and no one says, 'You are misbehaving. Would you leave.' I had a wonderful mad evening there with Rowley Leigh, who is one of the most intelligent chefs and writers on food, a rebel against the bullshit of haute cuisine and like all great cooks generous to a fault when it comes to sharing ideas. He has come out the other side of twenty-odd years at Kensington Place into his new restaurant, Le Café Anglais, like a car with a new engine and a re-spray, and we were enjoying ourselves so much we got a bit boisterous, but a woman came up and complimented us on having such a good time. She said we reminded her of even earlier happy days at Ballymaloe.

I look at Myrtle and what she has built, and I think the way forward for everything I want to achieve and the whole inspiration for trying to bring the small artisan producer directly into my kitchen just shines out like a beacon from her table at Ballymaloe.

Fish

A beautiful piece of simply roasted or steamed fish is pure magic, one of those things that makes you question the whole idea of ambitious chefs. What's the use of chefs at all, I sometimes wonder, when there is food as simple and gorgeous as a Dover sole or a native oyster out there? I think of sitting outside in summer late at night with a plate of oysters, a good bottle of wine and a steak tartare for afterwards. No chefs, just 'Thank you, Mother Nature'.

It's not that I'm trying to put myself out of a job, but after thirty-odd years in this business, I have reached the point where I don't want a mass of hands messing with produce that is beautiful and fresh. Over the years the penny has been dropping more and more that, especially where fish is concerned, the true value of the chef is in seeking out and choosing the best fish, the whole craft of preparing it, using your intelligence and your palate to marry flavours and make things happen, then knowing when to stop fussing and leave well alone.

That doesn't mean I want to stop experimenting with food. I'm not saying we should be just poaching or grilling fish and serving it with hollandaise sauce on the side. Far from it. My mind is busy all the time with ideas; the quest never stops. In my kitchens we are always reading and learning. I have a notebook in my back pocket and I'm forever jotting ideas down as they come into my head. I'll be on my bike to work thinking about octopus with a salad of blood oranges, or a kind of Scotch egg made with brandade. I just want things to always move on and not get stale. I hate going into kitchens where everyone comes in and does the same thing over and over again.

At Bentley's things evolve all the time with different dishes chalked up on the blackboard every day. That makes things exciting for chefs, but it's tough for them as well, because I want them to look at their ingredients and cook on the hoof. You get young chefs coming into the kitchens who don't know how to fillet a fish because they are used to everything arriving already done from the supplier, who think green asparagus flown in from Chile twelve months of the year with a fillet of sea bass sitting on top of it and loads of purées and artistic garnish is what it's all about. So they just don't get it at first.

Anyone can just serve the prime cuts, the fillet of sea bass, the lobster, but what about the rest of it, the shells and bones? Everything I do in the kitchen is governed by a policy of no waste. It's the way I was brought up. We cook and dress our own crabs, and then the shells get smashed up to go into a bisque. We store all the lobster shells and fish heads in the freezer to make our fish soups. If I see fresh, gelatinous bones and trimmings going in the bin, I am apoplectic.

What we are doing is exactly what a good home cook does or should do: you look at what you've got, and think, what can I do with it? And how can I use every bit of it, so there is nothing wasted?

The pure light of Bentley's, my little brasserie of fish, is shining very brightly for me. I had my first taste of cooking there in 1992. I had been in charge of the kitchen at Mulligan's in Mayfair, and much as I enjoyed it, it wasn't stretching my imagination, so when the opportunity came up to go to Bentley's, the famous old fish restaurant in Swallow Street, off Piccadilly, I took it. The restaurant was going through a bad patch; there was a bit of ill-discipline about the place, and I was let loose on it for a year, like a whirlwind. I cracked the whip hard, badgered and turned things around, and the business flowed back. When I handed in my notice a year later to head up the kitchen at the Fulham Road restaurant they held a party: I don't know whether it was for me, or for them; I'd given them such a hard time! I felt a bit like a mercenary, brought in to do a job, but at the same time, I learnt so much about fish from the customers and the suppliers, and there was something special about this old place that made me snap it up when I had the chance to take it over in 2005.

It is partly coming back to Bentley's years later that has reminded me of the happy truth of simplicity. Bentley's might be an institution, but to me it is a busy tavern with a brilliant ethos, full of enthusiastic happy people having a nice time: not a transient crowd there to make a fashion statement, but people who come to eat fabulous, fresh fish. You can sit at the bar and have a plate of oysters and a glass of wine, a bowl of fish soup or a dressed crab, or you can sit upstairs in the restaurant and have a whole fish taken off the bone in front of you, or a Dover sole done in four different ways. In the bar you can have a gorgeous, comforting fish pie made with smoked haddock, or upstairs a truly decadent royal fish pie, for a royal price – with lobster and scallops bound with Sauce Americaine. And I think they are equally good, because everything is based on the same respect for freshness, simplicity and deliciousness. When Fay Maschler came in to review Bentley's she thought it didn't seem quite right to serve Thai crab and mussel soup in the restaurant, but the funny thing is it has gone on to be one of our best-selling dishes. The joy of it is we have no boundaries, no fences; we're not afraid to serve anything, as long as I can look a customer in the eye, and say, 'I think this is great.'

What none of us can ignore, however, is that there are some species of fish that are in crisis. We've all had to learn the hard way that you can't treat fish like a commodity. It's not like planting wheat and corn. We can only have what the sea can give us, so let's start respecting nature, and the seasons, and rethinking our attitude to different species of fish, before it is too late and nature has nothing left to give us.

When I buy fish I listen to the guys in the ports who have known the fishermen for decades, because they know what is going on: which fish we should be buying, and which stocks are in danger. Before I took over at Bentley's, we invited Matthew Stevens to come in and chat to us. We were one of the first restaurants to buy our fish from Matthew Stevens & Son down in St Ives, a family business that has been handed down through three generations over sixty years. When we first started doing business with Matthew he had six people working for him. Now he has a brigade, and a business that can send fish straight from the local boats out to customers all over the country. I like that. I like the idea that my London pound is going into jobs for fishermen and local people in St Ives and not into some internationally owned Canadian lobster farm or Norwegian salmon farm. And I like the fact that everyone can have really fresh fish delivered straight to their door.

At the time I didn't realise that skate, for example, was in so much trouble. I had it in my mind that skate in black butter would be a menu classic. But Matthew was shocked at the thought. So we'll maybe serve it in the summer if there is enough of it around, but I see it very much as a seasonal fish now.

I've started looking at different fish like gurnard and, in particular, grey mullet. Yes, it is the wolf of the sea, and because it has a scavenging reputation, we tend to think we wouldn't want to eat that, but a big line-caught grey mullet when it is in season in July, caught out in the deep sea, especially around the south coast of Ireland, is as good as a sea bass, no question. In fact, the Chinese rate it higher. Huss is another meaty fish that is worth looking at: somewhere in between a sea bass and a cod in flavour, though not quite so tasty. Or how about pollack, third cousin of cod; rock salmon, or dogfish? I'm trying to convince my chefs that there is merit in all of these.

We're a bit lazy in this country; we have a typical island culture in that we only want to eat the fish we've always eaten, but diversity is the future. Let's have another look at the bounty of each season. I hate to use the expression diver-caught for plaice, but when the large ones come into southern England around June and feed on the mussel beds in Cornwall, the divers go down with their spears and catch them that way, and that is the time to eat them. On the bone, steamed, poached or grilled, with peas and samphire, they are just great.

And let's look at the 'poor' fish that smart kitchens have snubbed for so many years in favour of the sea basses and the turbots.

I like the idea of exploring sustainably fished species like roach and pike, and I love oily fish like mackerel and sardines and herrings, which my dad used to bring home by the sackload from the boats coming into the harbour at Clogherhead. To my mind we don't use these kinds of fish nearly enough.

Oils

Sometimes I feel as though in my thirty years or so in this business I have tasted every extra virgin olive oil in the whole world: you can overdose on information about it, instead of just enjoying the beauty of it.

I had one of the best times when I was much younger, staying with an olive oil producer outside Rome in the hills of the Sabina, an olive-growing region full of medieval towns and small artisan producers. The family had been making oil since the fourteenth century, and my room was up in one of the turrets of their old castle on the estate, where they had around 16,000 olive trees and a small processing plant. I remember going out with them first thing in the morning in October when the first of the olive-picking began, freezing cold and with a hangover, because the local wine they poured at dinner was so good. You'd set up nets around the trees to catch the olives, and hand pick or rake off the fruit, using ladders to reach the higher ones, and stop for lunch to feast on sandwiches made from the big ham they would carve in the kitchen. That is how to learn about olive oil.

I love Italy, and the sharing of knowledge and understanding that small producers are so generous about. From them I learned all I need to know about olive oil: first, that the best extra virgin olive oil is always cold-pressed – that is, the olives are simply crushed in a press to release their oil without any heat treatment or processing that could affect the flavour or goodness. For an oil to be classified extra virgin it has to have less than 1 per cent oleic acidity. If you leave the olives too long after picking and before pressing, or if you handle them roughly, the acidity goes up as they begin to 'ferment', and you have an inferior oil. The oil that doesn't make the extra virgin grade is usually blended with a refined oil, and this becomes ordinary olive oil.

Second, I learned that the flavour and goodness of a beautiful extra virgin oil starts to deteriorate immediately, so you should buy it in small bottles and use it quickly, because light and oxygen will kill it. That's why good oil comes in dark bottles, and it's best kept in a cupboard, not out on show. What you would do if you were in Italy and lived near an olive oil estate, they said, was buy your cold-pressed oil immediately it had been made, take it home and put it in little containers in the freezer, then take it out when you needed it.

Extra virgin oil is beautiful stuff that can vary from estate to estate, region to region, from light and delicate to deep green, fruity, peppery and grassy, but whatever you prefer, or works best with what you are cooking, only use it for finishing dishes. When I see people frying with extra virgin olive oil I want to box their ears. What a waste of delicious Mother Nature.

For sweating vegetables, I would use an ordinary olive oil; for anything that involves high heat, like sautéeing a piece of fish, I would use a vegetable oil and then, if you like, once it is cooked, you can finish it with a drizzle of extra virgin olive oil.

Something I do like the idea of is cold-pressed extra virgin rapeseed oil. I'm not saying it equals that happiness you get from a beautiful bottle of extra virgin olive oil, but it has similar qualities, it works well in something like mayonnaise, where you want a more neutral oil, and the big advantage is that you can heat it to deep-frying temperature without it losing its natural antioxidants, flavour or colour.

There's also something deeply satisfying about a home-produced oil that doesn't have to travel thousands of miles to get to you.

Until a few years back most rapeseed oil was refined and used in blended vegetable oil or in processed foods; then a handful of environmentally aware farmers started cold-pressing it. What I like is that it all helps to reduce the carbon footprint, because what many of these guys do is feed the by-products of the oil production to their cattle, then pick up the oil from the restaurants after they have used it for deep-frying and convert it into bio-diesel oil to run their farm vehicles and vans.

Oilseed rape might not be the prettiest thing to grow in the countryside – I'm not mad about fields and fields of bright yellow – but there's plenty of it, and I just love the idea of an oil that you can use on your salad, in the deep-fat fryer and in your car. The idea is coming, slowly, but it's coming. Bring on the British and Irish oil barons of the future!

Oily Fish

I'm a big fan of the whole oily-fish ladder, from tuna at the top, through sardines and mackerel down to anchovies. A plate of fresh anchovies, dusted in breadcrumbs mixed with a little bit of chopped garlic and parsley, fried in a very hot pan or put under a hot grill, then just pulled off the bone with the fingers, no need for knives and forks … just beautiful.

You can add a little bit of grated lemon rind to the breadcrumbs if you want, but actually I don't think you need it. Too much citrus can take away from the flavour of the fish. I especially wouldn't squeeze lemon over a fried or grilled oily fish. Fish oil and lemon juice doesn't work for me. A splash of vinegar, yes. Lemon, no. With the exception of eels, that is. Crispy roasted eels with a squeeze of lemon, mmm … beautiful. As kids, we used to have them for breakfast or tea, with salad from the garden. All our family love eels to this day. My dad used to put a line out and catch half a dozen, which we kept alive in a bath in the river, and when we wanted one we used to go out, bring it in and chop it up on the kitchen table.

Everyone says you have to skin eels, but, with small ones at least, if you roll the pieces in flour and fry them really, really hard in the tiniest film of oil in a hot cast-iron skillet, the fat under the skin disperses, and they get crispy, crispy. We used to hold the pieces at each end like corn on the cob, nibbling along the backbone. I liked the bit of tail best, which was mostly cartilage and bone, but it would be as crunchy as a cracker.

When I was cooking in the Netherlands, where the cuisine is simple and tasty and reminds me a lot of the cooking I was brought up on in Ireland, you'd be waiting with huge anticipation for April when the white asparagus came into season to eat with smoked eel; then in May you'd have the *maatjesharing*, the beautiful Dutch speciality of new season's salt 'maiden herring' – just before they breed they put on a lot of fat out at sea, so they are really tasty. The arrival of the *maatjesharing* is a cause for celebration and they would be sold on the streets, the herring straight out of the barrel on a white bread roll, with some chopped onion and a bit of gherkin. Or you'd maybe eat them with a shot of the gin-like Jenever, made with juniper berries.

There is something deeply pure about the fish culture of northern Europe, the whole cycle of salting and brining and marinating and potting, which is how people fed themselves before refrigeration.

One August I was on holiday in Ireland, out fishing for mackerel. It's not a hard job to catch mackerel when there are shoals of them about. They nearly jump into your boat. I caught ninety of them in a day, which was quite embarrassing, and I didn't know what to do with them all. Because I could never throw away a fresh fish, I stayed up all night filleting them and salting them. I looked in the cupboard and saw I had soy and ginger, so I made up a sweet pickle, and finally I put them in big jars under the pickle and passed them round to all the locals. I just love that way of dealing with fish, and we've spent a lot of time getting the process right at Bentley's.

Now we are even going to smoke our own mackerel and herring out on the roof, using a special smoker I've bought. We'll fillet and salt them one day, smoke them the next, and pack them in jars under oil, the way the Spanish do in Galicia in the north of Spain.

Home-cured Herring

This is fantastic with rye bread or crunchy, homemade Swedish-style crisp bread (see page 315). It's a little snack really, something to get out of the fridge when you come in from work or the pub, or to serve as a starter. The sauce is poured over the herrings just before you serve them.

Serves 4

4 herrings, scaled, gutted
  and filleted
10g sea salt
a pinch of sugar

Marinade:
450ml white wine
  vinegar
300ml water
250g sugar
14 allspice berries
14 black peppercorns
1 bay leaf
1 carrot, sliced
1 red onion, sliced
1 tablespoon grated fresh
  horseradish

**Honey, mustard and dill
  dressing:**
100g honey
100g English mustard
100ml white wine
  vinegar
350ml vegetable oil
1 tablespoon chopped
  dill

Put the herrings in a rectangular casserole dish.

Combine the salt and sugar and cover the fish with the mixture. Leave to cure in the fridge for 48 hours then lift out the herrings, brush off the salt and return to the dish.

Put all the marinade ingredients into a pan and bring to the boil, then take off the heat and leave until completely cold – it must be cold. Pour over the herrings.

When cold, transfer the fish and its marinade to sterilised preserving jars. Seal and put in the fridge for up to a month.

Mix together the honey, mustard and vinegar and whisk in the oil, gradually, until the sauce emulsifies. Add the chopped dill. Serve over the herrings.

Mackerel
Tartare

You want small mackerel for this. The flesh on small mackerel is different to that on the bigger ones. It's darker and firmer and it holds together more, and when you cut into it, it has an almost bluey tint, whereas the larger mackerel have much whiter flesh. This tartare veers towards sashimi with its Japanese-style dressing. This is a great little universal dressing or dipping sauce for anything Japanese in style. It is made with rice wine vinegar, which is quite gentle and fragrant, and mirin, which is a sweet Japanese cooking wine. The best pickled sushi ginger is white rather than bright pink, which is usually artificially coloured.

Serves 4

8 very fresh small
    mackerel fillets
2 shallots, finely diced
a small bunch of chives,
    finely chopped
a small bunch of spring
    onions, finely chopped
a squeeze of lemon juice
a little salt, optional

Japanese-style dressing:
1 tablespoon Kikkoman
    soy sauce
2 tablespoons mirin
2 tablespoons rice wine
    vinegar
2 teaspoons pickled sushi
    ginger with juice, plus
    a little extra to garnish

First make the dressing: mix the soy, mirin, vinegar and pickled ginger together.

Place the mackerel fillets on a chopping board and with a sharp knife cut in half lengthways, along the line where the bone would have been, then slice crossways into strips of about 5mm. Put into a large, cold bowl.

Add the shallots, chives and spring onions, a squeeze of lemon and a tablespoon or so of the dressing and mix everything lightly together. Taste and add a little salt or a little more dressing as you think necessary. You may not need any salt as the soy sauce may provide enough. Garnish with pickled ginger and serve straight away.

Mackerel with Rhubarb and Horseradish

I can never get tired of fresh mackerel, fried in a pan, the way we used to have them for breakfast as kids. This is loosely based on a wonderful old Irish seafaring recipe for mackerel and rhubarb compote, which was picked up by Alan Davidson in his book *North Atlantic Seafood*. Alan was born in Northern Ireland, and he found this in an old book put out by the Bord Iascaigh Mhara, the Irish Sea Fisheries Board, who were collecting recipes from women around Ireland at the time, and this is a classic. I love exploring the paths of seasonality, and new season's rhubarb with mackerel in February is perfect, as is gooseberry and mackerel a bit later on. There's something about that slightly mouthpuckering sourness of the fruit that just works with the oiliness of the fish. We add onion and garlic to the rhubarb, which gives it a bit of earthiness and stops it from being too sweet and jammy, and then we serve it with crème fraîche mixed with horseradish to give it a bit of a kick. It's a funny recipe really, a kind of savoury version of rhubarb and custard with a piece of fish, but it's a great combination of flavours.

New season, or forced, rhubarb is extraordinary stuff, something we never saw in Ireland, and something I definitely think has one over on summer rhubarb. The idea of a food being 'forced' would normally make you think of something industrialised and unnatural, but in the case of rhubarb it is fascinating to see how a clever idea can give you a better product. It's grown in pitch-black forcing sheds in the 'Rhubarb Triangle' in West Yorkshire, between Wakefield, Leeds and Bradford. The farmers there believe that what they grow is so special and distinctive to their part of the world, and so superior to any imported equivalent, that they have applied to the EU for PDO (Protected Designation of Origin) status, in the same way as Parmesan cheese, or Cornish clotted cream.

The story of the rhubarb is that at the Chelsea Physic Garden in London, back in the early nineteenth century, a gardener accidentally covered one of his rhubarb plants with soil in the winter, which kept it nice and warm, and because no light could get to it, instead of producing green leaves it put all its energy into its shoots, which came up bright pink and tender. Rhubarb wasn't that popular at the time, but this new stuff was. In the north of England people started looking at this 'blanched' rhubarb and experimenting with a different way of producing it: lifting it from the soil and forcing it without light in sheds heated by coal from the local pits. The history of forced rhubarb as we know it today is directly tied into the history of coaling and coking and smelting in Yorkshire, which made the local land quite acidic and perfect for growing rhubarb in the first place, and then supplied the fuel needed for the forcing process.

The basic technique hasn't changed for two centuries. The rhubarb plants are grown in the fields for two years, but they aren't harvested, so they build up a store of excess energy. Then they are lifted very carefully and taken into the dark forcing sheds. Once in there the warmth makes them think it's spring, and the buds start growing without any soil or light, just using the energy reserves they have built up. The farmers say you can hear the buds popping in the dark as they stretch and the long pink shoots start to grow.

The workers still move round in the dark by candlelight, though these days the sheds are heated by warm air instead of coal fires, and nowadays when the rhubarb is growing out in the fields for the second year, the farmers put special thermometers in the soil ready for when the frosts come, and when they show the exact number of frost units that will convert the plant's energy into glucose, they know it is time to lift the roots and take them into the sheds.

This makes a great lunch or light supper.

Serves 4
a little butter
1 small onion, finely
    diced
2 cloves garlic, sliced
a knob of fresh
    horseradish
about 10 sticks of
    Yorkshire forced
    rhubarb
about 1 tablespoon sugar
100g crème fraîche
1 shallot, finely diced
a small bunch of chives,
    finely chopped
8 large fresh mackerel
    fillets
sprigs of watercress,
    to serve

Heat the butter in a pan, add the onion and garlic and sweat lightly and gently to soften. Grate the horseradish finely. Add most of it (reserving a little) to the pan with a pinch of salt.

Wash and thinly slice the rhubarb, add to the pan, together with the sugar, and cook over a gentle heat for 10 minutes or so until the rhubarb is tender but still holding its shape.

Taste and add a little more sugar if you think it needs it, but not too much; it should taste quite earthy and tart.

Whip the crème fraîche until it thickens. Fold in the shallot, chives and the rest of the grated horseradish, and season with salt and pepper to taste.

Season the mackerel fillets and place under a hot grill, skin-side up, for 4–5 minutes, until just cooked.

To serve, spoon some warm rhubarb on each plate, alongside the fillets of mackerel. Add a spoonful of crème fraîche and a sprig of watercress.

Grilled Sardines with Runner Beans, Tomatoes and Basil

This is a great summer dish; or even if it isn't summer, it will cheer you up. You can have the salad ready, then all you have to do is grill, or barbecue, the sardines. You'll usually find sardines already scaled at the fishmongers – if they haven't been scaled, ask for it to be done for you. And ask for them to be gutted and cleaned – it's up to you whether you want the heads left on or not. I'd slice rather than finely chop or crush the garlic, as it doesn't want to hide in this dressing – it will kick the salad ingredients together.

Use a good sherry vinegar if you can – the one I've been using for years is Valdespino, which is about eight to ten years old and is made by a family-owned bodega in Jerez using the traditional solera system, in which the vinegars are aged for different times in barrels. The idea is that over months or years you draw some vinegar from the last barrel, top it up with some younger vinegar from the next one, top that one up with the next one in which the vinegar will be younger still, and so on, refreshing each barrel with new vinegar, which blends in with the older vinegar and keeps the quality going.

Serves 4

500g young runner beans
150ml extra virgin olive oil
50ml good sherry vinegar
1 clove garlic, finely sliced
8 really good ripe tomatoes
a bunch of basil
a little olive oil, for frying
8 sardines, cleaned and scaled (see method)

Cook the runner beans in heavily salted boiling water until tender.

Whisk together the extra virgin olive oil, vinegar and garlic to make the dressing.

Chop the tomatoes and add to the beans. Tear a handful of basil leaves (keep some back) and mix in. Toss with a little of the dressing (keep some of this back, too) and season to taste. Pile some salad on to your plates so that they are ready to go as soon as the sardines are cooked.

Heat a film of olive oil in a large non-stick frying pan. Season the sardines with salt and pepper and cook, skin-side down, without moving them, for about 2 minutes. Turn them over very briefly to seal the other side and remove from the pan. Serve on top of the salad, finish with some more torn basil leaves and a final drizzle of dressing.

Rare Grilled Tuna
with Scorthalia
and Gremolata

Yellowfin are fast-growing tuna that mature at between two and five years old, which means they are more sustainable than other fish in the tuna family. Look for ones that are caught by pole and line or hand-line, so that the dolphins that swim with them don't get caught in the nets.

Scorthalia is a traditional thing to have with amberjack, which is a little like tuna, in Greece. It's akin to an almond mayonnaise but made without eggs; it has similar flavours to the Spanish white gazpacho. It's worth buying good big fat almonds for their extra flavour. Blanching them in milk is the traditional way of softening the skins so you can peel them. It keeps in the flavour and the almonds stay really white. When we take out the almonds, we keep the flavoured milk and use it to make almond ice cream. Or you could use it to make a lovely almondy rice pudding.

Verjuice is just pure grape juice, made from pressing unripe grapes, and it was used in medieval times to do the job of vinegar. It has a nice touch of acidic bitterness that works well, but if you can't find it, use white wine vinegar.

Serves 4
a handful of whole
 almonds
a little milk
a handful of stale bread,
 crusts removed
3 cloves garlic
1 tablespoon verjuice or
 white wine vinegar
250ml good olive oil
4 yellowfin tuna steaks

Gremolata:
a bunch of flat-leaf
 parsley, chopped
zest of 1 lemon
2 cloves garlic, crushed
about 50ml olive oil

Put the almonds into a pan with enough milk to cover. Bring to the boil, then remove from the heat and peel them while still warm.

In the meantime, soak the bread in water and then squeeze it out.

Put the peeled almonds into a blender with the bread, garlic, verjuice or vinegar and a good pinch of salt, and whiz. With the motor running, add the olive oil, a little at a time, as if you were making a mayonnaise.

Preheat the grill.

To make the gremolata, mix all the ingredients together, and season with a little salt.

Season the tuna, and cook under a hot grill until charred on the outside but still rare in the middle.

To serve, spoon some scorthalia on to each plate, put a tuna steak on top and spoon some gremolata over the fish.

Eel, Cider
and Mussel Stew

This is a great little one-pot stew that's quite simple to make and is cooked in about half an hour. When I was growing up, eel was a free food. Now, as has happened to so many of our fish stocks, the populations are massively depleted, thanks to overfishing, climate change and too many elvers being sold to the Far East. The wild eel has an adventurous life. It spawns in the Sargasso Sea in the mid-Atlantic, then the larvae are carried by the Gulf Stream to Europe. When they get there they become elvers, also called 'glass' eels because they are transparent, and they start to swim upriver. By the time they are about four years old, they are completely covered in scales and called yellow eels. Between six and twelve years old for a male, and ten and thirty for a female, they change colour again. This time they become silver, and when they reach sexual maturity, those that aren't caught swim back to the sea to spawn and then die.

Our eels come from the Lough Neagh Fishermen's Co-operative in Northern Ireland, which is the largest wild commercial fishery in Europe. It was set up over thirty years ago by a priest, Father Oliver Plunkett Kennedy. They fish for eels on dark nights – the shoals move when there is no moon and when there is a high swell of water – and are careful to enforce the daily fishing quotas and replenish the stocks of elvers. To help keep the cycle of the wild stocks going, they have built-in escape routes at weirs so that some of the eels can swim on to the sea. If you can find an unfermented farmhouse cider it will make this dish really special.

Serves 4

1kg mussels

a little vegetable oil

1 onion, roughly chopped

1 head of celery, roughly chopped, leaves reserved

4 cloves garlic, chopped

1 bottle English or farmhouse cider, about 600ml

about 20 small potatoes, peeled

1 large fresh eel, gutted and cut into fillets (ask your fishmonger to do this)

Scrub the mussels well under running water, scraping off any barnacles and beards. Throw away any that are open, or won't close if you tap them.

To make the stock, heat the oil in a large pan, add the onion, celery and garlic and sweat for a few minutes.

Add the cider and then the mussels. Put on the lid and cook over a high heat until the mussels open, then lift them out and keep to one side, discarding any that haven't opened.

Add the potatoes to the pan, cook for 15 minutes, then add the eel. Cook for a further 15 minutes, topping up with a little water if necessary. By now the potatoes should be just tender, and if you insert a knife into the eel, the flesh should come away from the bone.

Lift out the eel and remove the bones and skin – the fillets will fall off the bone and the skin should come away easily. Discard the skin and bones and keep the pieces of eel to one side.

Taste your stock and season as necessary. Spoon some eels and mussels into the bottom of warmed soup bowls and scatter over some chopped celery leaves. Pour the hot stock and vegetables over the top and serve.

Smoked Eel

Smoked eel is gorgeous, and Frank Hederman, who smokes them down in Cobh, County Cork, has some of the best I've tasted. Frank is another, utterly charming, member of the colourful band of artisan smokers who are a bit of a law unto themselves, but consistently produce great food. I like the way he cures and smokes quite lightly, so he doesn't obscure the flavour of the fish. Sometimes eels can be a bit narrow and less meaty, but the ones Frank smokes are big and delicious. They're great cold, but it's also hard to beat smoked eels on the barbecue over some charcoal or wood embers.

Eoin Corcoran, who is in charge of the Oyster Bar at Bentley's, was the first chef in London to make a terrine of smoked eel, apple and foie gras, all layered up, based on something he saw in San Sebastian, in the Basque country of northern Spain, when he went out there a few years ago to Martín Berasategui's restaurant, which now has three Michelin stars. I thought it was fascinating at the time: eel and foie gras? But every chef in London seems to have done a version of it since, though a lot of them are more concerned with making the terrine look, rather than taste, perfect. It has become such a cliché now, and so overused. So we've moved on, though in a way we've moved backwards, because we just serve great smoked eel really simply with potato pancakes.

Smoked Eel
with Russian Salad
and Potato Pancakes

When I think of smoked fish, I think of Russian salad, made with peas, beans, carrots, potatoes and beetroot. It's one of those things people turn up their noses at because of bland processed versions you get in tins, but a freshly made Russian salad with some crunch and texture stands right up there gastronomically. A big bowl of it with some smoked eel is happiness on a tabletop. I'd gladly serve it with a cold poached blue lobster, too. And I like to put a bit of turnip in it, because I like that little bitterness in your mouth to offset the sweetness of some of the other vegetables and the creaminess of the salad cream. We don't have enough bitterness going on in our cooking overall.

The French laugh at things like salad cream but they have their own kind of salad cream in mayonnaise. I think the idea of a homemade salad cream – the kind that cooks like Mrs Beeton and Eliza Acton made, with milk and mustard and cayenne, long before Heinz put it in a bottle for the British market – is terrific, I really do. I particularly like the recipe from Constance Spry, who was the society hostess, cook, florist, writer and style queen of her day, and who gave us Coronation chicken to mark the Queen coming to the throne in 1952 (she did the flowers, too). A little bit of tarragon in the salad adds a slightly liquorice flavour that goes well with salad cream, and if you don't want the beetroot to stain your salad pink when you serve it, then do as I suggest here and scatter the beetroot over the top, then people can make their own streaks as they mix it in.

When you make the pancake mixture, if you add the egg white separately it just gives a lift to the mixture, so the pancakes will puff up in the pan.

To make the Russian salad, bring a pan of salted water to the boil, then put in the carrots and turnip. After about 5 minutes, add the green beans and peas and cook until all the vegetables are just tender.

Cool under cold running water, to halt the cooking, and drain.

Fold the salad cream and tarragon into the vegetables.

To make the pancakes, boil the potatoes in salted water, drain and mash them in a bowl. If you want to get the pancakes just right, weigh your mash at this point. You want 225g. It sounds a bit pedantic, I know, but if you have too much mash your pancakes will be more like potato cakes, and won't rise as well. If you have too little, they will be a bit tasteless. Add the flour, milk and egg yolks. Add a little nutmeg and salt.

Serves 4

250g smoked eel fillet, skinned and sliced into equal pieces

vegetable oil, for cooking the pancakes

Russian salad:

4 medium carrots, finely diced

1 medium turnip, finely diced

a handful of green beans

a handful of fresh peas (or frozen)

enough salad cream (see page 54) to bind

a little chopped tarragon

1 medium cooked beetroot

Potato pancakes:

4 large floury potatoes

125g plain flour

150ml milk

4 eggs, separated

freshly grated nutmeg

In a separate bowl, whisk half the egg whites (freeze the rest, so you can use them for another dish) until they double in volume and then fold into the mash mixture.

Heat a non-stick frying pan, brush with oil and, using a dessertspoon, drop small rounds of the mixture into the pan. Cook the pancakes for 2 minutes on each side until golden brown. Keep warm.

Serve immediately, with the eel and Russian salad. Sprinkle over the beetroot at the end (so that the colour doesn't stain the salad).

Salad Cream

Serves 4

1 teaspoon English
  mustard
1 teaspoon sugar
2–3 tablespoons white
  wine vinegar
¼ teaspoon white
  pepper
½ teaspoon salt
150ml evaporated milk
150ml olive oil

I love reading old books; you get so many ideas out of them, and this is based on a recipe from the *Constance Spry Cookery Book*, which Constance published in 1956 with her friend and fellow cook Rosemary Hume – together they had opened a domestic science school at Winkfield Place, near Ascot, after the war. You look at the ingredients and see evaporated milk and think, 'No!', but it's brilliant; genius.

Put the mustard, sugar and vinegar into a bowl with the pepper and salt and mix together. Mix in the evaporated milk. Gradually whisk in the oil until you have a nice creamy consistency. Check the seasoning, and keep cool.

Wild Salmon

Not many things stop me in my tracks and leave me stuck for words. But wild salmon … what can I say? A piece of wild salmon so good that you don't ever want to leave the table, you just want to carry on eating and eating it … well, it truly speaks for itself.

My wife Maria and I stayed in a guest house in Kenmare one time, and in the morning I was looking through the breakfast menu at the porridge, black pudding, crispy bacon and poached eggs, the same old Irish breakfast, and there was a special on: pan-fried darne of wild salmon with lemon butter and brown bread. I remember this piece of fish coming out, perfectly cooked so it was still a little pink in the middle, just gorgeous and pure, and when I'd finished it, like Oliver Twist, I said to the waiter, 'Could I have some more?' When I asked for it, I saw the chef put her head round the kitchen door, and she had a big smile on her face. When food does that to you, makes you feel that happy, that's really something. That piece of salmon was one of the greatest eating experiences of my life, partly because it reminded me of the wild salmon we used to have at home on the farm in County Meath. The taste of it has never left my memory.

Wild food was a big part of our lives. You'd see a hare popping around, bobbing from tuft to tuft of grass, and you'd think: he'd be tasty; where is the gun? And you'd be forever looking out for a brown trout or a salmon from the river. We were poachers, right enough, but you only took what you would be eating for your supper. Hunting what Mother Nature provides when you are hungry is a very different matter to putting out drift nets on the sea runs into the estuaries to catch the wild fish. I have no sympathy for the shocking pillaging and needless exploitation of wild salmon which has brought us to the point where we are today, where there is virtually no wild salmon to be had in Ireland, and will not be until the populations have been allowed to recover. You just can't take and take and take, because what is wild and natural can't replenish itself fast enough to keep up.

If the draconian measures put in place by the Irish government to limit fishing work, we may see the levels of wild salmon back again in the next 20–50 years, but it may not even be in my lifetime.

I remember when I was very small, being woken in the middle of the night by noises, half sleepwalking into the kitchen and seeing the flash of silver as a salmon was being gently removed from one of the old hessian sacks that came from the mill. It was probably only a matter of minutes since that fish had been swimming in the Blackwater river. There was my dad with the old carving knife that was used for nothing else but fish, carving it into thick steaks for what we called the 'poacher's cuts', which would be distributed scrupulously around the community in the spirit of proper, traditional poaching: what we liked to think of as a redistribution of natural resources.

Our portion would almost always be cooked for breakfast. Despite his late-night adventures, Dad would be down early, rattling the big cast-iron pan on the top of the Rayburn to melt the butter. When it was frothing, he'd put in the thick slices of salmon, fry them quickly on both sides then serve them up with slices of buttered soda bread. How decadent was that? Seven kids sitting down to a breakfast of wild salmon. But that was how we were: cash poor, food rich.

And the law pretty much turned a blind eye. Crime was no licence for your bull, no light on your bicycle, or not cutting thistles in your field, but not robbing a salmon from the river – or 'acquiring' it, as we preferred to say. Unless, of course, it was right in front of the noses of the Garda, as happened one night when my dad went out with one of his friends who was so short-sighted he wore glasses as thick as the base of a milk bottle. The story goes that it was a dark night, but suddenly the moon appeared from behind the clouds and my dad's friend found himself standing right in front of the local sergeant, clutching a fine salmon. It was a cut-and-dried case. He hadn't a leg to stand on. But strangely when the case came before the local District Justice, the prosecution were unable to find the key piece of evidence. Apparently it had been eaten.

The Wild
Side

Sally Barnes at Woodcock Smokery in Skibbereen is one of those rare, inspirational human beings you just take your hat off to. Sally is a law unto herself. Such an intelligent woman, with a profound understanding of the smoke, but what sets her apart is her absolute refusal to smoke anything other than wild fish. When the wild salmon all but stopped in Ireland, because there are now such strict limits on fishing to try to save the stocks, she was theoretically out of business and I was concerned for her, so I said, 'Sally, there's no wild salmon. Would you not smoke some organic salmon for me, because I really want to give you some business?' The look on her face. I swear she was about to box me on the nose. Such are her ethics and perfectionism she won't even use fish caught on the seven-day boats, because she won't smoke a fish that is over twenty-four hours old. 'If a fish stays on ice out on the boats I can't use it. It spoils before we can finish our process,' she says.

Instead, since drift netting for salmon in Ireland has been banned, she has to source sea-caught wild salmon from the east coast of Scotland. The salmon is blast-frozen, glazed with water and then blast-frozen a second time, which is the Japanese method, so it is kept in perfect condition until she and her daughter Joleine, who is taking on the business, and a couple of other workers, are ready to smoke it over native hardwood.

Like many of the artisans forging a future for great food in Ireland and championing small, local production in the face of demands for factories that meet endless rules and regulations, she isn't a local. She's a Scot who lived in London, moved to Ireland over thirty years ago and started out smoking the salmon that her husband, a fisherman, caught, using a pan in the bottom of a tea chest, because she had no freezer and no way of keeping what they couldn't eat otherwise. Then a bad debt led to her acquiring a mini-kiln, which she experimented with, smoking both cold, which means you cure the fish, keeping the temperature below 30°C, and hot, which involves smoking and cooking the fish at the same time. So she could learn everything about the fish and the process, she studied with the Open University. When she first set up she sold her salmon locally and at farmers' markets, and if proof was ever needed that you can go to the hills and make a living, she is now known all over the world in fish circles. Wild Alaskan fishermen ask her to come and smoke their fish, and she is on first-name terms with marine biologists all over the world. Incredible.

Being married to a fisherman for almost thirty years, she knows the fishing way of life and its vital importance to rural communities. 'We are an island; we should be connected to the sea. If we only looked after it, and our rivers,

and were properly mindful of not killing so many small fish as "by-catch", we wouldn't need to farm fish,' she believes. 'Yes, farms create wealth, but not necessarily for the local people, and the BSE crisis should have taught us to be wary of fish grown quickly for profit or eating bagged food that often contains dyes. It's all too new and imperfect as a science; whereas in nature everything is tried, tested and proven. The baseline for me is that the wild salmon chooses what it wants to eat (assuming its natural food isn't being plundered for fish meal for farmed fish, or raked up indiscriminately by the big trawlers). You get quite a variation in its natural colour, because each fish will be on a slightly different diet. And we have thrived and evolved on this planet consuming these wild creatures; we are physically geared up to absorb and utilise that incoming food material, so in the end, are we changing ourselves?'

'What other form of farming would be considered economically viable that requires 3½ to 5lb of wild fish to be caught to make the feed to put on 1lb of farmed fish flesh?' she wants to know. 'What is sustainable about that? Sustainability is becoming a word that is bandied about like 'traditional' or 'organic', but if you are really talking about sustainability, you have to follow it through to the nth degree. Drift netting might have been banned in Ireland (although not elite, leisure fishing on rivers) but we are still not properly addressing the fact that salmon rely on pure water and a whole eco-system that is in trouble. A big problem is that much of the gravel which was formed back in the ice age, that naturally lines the rivers and is crucial to the spawning process was taken away for building projects over the years. The particulate matter is the same size as the salmon eggs. The female makes a scrape, sprays in the eggs, the male fertilises them, the female covers the eggs with the gravel, and that's it, they hatch and they are off on their way looking for food, little nymphs and larvae, but these are also in limited supply because of pollution.

'100 years ago salmon were so plentiful – a bit like oysters in England – that according to Dr David Piggins, who was the Director of the Salmon Research Trust in Mayo, they were considered "verminous" fish. The beginning of the end was not only over-fishing,' she believes, 'but when Ireland acceded to the EU and farmers got grant aid to neutrify the land with fertilisers and use pesticides and herbicides which all end up in the water. Human waste, all our chemical cleaners for getting our baths and sinks shiny and bright, they all get into water systems too, but if all agriculture went back to being truly organic, not organic as in allowing certain chemicals, but the way it was seventy years ago, Ireland could turn itself into the organic salad bowl of the world, and that would help clean up the water for the salmon, too.'

She knows, though, through her constant dialogue with fishermen and marine experts, that there are no such simplistic answers. 'One expert, T. P. O'Connor in Dingle, cited thirty-nine issues,' she says. 'For example, you now have seals coming swimming right into fresh water chasing salmon.'

Sally's whole ethos is that the best things take time. At the smokery each fish is treated as an individual, hand-filleted and dry-salted for the right amount of time to suit its size and fat content. After that it is smoked slowly. Again, for how long is down to the temperature and humidity. After the first stage of smoking, it is pinboned again, by hand, and put back into the kiln again to finish smoking. Some of the salmon is kept back and matured for three months before being sold.

Because of the scarcity of the salmon, she now also smokes tuna, mackerel and herring. Then there's the pollack, which is such a delicious secret, I hardly even want to tell anyone else about it, because I truly think she's found a new corner of the market.

But it is the wild salmon, which poets have eulogized as the soul of the Irish land, that she will continue to fight for, for future generations to be able to enjoy. 'I just love salmon as creatures; adore them; they are amazing, so athletic,' she says. 'It's probably very telling that what I especially admire is the way they continually fight the current and go against the flow!'

Farmed Salmon

Wild salmon and farmed salmon are two entirely different things. When I first came to London, I used to feel murderous about the quantity of farmed salmon from Norway being passed off as wild salmon in hotels and restaurants at the time. In one restaurant I worked in, forty sides came in, supposed to be wild salmon. Did they think I wouldn't know the difference? I called up the suppliers and told them, 'Get this stuff out of here.' I hate that lack of respect.

I don't think a farmed salmon, organic or otherwise, should be called salmon at all. It might have been hatched as a salmon, but the whole nature of a salmon is that it makes its great journey from river to sea and back. Its character depends on the colour and flavour of the shellfish it eats in the open seas to fatten itself up and build up its strength and muscle for the long swim back to the river to spawn. All those things make a salmon what it is. A farmed fish, stuck in a cage, even in fast-flowing, deep seawater, is still a farmed fish in a cage, not a salmon.

Of course, there has to be room for farmed fish if we want to carry on eating salmon at the rate that we do, and many farms are getting much better at raising fish in a way that is more ethically and ecologically sound. I'm happy to hear that, because where is the morality in plundering the fish stocks off Greenland to turn the catch into fish meal pellets to feed farmed fish? Or in washing the lice off the fish with chemicals, which then fall to the bottom of the sea and kill everything down there? All this for a market that wants cheap smoked salmon.

I need to have salmon, especially smoked salmon, and so I do buy organic Irish farmed salmon from Clare Island and Glenarm in the north of Ireland, a smaller, individually owned smokery and hatchery, which nearly went out of business when a freak shoal of jellyfish attacked all its fish in 2007. But I will only buy organic salmon, because what really worries me about farmed salmon is the level of PCBs, industrial toxins that are out there in the environment and have been found to be higher in farmed fish than wild. How are they going to affect our bodies over time? I see people paying a fortune for imported pure Fijian water and then eating farmed salmon: how crazy is that?

What can we do? Stop going to the supermarket and filling up our trolleys with a huge weekly shop, and cramming our big American fridges – yes, I like mine, too – so that we can't even see what we have bought, and food like smoked salmon ends up in the bin. We have to get back to eating wild salmon just when we can and treating it with reverence.

Bentley's Gravadlax with Pickled Cucumber

There is a bit of sneering that goes on sometimes about gravadlax because it was quite a 1970s thing, but this is up there with the best Japanese sashimi and it looks beautiful with its covering of bright green dill. I also like to make a version of the dish with fresh mackerel instead of salmon. There's nothing fiddly or complicated about gravadlax, but you do need to allow 24 hours for the salting. We use Maldon sea salt, because the grains are bigger and won't melt and burn into the fish.

Eat the gravadlax just as it is, or with a duck egg omelette (see page 310). It will keep for a week and you can freeze it, too.

Serves 4

about 900g fresh salmon (half a side), skinned, pinned and trimmed (ask your fishmonger to do this)
20g sugar
40g sea salt
a little English mustard
a bunch of dill, chopped

Pickled cucumber:
1 cucumber
50ml white wine vinegar
25g caster sugar

Wash and pat the fish dry then lay it on a tray, skin-side down (make sure the tray fits in the fridge). Combine the sugar and salt and rub the mixture over the fish. Wrap it in clingfilm. Weight it down lightly (a heavy plate on top is fine) and put in the fridge for 24 hours.

To make the pickled cucumber, peel the cucumber, cut in half lengthways and take out the seed section, then slice finely. Sprinkle the cucumber slices with salt and leave to stand.

Meanwhile, put the wine vinegar in a heavy pan with the sugar. Heat gently until the sugar has dissolved. Remove the pan from the heat and leave to cool.

Rinse and drain the cucumber, then wrap in a clean tea towel and squeeze out as much liquid as possible. Add the cucumber to the cold vinegar mixture and keep in the fridge.

Take out the salmon from the fridge, drain away any liquid and then wash and dry the fillet again. Brush with mustard and then cover completely with the chopped dill.

Carve crossways into thin slices and serve with the pickled cucumber.

Whole Poached Wild Salmon with Duck Egg Dressing

This is a special occasion dish; and worth buying a salmon kettle for. Serve this with Bentley's soda bread (see page 312) and country butter, with the dressing, which is like soft scrambled egg flavoured with capers and parsley, on top.

This is a big fish, but the beauty of it is you will probably have some left over to serve cold.

Serves 10
1 whole wild salmon, 2–3kg, gutted and scaled
watercress, to serve

Poaching liquor:
1 bottle dry white wine
a bunch of parsley
2 small leeks, sliced
2 sticks celery, sliced
2 onions, sliced
2 tablespoons sea salt
6 black peppercorns
2 bay leaves

Duck egg dressing:
4 duck eggs
50g good-quality butter
1 tablespoon capers, rinsed
a small handful of parsley, chopped
lemon juice, to taste

Put all the ingredients for the poaching liquor into a large oval pot or fish kettle. Bring to the boil.

Lower the salmon into the poaching liquor. Add enough water to cover completely, put the lid on and simmer gently for half an hour. Turn off the heat, and leave to cool until warm.

Meanwhile, make the dressing. Lower the duck eggs into a pan of boiling salted water and simmer for 5 minutes. They should still be soft. Lift the eggs out of the water using a slotted spoon and cool a little under running cold water, then carefully peel off the shells.

Melt the butter.

Crush the eggs in a bowl with a fork then mix in the capers, parsley and warm melted butter. Season with lemon juice, salt and pepper to taste. Mix well and keep warm.

Remove the fish carefully from its poaching liquor and break into pieces. Spoon the duck egg dressing on to the bread, as if it were scrambled egg, and serve alongside with a sprig of watercress.

Wild Salmon and Chopped Oysters

This is a really nice way to treat two of my favourite ingredients so they take on a bit of a sashimi-like quality. The wild salmon and oysters are chopped up and mixed together, as if you were making a tartare, but instead of piling everything up in a neat mound, I like to serve it loosely on a very cold plate. Obviously you need really, really fresh salmon for this. Try using green Tabasco sauce, as opposed to the red one – it is made with milder peppers.

Serves 4

about 400g wild salmon, skinned, pinned and trimmed (ask your fishmonger to do this)
8 rock oysters
a bunch of chives, finely chopped
4 shallots, finely diced
a squeeze of lemon juice
green Tabasco sauce

Cut the salmon into small dice.

Shuck the oysters (see page 122), retaining the liquor, and chop them into small pieces.

Mix the oysters and salmon together. Add the chives, shallots, oyster liquor, a squeeze of lemon and a couple of drops of green Tabasco. Serve straight away.

Brown Trout with German-style Potato Salad

One of the best brown trout I ever ate was straight out of Lough Derg by the Irish Seed Saver Association in Scariff, County Clare (see page 250), which we cooked on their woodburning stove with a big bowl of salad from their bio-dynamic garden. It was a whopping three-pounder, which you rarely see, big enough to cut into darnes, but the trout you will usually get from the fishmonger are much smaller, so I'd give a whole one to each person. The leaves included the appropriately named speckled trout, which were so good and so full of flavour you didn't need any dressing at all, though I would normally just dress the leaves with oil – there is enough vinegar in the potato salad, which also has a spoonful of mustard added to it, as you want that sharp-ish Germanic flavour.

Serves 4

4 trout, gutted and scaled

a few fennel fronds

2 lemons

flour, for dusting

50–75g unsalted butter

German-style potato salad:

450–500g new potatoes, or small waxy ones

4 tablespoons cider vinegar

1 large onion, finely sliced

1 tablespoon wholegrain mustard

1 tablespoon chopped dill

To serve:

mixed salad leaves

a little extra virgin olive oil and salt to dress

First make the potato salad. Wash the potatoes and boil them in their skins, then drain them and put them back into the pan. Put a clean tea towel over the top and replace the lid. Leave for a few minutes. The heat will steam off the excess moisture in the potatoes. When they have dried, peel them, while they are still hot.

While the potatoes are cooking, pour the vinegar into a non-reactive pan, bring to the boil and add the onions. Allow the vinegar to evaporate and the onions to soften.

When the onions are soft, stir in the mustard. Mix into the potatoes, season to taste, add some dill and stir through so that all the potatoes are dressed with the warm dressing.

Fill the cavity of each fish with fennel and lemon slices (use one of the lemons and reserve the other). Season well with salt and pepper inside and out.

Put some flour on a plate and dip each fish in it until lightly coated.

Melt half the butter in a heavy-based frying pan. When hot add the fish. Cook two at a time unless you have two pans. Cook for 5 minutes on the first side without disturbing. The skin should be nice and golden. Turn over and cook for another 5 minutes. To test that the trout is cooked, insert the tip of a knife. The flesh should be opaque all the way through, but still a little pink.

Serve the trout with a wedge of lemon, the warm potato salad and the salad leaves dressed with olive oil and a sprinkling of salt.

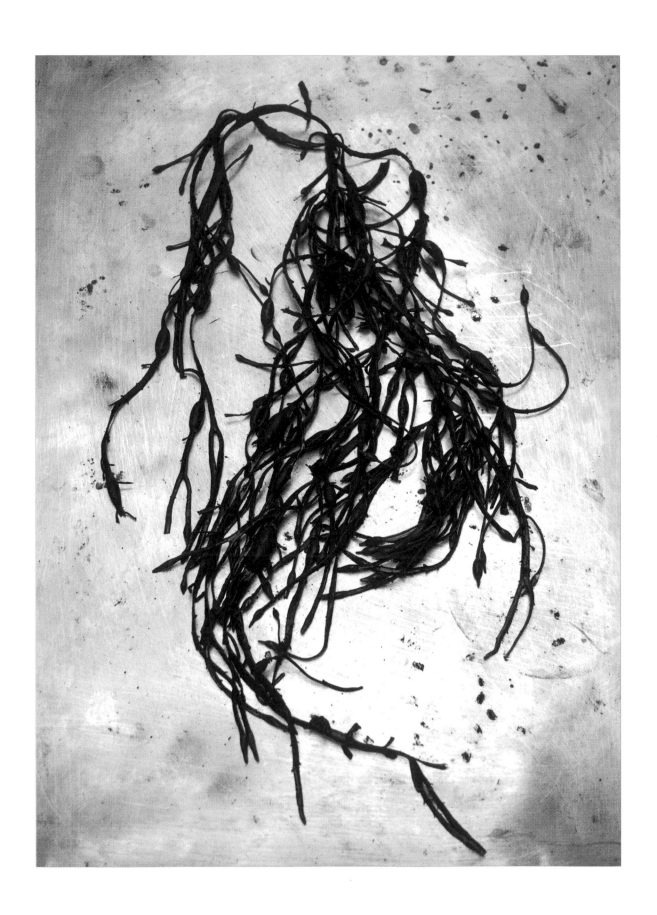

Whole Sea Trout
with 'Coastal Greens'

Sea trout is beautiful, it eats more like a salmon and there is more of a crustacea feel and colour to the meat, as opposed to brown lake trout, which also feed off things like plankton and insects: two different diets, two different characters to the fish. You could do this recipe with a whole sea bass, or any other similar fish. I'd serve it with a big bowl of new potatoes.

Serves 4

1 whole sea trout, gutted, scaled, fins removed, head on or off whichever you prefer (ask your fishmonger to do this)

a little vegetable oil, for frying

about 500g mixed coastal greens, such as samphire, sea purslane, sea beet and/or sea splurry

50g butter, cubed

a squeeze of lemon juice

Butter sauce:

1 shallot, finely diced

50ml white wine

50ml white wine vinegar

200g butter, diced

lemon juice, to taste

First make the butter sauce: put the shallot into a heavy-based pan with the white wine and vinegar. Bubble up until the liquid has reduced to a glaze. Turn the heat down low and vigorously whisk in the butter piece by piece. Season with salt and add lemon juice to taste. Pass through a sieve into a clean bowl and keep warm.

Preheat the oven to 220°C/Gas 7.

Season the fish. Use the biggest roasting tray that will fit into your oven. Pour in a little vegetable oil, put the tray on the hob and when hot put in the fish. Colour it on both sides, then transfer the tray to the oven and cook for 20–25 minutes. To check whether the fish is ready, insert the tip of a small knife as far as the bone, withdraw it and check that it is hot.

Have a pan of boiling salted water ready, and just before you take the fish out of the oven, lower the coastal greens in. Cook for 1 minute, then drain in a colander, put into a warmed bowl and toss with the butter, black pepper, salt and a squeeze of lemon juice.

Transfer the fish to a big carving board or plate, cut into pieces and serve with the greens, a bowl of new potatoes, if you like, and the sauce separately.

Pollack with Kohlrabi and Apple Gratin

I love a good gratin made with milk and cream, nice and garlicky. White turnip and potato is an old favourite, layered up and cooked really slowly, with a little bit of nutmeg in the sauce. With a chunk of beautiful bread it's a meal in itself. But what I also really like is kohlrabi, which looks like a cross between a cabbage and a turnip. Sometimes I poach it in ham stock, but I think it works especially well in a gratin with apple and potato.

This is best done in four individual pie dishes, though you could cook it in one big square or rectangular dish, and arrange your pieces of fish so you can easily divide it into four portions.

Serves 4
500g floury potatoes
1 head of kohlrabi
500ml single cream
2 cloves garlic, crushed
1 Bramley apple
a little butter, for greasing the dishes
4 pieces pollack fillet, about 200g each, skinned
a handful of fresh breadcrumbs
25g Gruyère cheese, grated
a handful of chopped parsley

Preheat the oven to 200°C/Gas 6.

Peel the potatoes and slice about half a centimetre thick. Peel the kohlrabi, discarding the shoots, and cut into pieces of a similar size to the potato. Put both into a pan of boiling salted water and cook until they just give when you insert the tip of a knife – you want them to keep their shape – then drain.

Put the cream and garlic into a heavy-based saucepan and season. Bring to the boil, then take off the heat.

Peel the apple and grate into the cream. Add the drained potatoes and kohlrabi. The potato will start to thicken up the mixture.

Butter your dishes and spoon in the creamy mixture. Place a piece of pollack on top, sprinkle with breadcrumbs and cheese and bake in the oven for 20 minutes, until golden brown.

Sprinkle with chopped parsley and serve.

Angry Hake

The French call this *en colère* because the way the tail is held in the fish's mouth as if it was biting it makes it look angry. Ask your fishmonger to skin and gut the fish for you and remove the eyes. The best way to serve the fish is one at a time, as soon as each is ready, as you would omelettes. Alternatively, preheat the oven to 150°C/Gas 2, and keep the first ones warm until you are ready to serve them all.

We serve this with anchovy and rosemary mayonnaise. Make some mayonnaise as on page 138, then just mix in a couple of sprigs of chopped rosemary leaves and chopped salted anchovy fillets.

Serves 4

4 small hake, head on, but skinned and gutted, eyes removed (see above)

8 eggs

200g flour, well seasoned with salt and pepper

about 500g white breadcrumbs

vegetable oil, for deep frying

anchovy and rosemary mayonnaise (see method), to serve

4 wedges of lemon and sprigs of watercress, to serve

Curl each hake and put the tail into the mouth, pressing the jaws down to hold it in place. Secure with a cocktail stick.

Beat the eggs in a shallow bowl, and have the seasoned flour and breadcrumbs in similar separate bowls. Dip the hake into the flour, then into the egg and finally into the breadcrumbs, turning to ensure the fish is evenly coated.

Preheat the oil to 160°C in a deep-fat fryer or a large pan filled no more than one-third full.

Deep-fry the hake one at a time for around 6 minutes, until golden brown and crisp, and serve each one as it is ready, with anchovy and rosemary mayonnaise, a wedge of lemon and watercress.

Whole Roast Gurnard with Coriander Mash, Saffron and Olive Oil

I get really excited about whole roast fish, and gurnard is a fish I especially like – it's very underrated and underused. Most people buy gurnard fillets, so your fishmonger should be able to give you some extra heads to make the lovely, rich, reddish-orange bisque-like sauce, which looks great against the white fish. Alternatively, you can just take the heads off your whole fish. A bed of greens, such as wild fennel in season, and a bowl of coriander mash to go with it is one of my favourite things. The mash is really light and fresh, no potatoes, just carrots, parsnip and coriander.

Serves 4

4 whole gurnard, gutted, plus 4 extra heads (or heads removed and reserved)
olive oil, for frying
sprigs of thyme
slices of lemon

Marinade:
6 cloves garlic, sliced
2 star anise
1 onion, roughly chopped
1 head of fennel, roughly chopped
500g plum tomatoes, chopped
2 tablespoon Pernod
125ml white wine
a good pinch of saffron
1 teaspoon sugar

Coriander mash:
4 carrots, chopped
4 parsnips, chopped
a good knob of butter
1 tablespoon chopped coriander

Put all the marinade ingredients into a bowl, add the fish heads and set aside for a minimum of 1 hour.

Remove the fish heads from their marinade and sear them in a frying pan with a little olive oil until nicely browned.

Pour the marinade into a pan, bring to the boil, add the fish heads and cook for a further 15 minutes. Push through a sieve, pressing down with a ladle. Taste, season as necessary and reserve.

Preheat the oven to 200°C/Gas 6.

To make the coriander mash, bring a pan of salted water to the boil and put in the carrots and parsnips. Cook until tender. Crush with the back of a fork, add the butter and coriander and season to taste. Cover and keep warm while you cook the fish.

Stuff the fish cavities with thyme sprigs and lemon slices. Tie with a little string and season well.

Heat a little olive oil in a large roasting pan. Brown the fish on both sides and transfer to the oven for 10–12 minutes until just cooked through.

Serve with the sauce and coriander mash.

Natural Smoked Haddock with Poached Egg, Kale and Scallions

This is the ultimate lunch dish, which has been on the menu at Bentley's for a couple of years now and is so popular we can't take it off. The egg is the star of the show. You cut into it and the egg yolk oozes out and destroys the perfect whiteness of the fish: it looks terrific. Frothing up the cooking liquor to spoon around might sound a bit cheffy, but again it looks good. You have this veil of froth with the green of the kale and scallions shining through. I love it. You want a good heritage potato for this, something with a depth of flavour, and of course, natural haddock, which hasn't had food colouring added to dye it a garish bright yellow.

Serves 4

500g small potatoes, preferably heritage

500g kale, stems removed

200g butter, plus a knob of butter for the mash

a bunch of spring onions (scallions), thinly sliced

2 litres water

2 tablespoons white wine vinegar

500ml milk

4 pieces natural (i.e. undyed) smoked haddock fillet, about 150g each, skins reserved

4 eggs

Cook the potatoes in boiling salted water until tender. Drain.

Cook the kale in boiling salted water until tender. Drain.

Melt the knob of butter in a pan, add the spring onions, potatoes and kale and mash with the back of a fork until well mixed together. Season to taste.

Put the water in a big pot and add the vinegar, ready to poach the eggs. While it comes to the boil, cook the haddock.

Bring the milk, 200g of the butter and the haddock skins to a simmer in a wide-bottomed pan, large enough to take all the fillets side by side. Discard the skins (they will have added some of their flavour to the milk). Add the haddock fillets and remove from the heat straight away. Leave to sit in the pan for about 4 minutes, during which time the haddock will cook through. (Remember the haddock has been smoked, so it is already cured, and needs very little cooking.)

Break the eggs into 4 cups and tip them gently into the boiling water, one at a time. Poach for 3 minutes. Remove with a slotted spoon.

To serve, spoon some of the potatoes and kale in the centre of your serving bowls or plates. Lift the pieces of haddock out of the cooking liquor and place on top, upside down. If you arrange the fish this way up, you will find that its natural curl makes a perfect little shallow bowl into which you can put the poached egg and it won't slide off. Spoon around some of the cooking liquor from the haddock – if you like, froth it up first with a hand-held blender.

Baked Red Mullet
with Crème Fraîche
and Mashed Fennel

I love the whole idea of poaching in crème fraîche. Along with poaching in milk, it's a way of cooking I've often come across in my travels in Scandinavia. Milk, especially, is used for gently cooking pork and elk, and it has a way of tenderising the meat. With fish it lends a clean, citrussy, creamy acidity, which is also great with the delicate taste of the fennel mash. When you put the fennel fronds into the mash at the end, you get a wonderful, natural green colour that is quite stunning against the reddish skin and white flesh of the fish. Ask your fishmonger to pinbone the fish for you.

Serves 4

a good knob of butter

1 onion, chopped

2 cloves garlic, chopped

4 heads of fennel, finely chopped (fronds reserved)

150ml good-quality crème fraîche

4 large red mullet fillets, skin on and pinboned

1 tablespoon dill leaves

Preheat the oven to 180°C/Gas 4.

Heat the butter in a pan, add the onion and garlic and sweat very slowly until tender. Add the fennel, and put a circle of baking paper on top (a cartouche) to create some steam inside and cook the fennel more quickly. Cook gently until the fennel begins to soften.

Transfer the contents of the pan to a blender or food processor and whiz, adding the fennel fronds, until roughly mashed.

Warm the crème fraîche until it melts. Pour into a shallow ovenproof dish. Season the red mullet and place on top. Bake for about 5 minutes, until the fillets feel just firm.

Spoon some of the fennel mash into the centre of each warmed plate. Carefully lift out the fish, skin-side up – the colour will look amazingly red. Season the crème fraîche, add the dill, and spoon a little around and over the fish.

Dover Sole
with
Brown Butter

In Ireland we call Dover sole black sole, and I can't think of many things better than a whole one, cooked simply in a pan in the classical way with a little brown butter.

We have two unwritten rules at Bentley's: don't ask for cheese on your fish soup (I think it's rich enough without it), and don't ask for Dover sole off the bone. Yes, of course we'll take it off the bone for you at the table if you want, but the way we like to serve it is whole, in all its magnificence; I just think that is perfection on a plate. There is a pathetic restaurant tradition of serving whole sole with the skirt untrimmed on a silver platter so that the fish looks bigger, but that's bullshit. We trim the skirt as close as we can to the fillets, with a pair of scissors, so the customer can take out the bone without the skirt getting in the way. And it is a very straightforward thing to do – you just have to run your knife down either side of the central bone, and lift it out.

I wouldn't even think about trying to cook Dover sole this way for a family – for a start the fish can be astronomically expensive, and because of the size of them you really need a pan for each one. I would keep it as a special dish for two, and cook the soles simultaneously in two pans. If you don't have two pans, keep the first sole warm in the oven while you cook the second one.

Dover sole on the bone is more and more the direction I want to go, with the exception perhaps of sole fillets *bonne femme* or the rolled and steamed fillets with crab, coconut, apple and lemongrass on page 82. I was having a discussion about the old fish classics with Simon Hopkinson one time in the bar at Bentley's, and we were talking about bonne femme, which is sole fillets with a white wine and butter sauce and mushrooms, called after the 'good wife' because it was supposed to be a family-style dish, and we came up with a kind of variation.

I sautéed some shallots and mushrooms slowly in butter, added some white wine, then puréed them up and folded in a little hollandaise sauce, put a little mound of it in a dish, the fillets of Dover sole on top, baked it in the oven, then put a little more hollandaise on top and put it under the grill. I scattered it with some soft fresh herbs and grated truffles, which happened to be in season, and it was just beautiful.

Serves 2

olive oil, for frying

2 medium black (Dover)
   soles, the 'skirt'
   trimmed and dark skin
   removed

50g butter, cut into
   pieces

juice of 2 lemons,
   1 juiced, 1 segmented

1 teaspoon capers

chopped parsley

Heat 2 large non-stick frying pans with a film of olive oil in each. Season the fish and put one into each pan, white skin-side down, and leave without touching for 4 minutes.

At this point, if you lift an edge, the underside of the fish should be golden brown.

Turn the fish over carefully, and add half the butter. Leave to cook for around 4 more minutes.

Insert the tip of a small sharp knife into the fish and when it is done you should see that the bone is clear and transparent, and no longer pink.

Remove the soles to serving plates and keep warm (resting briefly relaxes the fish and makes it easier to take out the bone).

Transfer the juices to one pan, add the rest of the butter and cook until it turns nut brown and smells fragrant. At this point add the lemon juice, which will stop the butter from cooking further – because the next stage after perfect brown is black!

Add the capers, chopped parsley and lemon segments, season to taste, pour over the sole and serve immediately.

Steamed Black Sole with Crab, Coconut, Apple and Lemongrass

This is another way of serving black (Dover) sole, unusual, but brilliant, rolled up around a filling of crab meat, apple, spring onions, chilli, mint and coriander. To make the green curry sauce in the authentic way – using the fatty cream of the coconut milk to fry the spice mix, rather than adding any oil – don't shake the cans of coconut milk or turn them over before you open them. You'll find when you open them that the milk has separated and settled into solid cream on top and liquid underneath, and you can easily spoon off the cream.

Although I love steaming fish, you could also bake the rolled, stuffed fillets in a lightly oiled ovenproof dish, with a good splash of white wine over the top. Cover the dish loosely with foil and put into a hot oven: 200°C/Gas 6. The cooking time will be the same as if you were steaming them: 8–10 minutes.

Start making the sauce. Put the ginger, lemongrass, garlic, chillies, shallots and coriander stalks into a blender and blend to a paste.

Smash up the crab shells and fry them in a large saucepan with a little vegetable oil until they are nicely coloured.

Carefully open the tins of coconut milk (do not shake them, and keep them the right way up). Spoon the cream from the top of the tins into a wok or large saucepan. At the same time, add the coconut water from the tins to the pan with the crab shells, bring to the boil and simmer for 5 minutes.

While the shells are simmering, heat the coconut cream over a gentle heat and let it melt. Add the spicy paste and cook gently for a couple of minutes until the spices release their aromas, taking care that the mixture doesn't catch and burn (if you are worried, you can add a touch of vegetable oil).

Tip the contents of the crab pan into the wok or pan with the paste, and stir well to combine. Simmer together for 5 minutes, then pass through a sieve. Check the seasoning and keep on one side.

Meanwhile, put the white crab meat into a bowl, checking carefully for any bits of shell.

Peel and grate the apple, finely chop the spring onions and chilli, and chop the mint and coriander (reserving a few leaves of each).

Serves 4

- 1 medium crab, cooked, claw meat removed and the body and shells reserved for the sauce
- vegetable oil, for frying
- 1 Granny Smith apple
- 2 spring onions
- 1 small red chilli, deseeded
- 2 sprigs of mint
- a small bunch of coriander, leaves picked, stalks and roots reserved for the sauce
- juice of 1 lime
- 2 black (Dover) sole, skinned and filleted (see previous recipe)

Sauce:

- 2.5cm piece fresh ginger
- 2 sticks lemongrass
- 2 cloves garlic
- 2 green chillies
- 2 shallots, chopped
- coriander stalks and roots (see above)
- 2 x 400ml tins coconut milk

Add all of this to the crab meat, mix well and season with a little salt. Add lime juice to taste, keeping some back for the sauce.

Lay the sole fillets flat with the skinned side upwards. Season lightly with salt and a little black pepper.

Place a spoonful of the crab mixture on each fillet, roll up tightly and secure with a cocktail stick.

Put the rolled up fillets on a plate, place in a steamer and cook for 8–10 minutes. Remove the cocktail stick from one of the fillets and make sure it is hot in the middle, which will tell you that everything is cooked through.

When the sole is almost ready, heat up the sauce and add lime juice to taste plus the reserved mint and coriander leaves.

Arrange the stuffed sole fillets on plates and serve with the sauce.

Poached Turbot with Grated Horseradish and Melted Butter

I always encourage the cooks in my kitchens to have a food book in their bags at all times; don't leave home without one. When I'm not working, a book or a food magazine is never far from my hand. No cook is born a genius; we all have to learn by sharing influences and ideas and recipes. You have to study and absorb in order to have opinions. I like people like Nigel Slater who have a profound understanding of their ingredients, or Richard Olney. I used to cut out pieces by Frances Bissell when she wrote for *The Times*, and I especially love to read the late Jane Grigson; such a scholarly writer. Elizabeth David was brilliant at getting the sheer pleasure of cooking and eating across, but Jane Grigson was hotter on theory and method and translating ideas to the table. Her little collection of books, are some of the best writing on food that has ever been produced.

Every time I open one of her books I discover a new recipe. Sometimes it will be something you might have glanced at a hundred times before it just jumps out at you. This one is based on a recipe from her beautiful *Fish Cookery* – she in turn based it on something she was served in a restaurant in Copenhagen: poached turbot, skin off, with some grated horseradish and melted butter poured over and hollandaise on the side. I'd serve it with a bowl of new potatoes, too.

To my knowledge, it hasn't appeared on a London menu before, but I'm sure that won't be the case soon: that is just the way ideas evolve and revolve in the big city, a great notion is never yours for very long. If you like, instead of the horseradish, you could serve it with a 'tapenade', of seaweed and olives. At certain times of the year seaweed takes on an almost liquoricey flavour, which makes the salad even more interesting, and a teaspoonful of English mustard really wakes up the flavour, in the same way as the Japanese might use wasabi. Dillisk is one of the seaweeds that works best, if you can find it.

Serves 4

40g butter, plus a knob for sautéeing

1 onion, finely chopped

1 leek, finely chopped

1 carrot, finely chopped

1 stick celery, finely chopped

1 bay leaf

a sprig of thyme

1 teaspoon fennel seeds

1 teaspoon coriander seeds

100ml white wine

50ml white wine vinegar

1 litre water

4 pieces of turbot, about 150g each

a good knob of fresh horseradish

To serve:

hollandaise sauce or seaweed tapenade (see opposite)

Heat the knob of butter in a large pan and sauté the onion, leek, carrot and celery for a few minutes. Add the bay leaf and thyme and stir in the fennel and coriander seeds. Pour in the white wine and vinegar and cook for a few more minutes. Add the water and bring to the boil, then turn down the heat and simmer for 30 minutes. Strain into a clean pan and bring back to a gentle simmer. Season the turbot, add to the pan, poach gently in the simmering liquor for 3–4 minutes, then take off the heat.

Melt the rest of the butter. Place the turbot on warm plates, grate some horseradish over the top, pour over a little melted butter and serve with hollandaise, or some seaweed tapenade alongside.

Hollandaise Sauce

Restaurant-style hollandaise is often made with a sabayon, which involves beating egg yolks and liquid in a bowl over a pan of simmering water to introduce air to the sauce and treble the mixture, making it foamy and quite light. This is fine for some recipes, but for something like the poached turbot what you want is a substantial, unctuous, velvety, buttery sauce that will coat the fish it is served with. It is also a much more straightforward method, which is pretty foolproof. The garlic béarnaise on page 214 is made in a similar way.

Makes enough for 6
225g butter
1 tablespoon white wine
2 tablespoons white wine vinegar
2 egg yolks
salt and cayenne pepper
lemon juice, to taste

To clarify the butter, melt it in a small pan, then carefully tip out the golden oil, leaving behind the milky residue, which you can throw away.

Put the wine and wine vinegar into a non-reactive pan. Bring to the boil, then turn down the heat and reduce until only a tablespoon is left in the pan. Take off the heat.

Stir in the egg yolks, then slowly pour in the clarified butter, whisking all the time, until all the butter is absorbed and the sauce starts to thicken.

Season with salt and a little cayenne. Taste, and if you want a little more acidity, add some lemon juice.

Seaweed Tapenade

Makes about 20 portions
250g mixed fresh seaweed, such as kelp, dillisk and laver
6 small shallots, finely chopped
a handful of good green olives
3 cloves garlic, chopped
100ml olive oil
1 tablespoon white wine vinegar
1 tablespoon English mustard

This will make around 500g, but what you don't use immediately you can keep in the fridge for a week. Eat it on toast, toss it through pasta – or it is brilliant on top of new potatoes.

Soak the seaweed to remove any sand, rinse under cold running water, dry in a cloth and chop very finely. Mix all the ingredients together in a bowl and keep in the fridge.

Fish and Chips with Mushy Peas and Hand-cut Tartare Sauce

I do think fish and chips, done right, is one of the most wonderful things in the world. There's nothing like it. But it has to have real character. Forget the chips for a minute: a piece of really fresh fish, in proper batter, with a touch of malt vinegar sprinkled over and hand-cut tartare sauce with hard-boiled egg grated in at the end – I'm sorry, that is one of the best things you'll ever eat. But it's a fine line you walk to get the balance right: the more you fry the batter, the crispier it gets (think of the little breakaway batter bits that have stayed in the hot oil through several fryings, that they sometimes serve you in bags in fish and chip shops). But the longer you fry your fish, the more you run the risk of destroying your great fresh fish inside. Cook your fish to perfection though and if you're not careful your batter won't be crunchy enough. That's why the batter recipe is so important.

As a rule you'd never ask an Irishman for a batter recipe. When I was young there were a few restaurants in Dublin where people might go for fish and chips, but overall it was never that big a thing in Ireland. But I reckon we now have the perfect batter, made with beer, in which the yeast works almost like it would in a bread mix and puffs up the batter – a thin, greasy batter is no good. In the oil it crisps up quickly and stays crisp. We use some rice flour in the batter, because it is very fine, doesn't have any gluten, and keeps the batter from getting too gooey and sticky; and as a result the batter is crisper. If you don't have any, substitute some more plain flour, but it is worth buying a bag of rice flour, as it makes a real difference.

This is such a favourite that we can never take it off the menu at Bentley's or change it. There was a day when I came in and one of the chefs wanted to do something different with the batter. We nearly had an official strike in the place, me included. Why, I said, would you want to tweak and tease and mess with it? Let tradition rule in these cases.

I've made fish and chips with gurnard recently, which is a much cheaper fish than haddock, and I was surprised at how brilliantly it works: no one would tell the difference.

But back to the chips. It isn't an easy thing to cook fish and chips perfectly for more than a couple of people, because unless you happen to have two fryers, you don't want the fish sitting around too long while you cook the chips. The best thing is to blanch the chips first at a quite low temperature, so they are soft but not coloured, then you can get them golden quite quickly in hotter oil when the fish has come out. If you need to keep the fish waiting for any longer than a few minutes you could wrap it in kitchen paper and put in a warm oven, but it really is best to eat it as quickly as possible after you've fried it.

Serves 4

4 pieces of haddock or
gurnard, skinned

vegetable oil, for
deep-frying

Batter:

10g fresh yeast

1 x 300ml bottle beer
(ale)

100g plain flour

80g rice flour

20g cornflour

10g salt

Chips:

1kg starchy potatoes

vegetable oil for
deep-frying

Mushy peas:

a little butter

1 onion, finely chopped

2 cloves garlic, crushed

1 stick celery, finely
chopped

250g dried marrowfat
peas, soaked overnight

1 teaspoon bicarbonate
of soda

100ml malt vinegar

Tartare sauce:

75g cornichons, drained
and coarsely chopped

75g small capers, drained

2 shallots, finely diced

1 tablespoon each finely
chopped parsley,
tarragon, chervil, and
chives

200ml mayonnaise

2 hard-boiled eggs

There are two secrets to great mushy peas. One is to resist stirring them as they cook (see below), the other is plenty of vinegar to lighten up the quite heavy pastiness of them. That vinegar flavour has a good old-fashioned rightness with the chips, too. If you like, you can cook the peas a few hours in advance, even overnight, and put them into the fridge. The taste will intensify and be even better, and as their starch cools they will thicken up even more, so when you reheat them, do it very gently, or they will burn.

For the mushy peas, heat the butter in a pan, add the onion, garlic and celery and cook gently until soft but not coloured. Drain the peas and add them to the pan, along with the bicarbonate of soda. Add enough water to cover by about 2.5cm. Bring to the boil, then turn down the heat and simmer for 1–1½ hours, topping up with more water if necessary. The crucial thing is not to stir the peas at all during cooking. Once you stir them, the outsides will start to break down, turning the water sludgy and unable to carry on cooking the peas properly. Stir them and you will end up with mushy outsides and hard insides. Once the peas are soft (test between your fingers), take off the heat and leave to cool. Now you can stir in the vinegar and a pinch of salt.

To make the tartare sauce, fold all the ingredients, except the eggs, into the mayonnaise and keep in the fridge until ready to serve.

For the batter, whisk the yeast into the beer, then whisk in the flours and salt. Allow to stand in a warm place for about 30 minutes, during which time it will puff up and bubble.

Meanwhile, peel the potatoes and rinse and dry them. Cut them as you like – we keep our chips quite chunky. Don't put the potatoes in water at this point or you will wash away the valuable starch that you need to prevent them cooking too quickly without softening properly. Preheat the oil to 140°C in a deep-fat fryer or large pan filled no more than one-third full. Put in the cut potatoes and cook for about 5 minutes, until they are soft but not coloured. Remove and drain on kitchen paper.

Reheat the peas if necessary and keep warm. Grate the eggs and mix loosely into the tartare sauce.

Increase the temperature of the oil to 170°C. Dip the fish into the batter and lower it into the oil. Because the fish is quite heavy in its batter it will want to sink at first, and the oil won't envelop it properly, so support it lightly with a fish slice or spider until the yeast in the batter puffs it up and it floats by itself. Fry for about 4 minutes, until golden and crispy, then lift out and drain on kitchen paper.

Increase the temperature of the oil to 180°C, put in the blanched chips, and cook until golden. Serve with the fish, mushy peas and tartare sauce.

Salt Cod
'Scotch Eggs'
with Aioli

I love the relationship between the Mediterranean and northern Europe: one had the salt, the other had the cod, so all over Europe you have salt cod recipes. In France salt cod is *morue*, in Italy *baccala*, in Spain *bacalao* and in Portugal *bacalhau*.

There are all kinds of recipes, from stewing the cod with tomatoes and onions or frying it, to poaching it and then puréeing it with milk and olive oil, in the French *brandade*. In some regions they also add potato to *brandade*, which I like, because I never need much of an invitation to add the spud. I was looking for a salt cod recipe, and then one day I was having a conversation with Mark Wogan, who is my agent and loves his food. He was talking about *bacalao* and poached egg, which got me thinking about moulding *brandade* around quail's eggs, as if you were making a Scotch egg, and deep-frying them. Having the potato in the mixture helps to bind everything and lets it cling to the egg brilliantly.

When you cut into them, you get the crunch of the breadcrumbs, then the flaky fish and mash, and then the beautiful soft yolk of the egg oozing out in the centre. You don't really need the twenty-four quail's eggs I've listed here, but they are tricky things to peel, once cooked, and you'll find you break some, no question … but think of them as the cook's perk, and just eat them with a bit of salt – delicious. Some time after my conversation with Mark I was chatting to the former head chef from Harry's Bar in Venice, when he told me he thought the secret of a beautiful tasting purée of salt cod was to use a really light, flowery olive oil; and he's right.

The salt cod really needs soaking over three days, so you'll need to plan ahead; however, you can make up the Scotch eggs the night before you need them, keep them in the fridge, and then all you have to do is fry and serve them. Like real Scotch eggs, they are also good cold.

Every European country has its version of aioli. In parts of Spain it is traditionally thickened with stale bread soaked in water, but if you prefer, you can substitute a whole egg and egg yolk. I wouldn't use an extra virgin olive oil for this, as it is too heavy and might cause the sauce to split. A light olive oil is better.

Serves 4
500g dried salt cod
4 large floury potatoes
50ml light olive oil
24 quail's eggs
white wine vinegar
   (to help peel the quail's
   eggs)
4 hen's eggs
100g flour
200g stale breadcrumbs
vegetable oil, for
   deep-frying

Aioli:
2 slices of stale bread,
   crusts removed, soaked
   in a little water
2 cloves garlic, crushed
zest and juice of 1 lemon
200ml olive oil

Place the cod in a bowl of cold water and leave in the fridge for 3 days, changing the water at least once a day. Remove from the water and pat dry. Cut into cubes.

Cook the potatoes in boiling salted water, drain and mash.

Warm the olive oil in a pan, add the salt cod and cook for 2 minutes over a very low heat. Turn over and cook for another 2 minutes on the other side.

Add the mashed potato to the pan. Flake the fish with the back of a fork. It will fall apart and the potato will soak up the oil, so you end up with a thick paste. Now set aside to cool.

Bring a large pan of water to the boil, lower in the quail's eggs and cook for about 3 minutes – they should be just soft. Remove from the boiling water and put into a bowl of white wine vinegar, which will soften the shell and should make them easier to peel. Leave to cool. Once they are cool, peel immediately – they won't all be perfect, but hopefully you will end up with 12 good ones and you can eat the rest with a bit of salt.

Take a little of the salt cod mixture at a time in the palm of your hand, make a dent in the centre, put in a quail's egg, close up your hand so that you cover the egg with the rest of the mixture, and roll it in your hands into an egg shape. Lay on a plate or tray lined with clingfilm or parchment paper and put in the fridge for an hour to firm up.

Meanwhile, make the aioli. Squeeze the water from the bread and put it into a food processor with the garlic, a good pinch of salt and the lemon zest and juice. Blend together and then gradually add the oil a little at a time, as if making mayonnaise. Adjust the seasoning to taste. Keep in the fridge while you finish off the 'Scotch eggs'.

Beat the hen's eggs in a shallow bowl, and have the flour and breadcrumbs in similar separate bowls. Dip each 'Scotch egg' first in the flour, then into the egg and then into the breadcrumbs.

Preheat the vegetable oil to 175°C in a deep-fat fryer or large pan filled no more than one-third full. Lower in the 'Scotch eggs' and fry for about 2 minutes until golden brown all over.

Drain briefly on kitchen paper and serve with the aioli.

More than
Mediterranean

In the nineties we all fell in love with the food of the Mediterranean, but everything can't be about Italy and Spain. I like the influences of middle and Eastern Europe. I love the marinated herrings of Scandinavia and Latvia; the great cake making of Vienna. A chocolate éclair with a cup of coffee has to be one of the most delicious things in the world. I feel like a little boy that has just robbed the pantry when I put an éclair in my mouth. You know you shouldn't but…

In Poland I've seen fabulous sauerkraut soup being made in the traditional way: broth, with the leftover ferment from the rye bread whisked into it, to give it a slight sourness. I've also seen carp being smoked by fishermen around a lake; wonderful bread to rival Poilâne, made with mashed potato, that filled the kitchen with an alcoholic aroma (shades of poteen), and, in a defining moment, tapped fresh birch juice, which is like drinking an upmarket cordial, but for free, from a tree. Awesome. If that doesn't make you feel close to the earth, nothing will.

My first job outside of Ireland, where I had started cooking at the local Kirwan Arms, was in the Netherlands. I like the Dutch and their simple food and cooking. They tend to be straight-talking individuals who don't pretend to be great gourmands, but they have some wonderful delicacies that they are rightly proud of, like new season fat herring, and their liquorice, made in traditional sweet-making shops in Amsterdam. I went there when I was in my late teens and worked in a series of Michelin-starred restaurants for two or three years. It was in the Netherlands that I educated myself, not just about food, but about life. I was very aware that much as I was enthused about food, my education as a child in Ireland had come to a bit of a sudden end, and left a lot to be desired. When we moved out of the farm and into the bungalow, I went to school in the town of Athboy until I was caught red-handed, lighting up a cigarette under an oil tank. It was a miracle that I didn't blow the place sky high, and no surprise that I was thrown out. Amazingly, my parents never found out. I managed to get myself into the local Technical School. My sister, who was good at that sort of thing, wrote a formal letter to the principal and I was in. I still got the same bus every morning. I just went to a different school.

While I was there, I also worked for a neighbouring farmer, Frank Joyce. I helped with the milking, morning and evening. Frank was very organised. He taught me a lot, including the great lesson that it's a good idea to pay generously for good work. In 1978 I was making £70 a week as a part-time farm labourer and I was flush. I can still see the teacher's face when I pulled out a wad of notes to pay for the school trip to France.

By the time I was fourteen-and-a-half, I had had enough of school but had no idea of what to do next. Out of the blue, my dad said maybe I should think about working as a chef for his old friend Ray Vaughan at the Kirwan Arms Hotel in Athboy. We had been there once, when I was about ten, for a celebration dinner. I remember I had sat in the dining room and thought, 'Yes, I feel I belong here.' Besides which, nobody took jobs for granted in 1970s Ireland so I left school the following Friday and turned up for work in the kitchen on the Monday.

My first day was a bit of a disaster. I was a hard worker, but I wanted to be seen to be a hard worker. I was so enthusiastic, I managed to throw a bucket of mop water all over a guest who happened to be passing the back door just at the wrong time.

I was sure I was going to get the sack, but I survived. Ray believed that nobody can learn if he's terrified of making mistakes; I certainly made them, but he managed to make something good out of most of what I cooked, which only reinforced the values I had learned at home: that you never waste anything, if you can help it.

It was Ray who helped me to get the job in Amsterdam, and I was on a mission to learn as much as possible. I felt that to say I wasn't good at school or to blame my dyslexia was a bit of a poor excuse, frankly. Dyslexia is a curse but also a blessing. If you're dyslexic you learn to memorise huge amounts of information. You have to.

I do believe that ignorance is self-inflicted, because wherever you go you can immerse yourself in culture. I didn't want to be the kind of cook that wasn't able to discuss a novel by James Joyce or Flann O'Brien, and in Amsterdam the people I was hanging out with were smart dudes. The nights started after you finished work. We'd go to listen to music – jazz, folk – and talk about writers, poetry and politics. I was quite political in those days, but Amsterdam mellowed me a bit. I went out a Republican and came back a nationalist and a socialist.

I only really discovered the way I felt about my own country by living outside it. Being in a crazy place like Amsterdam, which had been a bastion for refugees, political, religious and otherwise, for many centuries, gave me time to think. Ireland when I left it during 'the troubles' of the seventies was as close to meltdown as any country in Europe could have been. Strangers can often argue and then sit down and do a deal, but when very close families squabble there is a lot of bitterness involved, and I think the Irish and the English are much closer than ever we imagined, which is why it took thirty-five years for everyone to sit down together aound a table. Certainly, now, the English artisans I meet who are living in Ireland are often more attracted to the country than the Irish themselves, and they lead the way in terms of alternative lifestyles. Like all incomers over the years, from the Vikings down, they usually end up more Irish than the Irish.

Amsterdam really defined me and the way I feel about things. I'm a working-class guy from a family who were never going to vote Fine Gael or Tory; I hate pretension and bullshit, and people who look down their nose at other races and religions. What's wrong with just being kind and hospitable and generous, and giving people, and countries who need it, a hand up?

I like a bit of adventure, I'm a bit of a wanderer, so on my day off I'd get on a bike and cycle around the country. On our nights off, though, we'd party all night, then we'd wind up at the Hotel de l'Europe, which was Freddie Heineken's hotel; the Amstel, or the American Hotel in Leidseplein, which were pretty posh places, for the massive buffet breakfasts in the morning. We were always polite and tipped well, and they got so used to us they would reserve places for us in the corner. 'Good morning, Mr Corrigan…' and we'd sit there drinking juice and tucking in for hours before we finally crept off to get some sleep.

In terms of cooking, I devoured the craftsmanship, the spirit of the kitchen. I still have all the notes. Game in particular was fabulous. One dish stands out from my time cooking at the restaurant Les Quatre Canetons: saddle of hare with a soft stuffing of chestnuts and breadcrumbs, browned off, tied up beautifully, roasted, brought to the table in a big copper pan, and served with Brussels sprouts and pumpkin. I had never tasted food as accomplished as that. There was a great pheasant dish, finished with apples and Calvados. Many of the dishes were ahead of their time, but for all their haute cuisine status, it wasn't fine art, just good food you really wanted to eat.

My sister was over in Amsterdam for a while, too, with her friend Maria, a student nurse who is now my wife… and the reason that instead of going off to cook in Geneva, I came home. I went back to Ireland in late '87 for about three weeks, but nothing much was happening there at that time. There was a real sense of people just living on their survival instincts, very little money and a lack of real energy and decision-making. So I decided to head for London.

I had a job at the Sheraton Park Tower Hotel in Knightsbridge, and I arrived in the week of the great storm. I was living in Hanwell, and I walked all the way to Knightsbridge. I was the only person who turned up in the kitchen. The manager brought me a bottle of Champagne to say thank you for coming; but we're not opening today. I guess that tells you something about my instincts for getting on with the job. I wasn't about to let a load of fallen trees and no public transport stop me.

How to Prepare
Octopus and Squid

Squid

Put your hand inside the body and pull out the tentacles. The innards, including the plastic-looking quill, should also come out. Cut off the tentacles from in front of the eyes, squeeze out the beak with your thumbs and discard, along with everything else, except the tentacles. Pull away the two wings attached to the body. As you do this the membrane will probably come away too, otherwise pull it off. Wash well. If you are opening up the squid to grill or barbecue, slit the body lengthways along the 'seam' and open out (if you are doing this it is easier to open it out first, then wash it). If you like, you can score the body in a criss-cross pattern with a sharp knife – but be careful not to cut all the way through.

Octopus

Cut the tentacles from the head, just in front of the eyes. Cut off the 'swimming cap'-like head above the eyes. Turn this inside out and pull away the innards, including the stomach sac, and the bone-like sticks. Remove the membrane. It should come off in one easy pull. Turn it back again, right side out, and keep to one side.

Find the beak in the middle of the tentacles and push it out with both thumbs. If it is a big octopus, remove the heavy membrane from the tentacles. It won't all come off, but don't worry. It will soften during cooking, and it is the bits of membrane that give the octopus its lovely purpley colour. Wash well, drain and chop.

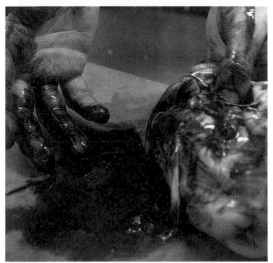

Stuffed Baby Squid with Chorizo and Feta-style Cheese

When I buy uncooked chorizos I like to pre-cook them a little, just heating them through in a pot of water or wine, to draw excess fat off them before I carry on with whatever dish I am doing. I used to watch my mother and my auntie doing the same thing with fresh sausages in Ireland. They would always pre-cook them briefly, and then put them into the fridge. It made them keep a little longer and gave them a slightly different texture, which was very enjoyable.

In this recipe, as well as the chorizo we use a feta-like, barrel-fermented sheep's cheese from the Pyrenees. You can no longer call cheeses like this 'feta', because in 2005 Greek producers won their case for Protected Designation of Origin status, and now within the EU a cheese is 'feta' only if it is made in Greece from ewe's milk following traditional methods.

In the restaurant we sometimes serve the squid complete with tentacles with garlic butter and mussels, but they are good with a big bowl of salad and potatoes.

Serves 4

200g uncooked chorizo

white wine, for cooking the chorizo

200g feta or feta-style cheese

20 baby squid tubes, cleaned (see page 96)

vegetable oil, for frying

1–2 tablespoons good extra virgin olive oil

Preheat the oven to 180°C/Gas 4.

Put the chorizo into a saucepan with enough white wine to cover, bring to the boil, then turn down the heat and simmer for 5 minutes. Leave the chorizo to cool down in the pan.

When cool, take out the chorizo, peel off the skins and chop into small dice. Chop the cheese into similar-sized dice and mix with the chorizo. Spoon the cheese and chorizo into the squid tubes, to about three-quarters full.

Have an ovenproof dish warming in the oven. Heat a large frying pan that will transfer to the oven, put in a film of vegetable oil and when fiercely hot cook the squid in batches, searing them for 1 minute on one side, then turning them over for another minute (if you try to cook too many at once, you will bring the temperature of the oil down and the squid will boil and toughen, rather than sear). Sear the tentacles if using.

As each one is done, transfer it to the dish in the oven. When the last squid are cooked, transfer them in their frying pan to the oven and leave them for a final 2 minutes, then drizzle them all with a little olive oil and serve.

Chorizo and Seafood

Spicy, complex sausages and seafood are one of those happy little culinary marriages that really wake up the palate. A bowl of mini chorizos with a plate of rock oysters on a summer evening with a nice bottle of wine: perfect. I wouldn't use natives, because the sausage would kill their flavour. Chorizo is great with squid, too. The little chorizos are by far the best. We get ours from Brindisa, who now have shops in Exmouth Market, Borough Market and Kensington in London. The company was started twenty years ago by Monika Linton and her brother Mark Lavery. Mark was working in Barcelona, while Monika was teaching in the foothills of the Pyrenees. When she came back home Monika was frustrated that there was nowhere to buy the cured meats and cheeses and oils that she had been enjoying in Spain. So, on a shoestring, with an early band of Brindisa devotees, and with Mark's help, she started bringing over foods from small artisan producers. As much as anything, the teacher in her wanted to educate people about great Spanish produce.

When I was cooking with Stephen Bull at Blandford Street, we were one of the first to open an account with Brindisa, along with chefs like Alastair Little and Simon Hopkinson. At the time, to see all this food being brought into their warehouse in Bankside, ingredients that were definitely not aimed at the Torremolinos brand of customer, was fascinating, and to be able to put out plates of pata negra (black pig) ham and fat anchovies was very exciting.

I have attempted to make chorizo myself, and the result wasn't too bad, but you really need that cool, dry, local Spanish air to dry the sausages, and the particular local *pimentón* (paprika) that has been used for generations and gives the chorizo its special aromatic flavour and natural coppery-rust colour.

The best meat for chorizo, according to Monika, is the redder lean meat from the rib area of the pig, between the belly fat and the ribs, as well as cuts from the fore leg, which is juicier than the hind leg. The best producers cut their meat by hand and then add some belly fat, because you need about 30 per cent fat. Cheaper chorizos tend to be more gristly, she reckons, because they have been made from less fine cuts of meat. Many consider Iberico chorizo, so called because it is made from the Iberian pata negra pig, which feeds on acorns, to be the best quality, though you can also find good ones from Rioja, León and Asturias.

When you buy chorizo, look for ones made with traditional animal intestine, which will be quite thick and the sausages will be irregular in shape. Because the intestine is permeable both ways, the sausage is able to cure naturally over a long time and will have a more intense flavour than industrially made chorizos, which are fast-cured inside man-made casings, uniform in shape and often contain preservatives, flavourings and colourings, resulting in a garish pinky-red colour and sometimes what Monika calls a 'petrolly, chemical aftertaste'.

You can buy fresh chorizos, which have been cured for only a few days and need to be cooked. Because they haven't dried out through long curing, their juices come out into the dish better. Other chorizos, usually the hoop-shaped ones, have been cured for a relatively short time, about a month, and can be used for both cooking and eating as they are. Longer-cured chorizos (often up to five months) tend to be firmer and more expensive and are best simply sliced and eaten as they are with good bread.

Braised Octopus

This is the best way to cook an octopus, steaming it very slowly in olive oil, white wine and vinegar, which tenderises it and infuses it with flavour. Once it is cooked you can eat it hot, leave it to get cold and serve it with a salad, or keep it in the fridge and braise it again the next day in a little stew with chickpeas, beans or tomatoes, whatever you like. A great way to eat it hot is to mix in some chopped parsley, chopped chilli and lemon zest, and serve it as a tapa.

The way they do it in Galicia in northern Spain is to boil or steam some small potatoes, peel and slice them, then warm a little of the liquor from cooking the octopus in a pan with some paprika, pour it over the potatoes and serve the octopus on top.

If you let the octopus cool down you could serve it with a little salad made with about three blood oranges, segmented, and some mixed leaves, including peppery rocket. Use the juice of another blood orange to make a dressing, mixing it with a spoonful of the octopus cooking liquor (which contains oil), a pinch of sea salt and some black pepper. Toss the orange segments and leaves through the dressing, along with a handful of salted almonds and some chopped up, sharp little cornichons, and serve with the octopus.

Serves 4

1.5kg octopus, cleaned (see page 96) and cut into large pieces
300ml olive oil
100ml white wine
100ml white wine vinegar

Preheat the oven to 150°C/Gas 2.

Put the octopus into a large pot and add the rest of the ingredients. Lay a 'cartouche' (a circle of greaseproof paper), on top of the ingredients, then cover the top of the pot with tin foil so that it is completely sealed. The idea is that the cartouche keeps as much moisture as possible inside the octopus as it cooks but also protects it from any 'taint' from the foil, which, in turn, helps keep an even temperature inside the pot and creates a perfect steamy atmosphere for the octopus to cook.

Put into the oven for about 3–4 hours, until the octopus is tender. If you insert the tip of a knife it should go into the flesh easily, but with just a bit of resistance. Take the pot out of the oven and leave the octopus to cool down in the cooking liquor.

Mixed Steamed Fish and Green Curry

When I bought a little electric steamer for Bentley's there was nearly uproar from all the cooks. They thought I was taking their skills away from them. Now it's there they think it is the most fantastic thing that was ever put in a kitchen, because when you are running a busy service and you have to keep an eye on everything, you can't go wrong with it: it's out of the way of the stoves, you set a timer and you get a perfect piece of steamed fish every time.

Steamed fish is the most fantastic thing: it tastes great and it gives you such a good, healthy feeling when you eat it. This recipe is one of Brendan's ideas. Brendan Fyldes is the head chef of the restaurant, and he spent some time in Thailand soaking up ideas. Everyone loves it, and it is so easy to do, with or without an electric steamer. It's worth buying some cheap bamboo steaming baskets (as used for Chinese dim sum) because they look fantastic when you bring them to the table.

We make the green curry sauce in the same way as for the black sole recipe (see page 82). Then we make a bed of lemongrass, shredded ginger, spring onions and coriander in the base of the steaming basket and put a selection of bite-sized pieces of fish and shellfish on top: red mullet, sea bass, gurnard steaks, pieces of squid, some scallops and king prawns.

We steam everything for about 2 minutes, then serve the fish with lime juice squeezed over it and coriander leaves scattered over the top, with the green curry sauce and sticky rice on the side.

Bentley's
Fish Soup

This is such a rich soup, you really don't need cheese sprinkled over the top the way the French like to do it. Go to your fishmonger and ask for fish heads, which are wonderfully gelatinous and full of fleshy bits around the cheeks. This is what gives the soup its flavour, rather than big pieces of fish, which can give a stewed, sardine-paste taste to the soup, especially if it has been simmered for ages. If you want to add larger pieces of fish, they really have to be cooked separately and added in at the end. The main thing is not to overcook the soup. A great fish soup should taste freshly of fish.

Serves 4

1kg mixed fish heads and any bones your fishmonger may have

a little olive oil

500ml water

rouille (see opposite) and pieces of toasted bread (croutons), to serve

Marinade:

1 onion, diced

1 carrot, diced

1 head of fennel, diced

1 stick celery, diced

2 cloves garlic, crushed

2 x 400g tins chopped tomatoes

6 extra-ripe tomatoes, chopped

50ml Pernod

250ml dry white wine

1 teaspoon fennel seeds

1 teaspoon coriander seeds

4 star anise

1 tablespoon black peppercorns

a pinch of saffron

1 teaspoon sugar

1 teaspoon salt

Mix all the marinade ingredients, except the sugar and salt, in a large saucepan. Add the fish heads and bones and marinate for 24 hours.

The next day, preheat the oven to 200°C/Gas 6.

Remove the heads and bones from the marinade and place on a roasting tray. Drizzle with a little olive oil and roast for 20–30 minutes until nicely browned.

Add the water to the pan containing the marinade. Bring to the boil, then turn down the heat and simmer for around 15 minutes until the vegetables have softened. Add the sugar and salt and taste. The trick is to get the seasoning right at this point as it will bring out the flavour of the fish better, and you don't want to find yourself having to add salt at the end.

Add the roasted fish trimmings to the pan and simmer for another 15 minutes, no longer. Put through a large sieve, pressing the fish trimmings through with the back of a ladle or the end of a rolling pin.

Keep the soup hot while you make the rouille to serve with it, along with the croutons.

Rouille

If you are making this to serve with fish soup, it really makes it quite special if you mix a little of the finished soup into the rouille. At any other time, just leave it out.

Makes enough for 12
100ml fish soup
  (optional, see opposite)
a pinch of saffron
1 tablespoon mashed
  potato
2 egg yolks
1 clove garlic, crushed
a pinch of dried chilli or
  a few drops of Tabasco
250ml olive oil
lemon juice

Pour the fish soup into a small saucepan and reduce by half to intensify the flavour. Add the saffron. Allow to cool, then put into a food processor along with the mashed potato, egg yolks, garlic and chilli or Tabasco.

Blend together and, with the motor running slowly, pour in the oil, as if making mayonnaise.

Add lemon juice and salt to taste.

Bentley's
Fish Pie

Our fish pie has been voted the best in London, and I think it's a joy to eat: quite dry, floury mash covering oozy sauce, and the fish just cooked inside it.

If you like, you can make the sauce the night before. Put it in a bowl, cover it with clingfilm to stop a skin forming, and keep it in the fridge. Traditionally the mashed potato on top of a fish pie is piped, as it creates ridges, so you get nice crispy bits of potato, and it seals in the sauce neatly – it's worth doing because if you spoon on the potato, you tend to get sauce mixed into it. However, if you don't want to use a piping bag, spoon on the potato and run over it with the prongs of a fork. We make individual pies, which ensures that everyone gets a good mix of fish, and it's quite a craft making twenty or so of them a day, but of course you can make one large one instead, and cook it for a bit longer, about 30 minutes.

Remove the skin from the fish and cut into bite-sized pieces, reserving the skin of the smoked haddock for the sauce.

To start the sauce, heat a little butter in a saucepan, add the onion, garlic and thyme and sweat until softened. Add the white wine and the smoked haddock trimmings and cook for a few minutes to burn off the alcohol. Add the milk and bring to just under the boil, then take the pan from the heat, pass the contents through a sieve into a bowl and keep hot.

Melt the 100g butter in a heavy saucepan, add the flour and cook over a low heat, stirring well, for 5 minutes. Pour the hot infused milk into the pan and whisk vigorously until the mixture is smooth and thick. Taste to make sure you can't taste the flour. If you can, let it cook gently for a little longer.

Whisk in the mustard and add the chives and parsley. Check the seasoning and add salt and pepper and more mustard if you wish. Leave to cool down while you make the mash – it is best not to assemble the pie with hot sauce as it will cook the fish too quickly.

Preheat the oven to 180°C/Gas 4.

Peel the potatoes and cook in boiling salted water until tender. Drain in a colander and allow the potatoes to steam for a couple of minutes to rid them of excess moisture, then mash and season with salt and pepper. Add the egg yolks.

Serves 4

1kg fish fillets, including salmon, smoked haddock and white fish such as pollack and haddock (the smoked haddock trimmings will be used in the sauce)

1.5kg floury potatoes

2 egg yolks

Sauce:

100g butter, plus a little extra for sweating the vegetables

1 onion, diced

2 cloves garlic, crushed

a sprig of thyme

150ml wine glass of white wine

smoked haddock trimmings (see above)

2 litres milk

100g plain flour

1 tablespoon English mustard

a handful of chives and parsley, chopped

To finish:

a little lemon juice

a little green Tabasco sauce

a handful of fresh breadcrumbs

a little grated Parmesan

Scoop the mash into a piping bag – it needs to be hot in order to pipe easily. (If you prefer not to pipe it, spoon it on carefully, then plough lines across it with the prongs of a fork.)

To assemble, spoon a little of the sauce into the bottom of each of 4 pie dishes. Arrange a selection of fish on top of the sauce. Season with salt and pepper, a squeeze of lemon juice and a few drops of green Tabasco – the colour looks great.

Completely cover with sauce, then pipe or spoon on the mash. Mix together the breadcrumbs and Parmesan and sprinkle evenly over the pies.

Place the pie dishes on a baking sheet and cook for around 20 minutes until the top is golden brown and the centre of each pie is good and hot – push a skewer into the centre and it should come out hot to the touch. Serve immediately.

Bentley's 'Royal' Fish Pie

This is our truly decadent 'rich man's fish pie', as I call it, because we have to sell it for a royal price. It came about when one of our customers at Bentley's said, 'I love the fish pie, but if only you had lobsters and scallop in there … I'm not worried about the price.' So I said, fine, we'll put it on the menu. Now we probably make twenty-five a day and they sell out every time. In the restaurant we make good use of all the lobster shells to make the Sauce Americaine, but you could do a simpler version, using 2 lobsters, plus 2 cooked and peeled langoustines per person, 2 scallops per person, and some chunky white crab meat to give an extra sweetness.

Despatch the lobsters and cut up in the same way as for the sauté of lobster with chilli, garlic and coriander on page 147. Sauté them, shell-side down, in a film of olive oil in a large frying pan, to colour the shells, then take out the meat – it should come out easily.

Keep the meat on one side, then, to make the sauce, put the shells back into the pan, add a tablespoon of tomato paste, cook for 5 more minutes, then flambé with 50ml of brandy. Add 1 litre of double cream, bring to a simmer and cook for 15–20 minutes. Pass through a rough sieve, pushing all the liquid through, and cool.

Now you can assemble the fish pie in the same way as the Bentley's fish pie on page 108. I would make one big one. Yes, it's a bit pricey, but what a great dish to serve to friends when they come round to dinner. A big, sumptuous pie in the middle of the table with a big bowl of salad and a nice bottle of wine; great grub.

Shellfish

The coastal waters of Britain and Ireland, with their particular eco-system, are some of the best in the world for growing shellfish, from our lobsters and crabs in the south-west of England to our langoustines in the north, mussels and sea urchins from Bantry Bay, whelks from Wicklow, and oysters from Galway Bay to Colchester. There was a time when we rarely saw any of our native seafood, because it was all being exported. It's been a long time coming, but now at last there is a new awareness of what native treasure we have, and we are starting to grab more of this fabulous bounty before it leaves for foreign shores. And it's about time; it really is.

As always, though, we have to temper our enthusiasm with respect for what we have and what we could lose if we don't take care of the ocean. Scientists are concerned about seas turning more acidic as they soak up carbon dioxide emissions. That can alter the oxygen levels in the water, but also, when the carbon dioxide dissolves, it forms carbonic acid, which attacks calcium carbonate, the mineral in seawater that shellfish use to build their shells and skeletons.

And then there's our worldwide greediness, which is a problem for shellfish populations everywhere. You can harvest, but you can't just pillage on the scale that we have been doing. Whenever the super-trawlers go out fishing for prawns, they throw away about 10 kilos of other fish for every kilo of prawns they land. And to satisfy the demand for tiger prawns, thousands of miles of coastal mangrove forests have been destroyed and the eco-systems, and the fishermen and their families they support, have been ruined.

I met a guy down in Bantry Bay who is raising sea urchins. I've always loved sea urchins. The Japanese tempura them and serve them with pork belly, and you can put them with things like scrambled eggs, but I love them raw. You crack them like a boiled egg and scoop out the five yellow gonads, the reproductive organs, with a teaspoon. It's the most incredible delicacy.

This producer in Bantry grows the urchins from seeds in laboratory tanks, then plants out the hatchlings into rock pools. It's an awesome operation, but he admitted that he started doing it because he felt so guilty that he had spent the last twenty years or so selling hundreds of tonnes of urchins abroad, and then realised there were none left. It's the wild salmon scenario over again: we can't go on taking and taking, and expecting nature to keep giving.

Oysters

I'm very much an oyster snob, I'll be honest with you. Not in the sense of oysters being an elite food – I'm all for demystifying them and restoring them to their traditional place as a food of the people. But I'm snobbish about them in the sense of championing the wild oyster over the cultivated rock oyster. Wild oysters, or natives as they are known, rule the day. The native is just perfection. It has to be polished and loved and served on a bed of seaweed or ice, whereas I look at a rock oyster and I think, 'Cook you. You're for the deep-fat fryer.'

Don't get me wrong, we get really good rock oysters; we bring them in from Donegal as well as from English waters, but they just don't have that real marine flavour that a native has. The big advantage of the rock is that you can have them all year round, and some people even prefer them to natives, because they are bigger and not as expensive, but for me their true value is that without them we wouldn't have our hot oyster dishes, because I wouldn't cook a native. And cooked oysters are beautiful: deep-fried tempura rock oysters in a honey dressing with loads of black pepper mixed into it is one of the simple delicacies of life – gorgeous, really gorgeous. Bentley's was one of the first fish restaurants to serve the American style of hot oyster dishes back in the thirties, so we are proud to keep up the tradition.

The point is we are talking about two completely different products: the rock oyster is cultivated; the native is wild and only available in season. And I always have huge respect for food from the wild. Portuguese rock oysters were introduced to fisheries around the south coast and Essex in the early 1900s, but it wasn't until disease almost wiped out the native in the 1920s that the rocks were brought in in any quantity. This time they came from Japan and south-east Asia and they were such a success they took over the market. Rock oysters at first couldn't spawn here because the waters were too cold, so they had to be farmed, but they grow easily around our islands and they are quite hardy. For many years they were virtually all you could get, and people nearly forgot about the natives.

Rock oysters aren't intensively farmed, I know. We're not comparing them to industrially produced chickens here; they are more akin to farmed venison, where the animals are able to roam free. But who are we fooling? The flavours of farmed venison don't come anywhere near a piece of wild roe in my book, and nor does a rock oyster come near a native.

When Fergus Henderson and Trevor Gulliver of St John came to Bentley's, Trevor said to me he was surprised we didn't have a selection of French oysters on our list. Well, it might be an English tavern owned by an Irishman ... but to have French oysters! When the French go on about their oysters, I really have to stand up and say, 'Ours are as good.' Or actually I would say ours are better.

Fair enough, in reality you can't get too patriotic about your oysters, because the native oyster world is a big one around Europe and sometimes you have to bring them in from where they are best. But the coastal waters of Mersea Island, off the coast of Essex near Colchester, are perfect for growing oysters, and the ones we get from there are hand-picked for us and just magnificent. There have been oyster beds there since the days of the Romans, and in Victorian times they were so cheap and plentiful that even the poorest families would stew them, cook them in pies with beef, or pickle them. The original Bentley family had their own oyster beds in West Mersea, which is why they opened the restaurant, back in 1916, in the first place. Twenty years ago, though, you couldn't eat them, because pollution and disease and over-fishing had wrecked the beds. Scientists liken oysters to the canaries that used to be taken down the coalmines to test the conditions, because they are a barometer of the health of the sea. They feed by filtering phytoplankton from the water, so they contribute hugely to keeping the waters clean, and if your oysters are contaminated you know you have a problem. American expert Roger Newell reckons that in Chesapeake Bay, the biggest estuary in the US, back in 1879 the population of oysters was large enough to filter and cleanse the entire volume of the bay in three days.

In the days when you couldn't buy a native from around Colchester, I used to buy mine from Carlingford Lough or Strangford Lough in Northern Ireland. Ireland has always been a special place for oysters, and they have a special place in an Irishman's heart. In *The English, the French and the Oyster*, a lovely book written in 1995 by Robert Neild, who is a retired Cambridge Professor of Economics and a regular at Bentley's, he tells a story about how some years after the famine, when private oyster beds began to be allowed, Archbishop McHale of Tuam set up a fishery at Achill Sound thinking there was good money to be made, but of course everyone was robbing the oysters from under his nose, and the curate looking after the fishery just turned a blind eye.

Now you can't buy oysters from those loughs any more, actually because the area was plundered for whelks for the Asian market, rather than oysters, so much of the water has been turned into a conservation area. But, by contrast, around Colchester the oyster beds have been revitalised and we can carry on the great tradition of eating the bounty of the sea. The first thing I did when I came back to Bentley's was reinstate all those old contracts with the small companies that had been proudly selling oysters to us decades ago. It's great to have that kind of lineage reaching back to the past again.

I feel the same kind of reverence waiting for the natives as I do for asparagus. Waiting and waiting. Then the oysters arrive, and it is up to us to keep up their magnificence, which means doing very little to them. The ultimate for me is a plate of natives on their own, with maybe a bit of black pepper and a touch of lemon. That's it. Tabasco, tomato and horseradish, or sauce mignonette (minced shallot and red wine vinegar), are fine with a larger rock oyster, but nowhere near the native, please. When I first cooked at Bentley's years ago, it was the older customers, the ones who really know their oysters, and for whom I have the utmost respect, who showed me how to eat native oysters. To them, asking for mignonette with a native oyster would be as embarrassing as wanting ketchup with a lovely steak au poivre: 'Are you a philistine?' they'd say.

The French like to serve their oysters still attached to the muscle, but I like them to float off the half shell and into my mouth like a ship off the dock. And you should eat an oyster in three bites, not swallow it straight down. When you chew an oyster it's much more enjoyable, it really is.

I am very proud of the oyster bar we've created at Bentley's. A great oyster bar is pure indulgence, and there's a lovely buzz about the place. You can just come in, sit up at the bar, let the oyster barman open you up half a dozen natives, have a glass of Chablis and enjoy yourself. Of course, it doesn't have to be Chablis, but there is a perfect little harmony in the idea of eating oysters and drinking wine from vineyards that are founded on limestone rocks made up of fossilised oyster shells.

The *Sunday Times* critic Adrian Gill really summed it up for me when he came to review the place just after I re-opened it and wrote that, 'The room was full of fat men doing body maintenance, with beatific smiles on their many faces. It was the happiest bar in London.' It was a bit of a male kind of domain back then, but there are a lot more women coming in now and that's great. I really want to see oyster bars opening up again in London for a new generation, the way they used to be in the 1800s, before oysters ended up as a rich man's food. It's good to see seafood restaurants around the city looking at themselves and beginning to feel a bit unadorned if they haven't got an oyster bar.

Oysters are graded from 1 to 4 according to their size. We serve only the two largest grades, no. 1 and no. 2, which to me are the true tavern oysters of London, and I just want to concentrate on excellence. You don't need a huge oyster menu but what you do need is for the oysters to be taken from the sea and brought to the restaurant immediately. You can keep an oyster chilled for up to five days, but I don't want mine hanging around. Eating an oyster straight out of the water is like tasting a mouthful of the sea, very different from a four-day-old oyster, which just loses that beautiful sea-brine taste that stays around in the shell for a couple of days, no more.

It used to be that on the first of September, when the first cold spell kicked in, we would have our first natives. Now, though, climate change means the whole seasonality is shifting, and sometimes they won't come in until maybe the last week in September. There is an old act of Parliament that says natives can't be fished from May to August, to protect the breeding cycle, which is where the idea of eating them only when there is an 'r' in the month comes from, but we can't go on sticking to a rule when the seasons are changing and soon we could be having magnificent natives in May.

A year or so ago we had some fun when the natives were particularly late and not that plentiful. I was like an American gold magnate, buying up all the natives in the British Isles and cornering the market, because we sell more natives than anyone else in London – 8,000–10,000 a week in the run-up to Christmas, with another 1,000–1,500 rock oysters going into the kitchen for the hot dishes – and no one was going to stand in the way of my customers! And then I lowered the price. In seafood bars around London they were selling half a dozen natives for £20–£21, so we sold ours for £16.50, and we've kept the price down ever since. The devil in me loves to create a bit of a stir.

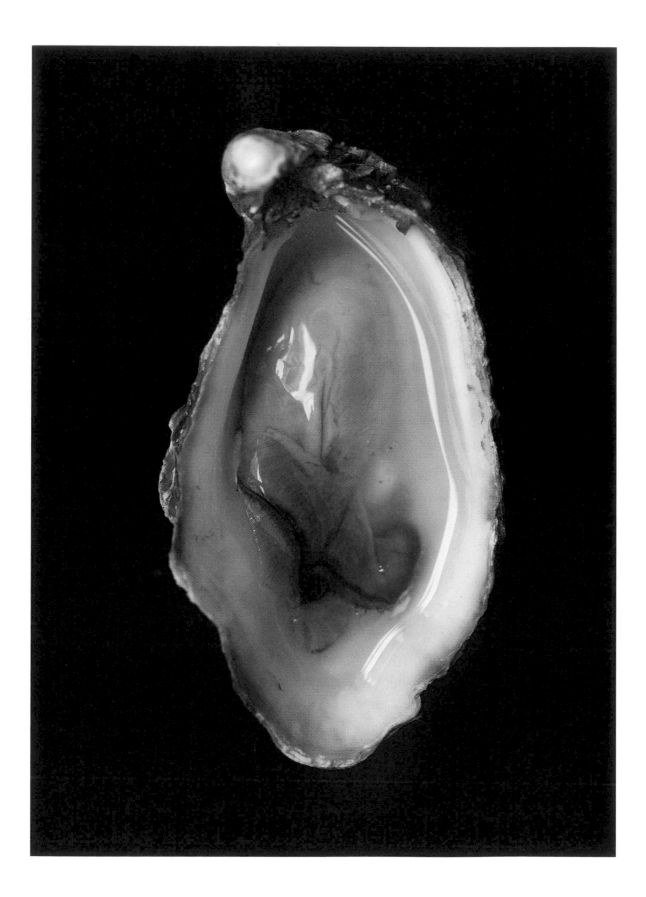

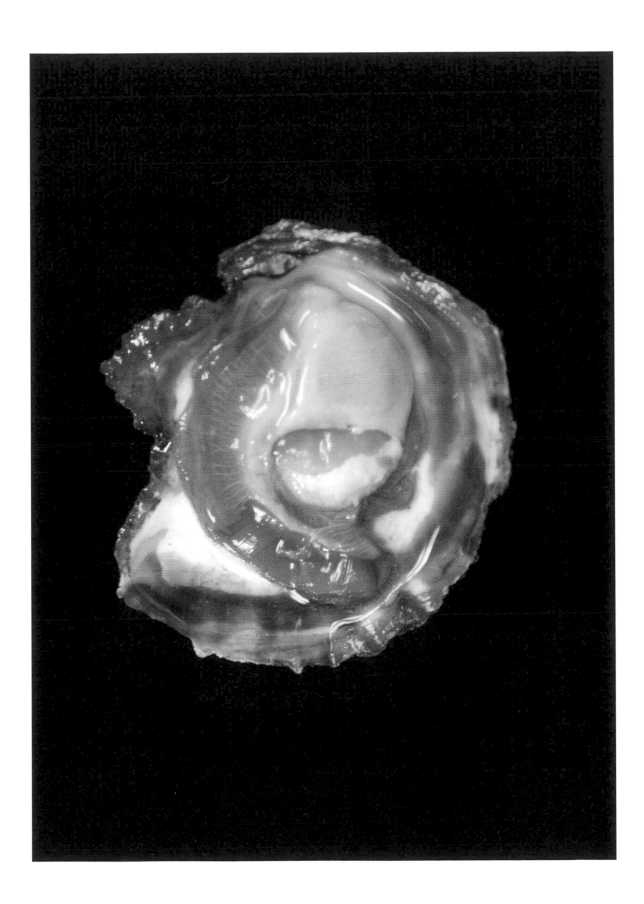

How to Open
an Oyster

At Bentley's oyster barmen open all the oysters, rather than chefs, because an oyster barman can tell immediately if there is a problem with an oyster. They are incredible, these guys, how quickly and deftly they work. The customers like the theatre of it, and the personal touch, because the barmen know which of the regulars like their oysters on ice, who prefers seaweed, etc. Apparently they still get asked all the time if they ever found a pearl.

The way an oyster is constructed is that a hinge holds the two shells together. In addition, the oyster inside has an adductor muscle that holds it to either shell. So you need to break the hinge and sever the muscle where it is attached to each shell. When you buy oysters the shell should always be closed, or it should close if you tap it, which shows the oyster is still alive. Another way to tell, when you open it, is to squeeze a little lemon over the oyster. If it is alive it will move slightly.

Always use a glove or wrap a cloth around your hand when you open an oyster. Some of the barmen do, some of them don't as they don't feel they are in touch with the oyster if they cover their hand, but most of them have scars around their wrists that tell the tale of a knife slipping.

With your gloved or wrapped hand, hold the oyster firmly, then insert the tip of a small sharp knife (preferably a small specialist oyster knife) into the hinge that holds the two shells together and wiggle it until you can break the hinge. Twist the knife through eighty degrees to prize the two shells slightly apart.

Slide the knife along the underside of the top flat shell, and cut the part of the muscle that is attached to the top shell. You could just serve the oyster as it is now, sitting on the cupped half shell, but to make it look neater and to enable the oyster to slide off easily into your mouth, we turn the oyster over. To do this, slide your knife underneath the oyster and cut the muscle that is holding it to the cupped shell, then flip it over, taking care not to lose any of the juices.

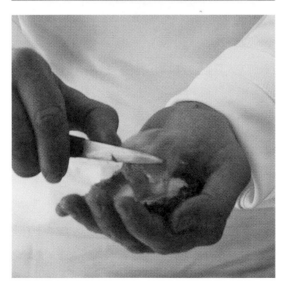

Deep-fried Oysters with Honey and Black Pepper Dressing

These are just beautiful, so easy to make – and a great way of introducing newcomers to oysters. Pick them up in your fingers, dip them into the dressing, and at the first bite you get the contrast of light, crispy batter and sweet hot pepperiness, then the flavour of the oyster comes through. To me that's gastronomy.

You don't even have to make the batter and deep-fry the oysters if you don't want to. If you prefer, you can just roll them in flour seasoned with a little cayenne pepper and fry them in a film of hot oil in a non-stick pan. But tempura batter does work beautifully with rock oysters. The key to the batter is the iced sparkling mineral water. Mark Edwards of Nobu is a good buddy of mine; I've been gleaning information from him over the years, and this is the way he makes his tempura. It really works, though I'm not sure why, to be honest; the bubbly water just seems to aerate the batter. You need it to be quite lumpy, so mix it with your finger, not a whisk or a fork, which will break it up too much.

And, by the way, you can make up a lot of the flour mix in one go – multiply this recipe by four, say – and keep it in a sealed container in the store cupboard, then just add water whenever you need it.

The idea for the honey and black pepper dressing came from a discussion with Frank Hederman, a passionate individual who smokes wild salmon (when he can get it) and wonderful eels at his little smokery at Belvelly, just outside Cobh in County Cork. Frank told me to try smoked salmon with honey and crushed black pepper, and I thought it was the most divine combination in the world: gorgeous, gorgeous – so why not have it with oysters? It's such a great dressing, you can keep a jar of it in the fridge and have it when you want, with whatever you want. I'd even put it with a piece of cold roast beef.

If the mood takes me, especially on a hot summer day, we might keep back the oyster shells, clean them, then make a little cucumber and melon pickle and spoon a little into each half shell before putting the deep fried oyster on top. There's something so tasty about the contrast of crispy hot oyster and refreshing, fridge-cool cucumber and melon. I've worked on the edge of Chinatown for the last ten years, at Lindsay House, so we'd often go down to eat there after finishing in the kitchen, and I think that whole Chinese experience of ordering a series of little hot dishes with cold pickled vegetable salads has rubbed off on me.

To make the pickle you just peel a cucumber, then slice it into long ribbons using a swivel-peeler and throw away the seeds. Do the same thing with a quarter of a melon, mix the two together, toss them with 50g of salt and leave them in

a colander to drain for around half an hour. Wash off the salt, pat the ribbons dry and put them into a bowl. Next, make a syrup by putting 100ml of mirin, 250ml of white wine vinegar, 150g of sugar and 5g of mustard seeds into a pan and bringing the lot to the boil. Take the pan off the heat, pour the syrup over the top of the cucumber and melon and leave to cool.

Another day I might feel like just grating some sharp Granny Smith apples and adding them to the honey and black pepper dressing. Or I might shred up some raw fennel, really finely, put it into a bowl of iced water, so it takes on a new level of crispy deliciousness, drain it and mix it with the sweet-sour apple, a touch of lemon juice and a pinch of Maldon salt. Serve it up as a little salad alongside the oysters, perhaps with some rounds of grilled, spicy chorizo.

To make the dressing, pour the cider and vinegar into a non-reactive pan. Bring to the boil and allow to reduce by two-thirds. Take off the heat and whisk in the honey. Stir in the lime juice and pepper, and a pinch of salt if you like.

With your finger, mix the ingredients for the tempura batter together until it is the consistency of double cream, but still lumpy. This batter doesn't hold well for long, so make it just before you are ready to fry the oysters.

In a deep-fat fryer, or a large pan filled no more than one-third full, preheat the oil to 190°C. Dust the oysters in seasoned flour, then toss them in the batter, shake off the excess and, with a slotted spoon, gently lower the first batch into the hot oil – fry only half a dozen or so at a time, no more, so as not to overcrowd the pan and lower the temperature of the oil. Fry the oysters until golden and crispy – they should take no more than 2 minutes. Drain on plenty of absorbent paper while you put in the next batch.

Serve with a little honey and pepper dressing on the side.

Serves 4

6 rock oysters per
    person, shucked
    (see page 122),
    bottom shells retained
vegetable oil, for deep
    frying
seasoned flour, for
    dusting

Tempura batter:
500g rice flour
50g cornflour
5g bicarbonate of soda
1 bottle ice-cold
    sparkling water

**Honey and black pepper
    dressing:**
165ml cider
125ml white wine
    vinegar
½ jar (about 220g)
    runny honey
juice of 1 lime
10g crushed black
    pepper
a pinch of sea salt,
    if you like

Oyster Plant with Smoked Salmon and Dill

Serves 4

4 sticks of salsify
  (oyster plant)
a squeeze of lemon juice
8 oysters
250ml good-quality
  crème fraîche
2 shallots, very finely
  diced
1 teaspoon chopped dill
150g smoked salmon,
  sliced into ribbons
½ bunch of watercress,
  leaves only

Salsify is known as the oyster plant, because its roots, which look a bit like parsnips, taste like oysters. We peel it into strips, so it looks like oyster plant tagliatelle, and blanch it, then serve it as a starter with lightly poached oysters and similar-sized strips of smoked salmon. Try to buy a good-quality crème fraîche, which won't split, but will be nice and creamy when you heat it – or if you prefer, you could use double cream.

Salsify turns brown and stains your hands almost as soon as you cut into it, so wear gloves and have a bowl of water with a squeeze of lemon juice in it ready. Peel the salsify and, using a swivel-peeler, slice it into long ribbons. Drop them into the bowl of water and lemon straight away, to help prevent them discolouring.

Bring a pan of salted water to the boil and blanch the salsify for about 30 seconds to 1 minute until just beginning to soften – it should be al dente. Refresh under cold, running water, drain well and reserve.

Shuck the oysters (see page 122) and pass their liquor through a fine sieve to remove any grit.

Pour the crème fraîche into a pan, add the shallots and bring to just below boiling point.

Simmer gently for 3–4 minutes, then add the oyster liquor and a couple of turns of black pepper. Continue to simmer for a few minutes more. Taste and add salt as necessary.

Add the salsify to the pan to heat through. Add the oysters and simmer for a minute more. Remove from the heat, stir in a little chopped dill and adjust the seasoning if necessary.

Serve in warmed bowls, garnished with ribbons of smoked salmon and leaves of watercress.

Oysters with Spinach and Tarragon Butter

This version of Oysters Rockefeller is based on Simon Hopkinson's recipe, which he doesn't remember making, but I do. The little spray of Pernod over them as they go out is a bit camp – but delicious. If you want to try it, you need a clean spray bottle, such as a disposable plastic perfume bottle.

Serves 4

150g butter, cubed

300g spinach

a handful of watercress, leaves only

1 stick celery, peeled and finely diced

3 shallots, peeled and finely diced

1 teaspoon chopped tarragon

1 teaspoon cayenne pepper

1 tablespoon fresh breadcrumbs

16–20 oysters, shucked (see page 122), bottom shells retained

1 tablespoon Pernod, to serve (optional)

Preheat the grill. Have the butter at room temperature.

Blanch the spinach in a pan of boiling salted water for 30 seconds, drain well under cold running water and squeeze out as much water as possible.

Put the butter, blanched spinach and all the other ingredients except the oysters and Pernod into a blender and whiz until smooth. Spread over the oysters and put under a very hot grill, until a crust forms. The oysters underneath will warm through rather than cook.

If you like, put the Pernod into a clean spray bottle, spray all over the oysters and serve.

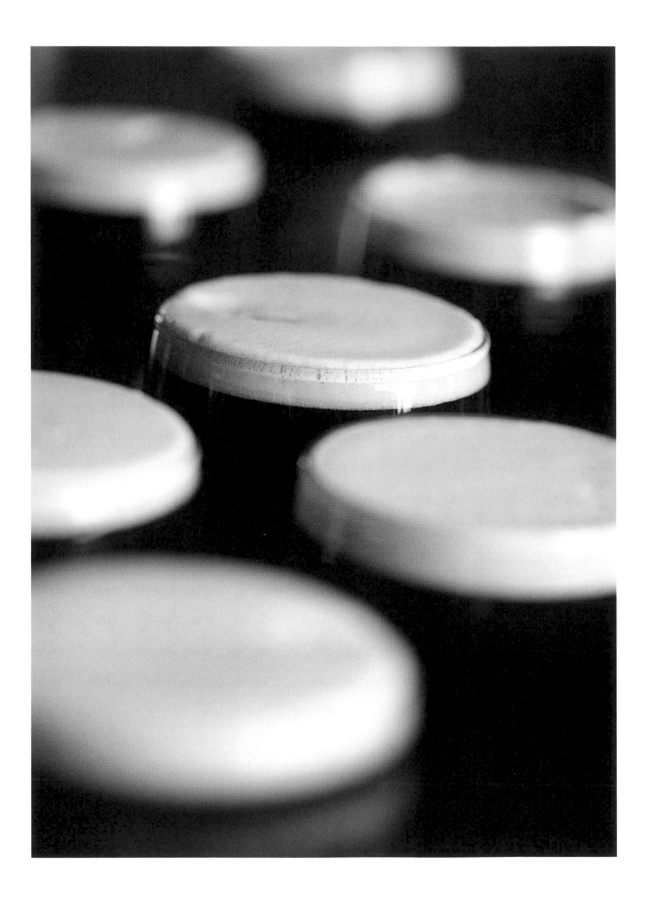

Oyster Stout Rarebit

Oyster stout is made by a friend of mine, Oliver Hughes, who co-founded the Porterhouse Brewing Company originally in Bray, County Wicklow, making beers with no chemicals or additives, just natural ingredients. Now there are bars in Dublin and one in Covent Garden in London, and we have the oyster stout on tap in the bar at Bentley's. Oliver is an ex-barrister, part of the Slow Food Movement in Ireland, another one who is a bit of a food and drink anarchist, a member of the whole sub-culture of producers who prize individual flavour above brands. Imagine launching three stouts in Dublin, home of the most famous stout in the world; you'd have to have some front. When they started in Dublin in 1996, they cheekily called one of their American-style lagers 'Weiserbuddy' – it had a label remarkably similar to a rather better-known American beer, and the slogan, 'You would be a wiser buddy for drinking this beer.' After they had had their fun and backed down and the writs stopped flying around, their next joke was to call one of their European beers 'Probably', with the slogan 'The Best Lager in the World'. The oyster stout really is made with shucked oysters. It is gorgeously smooth, and just slightly sweet from the oysters – you can't taste them, but you know they are there, and it makes a delicious rarebit with Mrs Kirkham's Lancashire cheese.

Serves 4
100g butter
100g flour
400ml milk
330ml bottle oyster stout or other stout
250g good Lancashire cheese, grated
1 tablespoon English mustard
100ml Worcestershire sauce
a pinch of cayenne pepper and a little salt
8 oysters
8 thick slices of good bread

Melt the butter in a pan and add the flour to make a roux. Cook for a couple of minutes, to get rid of the taste of the flour, then add the milk a little at a time, stirring constantly, and then the stout, stirring again as the mixture thickens: it must be very thick. Fold in the cheese, mustard, Worcestershire sauce, cayenne and salt. Don't worry about the colour; it will look very dark, because of the stout and the Worcestershire sauce, but once the cheese heats up under the grill, it will turn golden. Leave to cool and thicken up and set some more.

Preheat the grill.

Open the oysters (see page 122). Take them from their shells and pat dry with kitchen paper.

Toast the bread on both sides. Place an oyster on each piece of toast. Cover completely with the cheesy mixture. Put under the grill until the cheese is molten and golden brown. Serve with more good stout – in a glass this time.

Crab

When you taste a beautiful fresh crab that has been hand-picked and boiled in the morning and dressed in its shell by lunchtime, it's so deeply satisfying, and humbling. Food just doesn't get much better than that. A squeeze of lemon juice, some home-made mayonnaise and brown bread: what more could you want?

There are kitchens that have their crab meat pasteurised and delivered in bags, but we do everything ourselves. We even have one person in the kitchen whose job it is to crack and pick the crabs, separate the meat, and keep the leftover shells from the claws, which go to make soup.

They say the meat on a cock crab is often sweeter than on a hen crab, but then a large cock crab can be huge, sometimes around twice the size of a small cock crab, so the body meat tends to be more plentiful, meatier and more firm – but it is also expensive. For one person, a more affordable medium crab should be fine.

Cracking
and Picking
Fresh Crab

The first thing to do is to separate the claws and the legs from the rest of the body. Lay the crab on its back and twist off the claws first. Next, break off the lower sections of the legs, and pull the fatter top halves in towards the body and then outwards so they snap off cleanly.

Next, with your thumbs at the bottom of the hard shell, push upwards to lever out the body section. If it is being stubborn, insert the handle of a spoon into the base and use that as extra leverage. Put the body section to one side.

Take the feathery, pointed gills, the 'dead mens' fingers', from inside the shell and throw them away, along with the stomach sac, which is just behind the mouth. Scoop out the sludgy-looking brown meat and put into a bowl (strain this before you use it).

With the really big cock crabs, you can now pick the body section that you levered out, until it looks like a skeleton (with small hen crabs this might be too tedious, but if you make soup with the shells there will be lots of lovely meat to come out into it).

You'll see there are five rings around the body. Get a spoon handle underneath each one, and it will pop out, revealing lots of little cavities, like tiny rooms, full of tasty white meat, which you can pick and scrape out with the point of a knife. It's a bit of a time-consuming job, but worth it. Keep this white meat in a separate bowl.

Finally, crack the claws by knocking the shells with a hammer or the spine of a kitchen knife, and push out all the white meat with the end of a teaspoon or skewer. Put it into a bowl with the white body meat. Pick through it all carefully, to make sure there are no little pieces of shell in amongst the meat.

Now you are ready to dress the meat and put it back into the shell, or use it as you like.

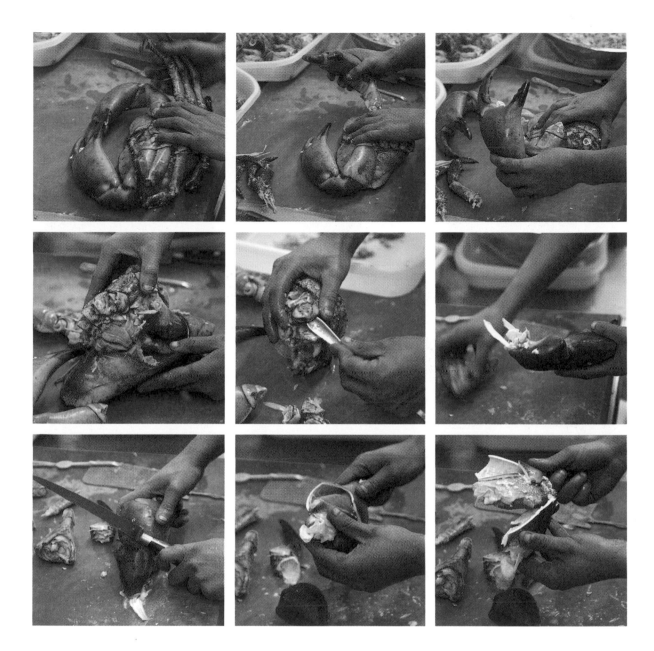

Dressed
Crab

Serves 4

4 medium hen crabs

1 teaspoon lemon juice,
plus lemon wedges
to serve

mayonnaise

4 hard-boiled eggs

4 teaspoons chopped
parsley

You could always prepare an extra crab and just add its meat to the rest, if you want to be extra generous.

Bring a pan of heavily salted water to the boil – about 200g sea salt to each litre of water.

Weigh the crabs and boil for 1 minute per 100g.

Have a bowl of iced water ready, and when you take the pan off the heat, drop the crabs into the iced water to prevent them cooking any more.

Prepare the crab as on page 134. Mix the lemon juice and a tablespoon of mayonnaise into the strained brown meat. Scrub the crab shells and dry thoroughly.

Separate the egg yolks from the whites and grate or chop them finely. Season each with salt and pepper.

Fill the sides of the crab shells with the white meat, leaving a space in the middle for the brown. Where the two meet, sprinkle a line of egg yolk, on one side, and egg white, on the other. Arrange a line of chopped parsley on top of the brown meat in the centre of the crab.

Serve with more fresh mayonnaise and lemon wedges on the side.

Mayonnaise

Makes about 20
portions

4 egg yolks
1 heaped teaspoon
   Dijon mustard
1 heaped teaspoon
   English mustard
1 tablespoon white
   wine vinegar
1 tablespoon lemon
   juice
1 teaspoon salt
a pinch of cayenne
   pepper
500ml vegetable oil

Unlike aioli, which should be green, peppery and garlicky and so needs an extra virgin olive oil with a bit of character, you want a neutral oil for mayonnaise. Sunflower oil is good, because it also has a high viscosity, which means the mayonnaise is unlikely to split.

Whisk together everything except the vegetable oil.

Slowly whisk in the oil a little at a time, until you have a thick emulsion.

John Wonnacott's Cornish Crab and Samphire with Soda Bread

Serves 4

200g samphire

8 slices soda bread

100g brown crab meat, strained and mixed with teaspoon lemon juice and tablespoon mayonnaise

400g white crab meat

House dressing:

2 shallots, finely diced

2 teaspoons wholegrain mustard

1 teaspoon English mustard

1 teaspoon honey

4 teaspoons white wine vinegar

a pinch of salt

250ml vegetable oil

So many of the dishes on the Bentley's menu have a little story behind them. This was something that the painter John Wonnacott (see page 143), who is a regular, requested, so we put it on the menu.

The dressing we use for the samphire is our house dressing – you can use it on salads, whatever you like.

To make the dressing, whisk together the shallots, mustards, honey, vinegar and a pinch of salt. Slowly whisk in the vegetable oil to emulsify.

Wash the samphire well in cold water and drain.

Toast the soda bread and spread with a little of the brown crab meat. Toss the samphire with the dressing and arrange on top of the brown crab meat. Top with a generous amount of white crab meat and eat immediately.

Crab, Scallion and Goat's Cheese Tart

Makes one 21cm tart
Serves 6–8

6 free-range eggs, plus
   1 egg beaten, for egg-
   wash
600ml double cream
250g goat's cheese,
   crumbled
250g white crab meat
2 bunches of scallions
   (spring onions),
   chopped

Pastry:
175g plain flour
75g cornflour
½ teaspoon salt
120g butter
2 egg yolks

Make the pastry. Whiz the two flours, salt and butter to fine crumbs in a food processor (or rub the butter in by hand). Tip into a bowl, then mix in the egg yolks and about 2 tablespoons of ice-cold water until you have a smooth dough. You may need some extra trickles of water. Form into a ball, wrap in clingfilm and chill in the fridge for a minimum of 20 minutes.

Preheat the oven to 160°C/Gas 3.

Roll out the pastry into a circle on a lightly floured board. You need a round large enough to fit a flan tin 21cm in diameter and 3cm deep. Roll it around your rolling pin, then lift it over the top of the tin and drape it over. Press it gently into the tin, taking care not to stretch the pastry. If it cracks, just press it together again. Don't trim the edges, leave them overhanging. Line with foil and dried or ceramic beans and chill for 15 minutes in the fridge to firm it up and help to stop it from shrinking in the oven. It may still shrink a bit, but if you don't trim the edges until after baking, you can compensate for this.

Put the flan tin on a baking tray and bake for 45 minutes, then remove the foil and beans and bake for another 5 minutes until the pastry is dry on the base. Brush the whole of the inside of the pastry with eggwash. Turn the oven up to 180°C/Gas 4.

Beat the eggs and cream together and season well.

Scatter the goat's cheese, crab meat and scallions evenly over the base of the tart. Pour over the egg and cream mixture. Return carefully to the oven and bake for 20 minutes, then turn down the heat to 160°C/Gas 3 and cook for another 40 minutes, until the top is pale golden and the centre barely wobbles. Remove from the oven and leave to cool to room temperature, during which time the eggs will have set and the tart will have firmed up.

When cool, trim the edges of the pastry, push the tart up out of the flan tin and slide on to a board or a flat platter.

Thai Crab and Mussel Soup

A big bowl of deliciousness. If you are feeling a little bit weary, this soup just dances on your palate and wakes you up. The painter John Wonnacott, whose fantastic pictures are hung around Bentley's, painted a picture of Stephen Evans, the producer of *The Madness of King George*, having a big bowl of the crab soup, which hangs in the Crustacean Room. He's just captured it beautifully: floating mussels, spring onions … you look at it and think, 'I want to eat that.'

Serves 4

500g mussels

100ml white wine

1 medium crab – cooked and prepared (see page 134), white meat and shells reserved

a little vegetable oil

4 x 400ml tins coconut milk

2 teaspoons Thai fish sauce

2 teaspoons palm sugar

fresh lime juice, to taste

½ bunch of spring onions, thinly sliced

coriander leaves (see below)

Paste:

50g fresh ginger, roughly chopped

50g fresh galangal, roughly chopped

2 sticks lemongrass, chopped

1 red chilli, deseeded

4 cloves garlic

2 shallots, chopped

2 kaffir lime leaves

a bunch of coriander, leaves picked, stalks reserved

Scrub the mussels in plenty of running water to remove any barnacles and beards. Discard any that are open or won't close when tapped. Put into a pan over a high heat with the white wine, cover with a lid, and cook quite fiercely until the mussels steam open. Strain the cooking liquor through a fine sieve and reserve. Discard any mussels that have stayed closed, and keep the rest on one side.

Setting aside the coriander leaves, put the rest of the paste ingredients into a blender and whiz until smooth.

Smash up the crab shells and fry them in a large saucepan with a little vegetable oil until they are nicely coloured.

Carefully open the tins of coconut milk (do not shake them and keep them the right way up). Spoon the cream from the top of the tins into a wok or large saucepan. At the same time, put the crab shells into a pan with the coconut water from the tins, bring to the boil and simmer for 5 minutes.

While the shells are simmering, heat the coconut cream over a gentle heat and let it melt. Add the spicy paste and cook gently for a couple of minutes until the spices release their aromas, taking care that the mixture doesn't catch and burn (if you are worried you can add a touch of vegetable oil).

Add the cooking liquor from the mussels to the pan containing the crab shells, then tip into the pan with the paste, and stir well to combine. Take off the heat.

Pass the soup through a fine sieve into a clean pan. Add the fish sauce and palm sugar. Taste, and if necessary add a little more of one or both.

To serve, arrange some white crab meat and mussels in each bowl. Pour the piping hot soup over the top, and squeeze in some lime juice to taste. Finish with the spring onions and coriander leaves.

Proper
Shellfish
Cocktail

The quantities of seafood you use are up to you: just try to get a good mix of everything. How much sauce you make is really up to you, too. Keep tasting it, and adjust it until it makes you smile. Simon Hopkinson had a nice idea of mixing a little cottage cheese into a cocktail sauce; it lightens it up a bit and takes that cloyiness off it, which part of you dislikes, but you just know that no one has ever come up with anything as good.

Serves 4

a mixture of seafood:
  picked white crab
  meat; Dublin Bay
  prawns; Atlantic
  prawns, the pink ones;
  cooked lobster tails;
  brown shrimps, peeled
extra virgin olive oil
a squeeze of lemon juice
2 baby gem lettuce
1 small cucumber,
  peeled, deseeded and
  diced

Cocktail sauce:
2 parts mayonnaise
1 part tomato ketchup
a splash of brandy
a dash of Tabasco sauce
a pinch of paprika
a squeeze of lemon juice

Mix together all the ingredients for the sauce. Take four old-fashioned cocktail glasses. Season all the seafood with a little extra virgin olive oil, salt and a drop of lemon juice.

To assemble, put some lettuce and cucumber at the bottom of the glass, which will give a lovely crunch, then layer up your seafood, put a dollop of sauce on top and let people mix everything up, or keep everything separate, as they choose.

Lobsters, Langoustines and Scallops

Sauté of Lobster
with Chilli,
Garlic and Coriander

If we are cooking lobster whole, we would put them into cold water and bring them up to the boil very slowly. If they are to be chopped up, we put them in the freezer briefly to send them into a trance first. The lobster is great with some simply steamed noodles.

Serves 4
4 small lobsters
vegetable oil
4 spring onions, sliced
4 fresh red chillies,
    deseeded and
    finely diced
4 cloves garlic, crushed
2 limes
a bunch of coriander,
    leaves only

Put the lobster in the freezer for about 45 minutes, then place one lobster at a time on a chopping board, and hold it steady. You will see that there is a perfect cross on the head of the lobster. Take a big, very sharp knife, insert it sharply, and then draw the knife backwards so that it splits the head cleanly. The lobster may twitch for a second but it is dead.

Cut off the claws and crack them with the back of the knife. Cut the tail crossways into slices, following the joints.

Heat a wok or large frying pan with a little vegetable oil, and when hot throw in the lobster pieces. Sauté briskly for a minute or two, then add the spring onions, chillies and garlic and continue to cook on a high heat for 2 minutes more.

Squeeze over some lime juice, finish with a handful of coriander leaves and serve immediately.

Salad of Couscous, Lobster and Citrus Juices

The citrus zest and juices lift the couscous from being just a grain to something greater, a kind of fragrant pillow that carries the shellfish quite magically. Sometimes I might put the couscous into the oven for a few minutes after it has taken up the water, just to dry it out a bit.

You can use this recipe with any number of dishes and enhance it as you like, maybe mix in some sautéed courgettes.

Serves 4

250g couscous

a little really good extra virgin olive oil

375ml hot water

zest and juice of 1 orange

zest and juice of 1 lemon

1 onion, diced

1 clove garlic, crushed

1 cucumber, peeled, deseeded and cut into small dice

harissa (see page 205), to taste

2 cooked lobsters

Citrus dressing:

2 tablespoons lemon juice

2 tablespoons orange juice

6 tablespoons olive oil

To serve:

a handful of chopped coriander

a handful of pine nuts, lightly toasted in a dry pan

Put the couscous into a bowl, add a little extra virgin olive oil, and rub it between your fingertips, which is a Moroccan trick to stop the couscous clumping together. Pour the hot water over and cover with a plate. Leave for about 10 minutes, until the grains have swollen up and softened. Fluff up a little with a fork, then mix in the citrus zest and juice.

Fold the onion, garlic and cucumber into the couscous. Add harissa to taste. Leave to cool completely.

Remove the shell from the lobsters and chop the meat. Mix together the lemon juice and oil for the dressing, season, and toss through the lobster meat.

Serve the lobster with the couscous, scattered with chopped coriander and pine nuts.

Lobster Bisque

This is a really luxurious and decadent soup, made entirely with cream, not stock.

Serves 4
1 large or 2 small live
    lobsters
a little olive oil
1 onion, finely diced
2 carrots, finely diced
2 sticks celery,
    finely diced
1 head of fennel, finely
    diced
4 cloves garlic, sliced
1 tablespoon tomato
    paste
100ml cognac, plus a
    little for the brandy
    cream
1.3 litres double cream
a little chopped tarragon

Despatch the lobster, crack the claws and cut it as for the recipe for sautéed lobster on page 147.

Heat the oil in a sauté pan, and when it is very hot put in the lobster and sauté briskly until the colour changes.

Add the vegetables and garlic and colour briefly.

Remove the lobster pieces from the pan. Take the meat from the shells and put a few of the larger pieces of shell back into the pan. Dice the meat and reserve.

Stir the tomato paste into the vegetables and shells in the pan, pour over the cognac and set alight. When the flames die down add 1.2 litres of the cream. Reserve the rest.

Simmer for around 10 minutes, until the vegetables are soft. Remove the shells from the pan and pass the liquid through a fine sieve into a clean pan, pressing the vegetables down with the back of a ladle. Season.

Put the soup back on the heat, add the chopped lobster and heat through.

Lightly whip the remaining cream with a dash of cognac, and add a little chopped tarragon. Serve the soup in bowls, with a spoonful of the brandy cream on top.

Langoustines with Chickpeas and Cumin

Serves 4

250g dried chickpeas
olive oil
1 onion, very finely diced
2 cloves garlic, crushed
1 level teaspoon
    cumin seeds
500ml water
100ml extra virgin
    olive oil
16–20 raw langoustines
lemon juice, to taste
a handful of chopped
    coriander leaves

Soak the chickpeas in plenty of water overnight, so that they will soften and cook properly, then drain and rinse.

Take a large pan and heat a tablespoon of olive oil. Add the onion, garlic and cumin seeds and sauté gently for a few minutes until the onions and garlic have softened. Add the drained chickpeas and pour in the water (don't salt it, as salt will toughen the skins of the chickpeas and make them wrinkly). Bring to a vigorous boil, then turn down the heat, skimming off any frothy scum, and simmer for around 2 hours, until the chickpeas are tender. As they cook, they will soak up the water and swell up, so add more water if necessary. Drain, return to the pan and stir in the extra virgin olive oil.

Preheat the grill.

Bring another pan of salted water to the boil, and have a bowl of iced water ready. Put the langoustines into the boiling water and cook for 1 minute. Drain immediately and refresh in the iced water. It is important to stop the cooking quickly at this point, otherwise the langoustines will turn disappointingly cotton-woolly in texture and lose flavour. Take off the heads and peel the tails.

Drizzle the tails with a little more olive oil, and flash quickly under the grill just to heat them through.

Season the chickpeas, add a little lemon juice and chopped coriander, and stir through. Serve in bowls, with the langoustines on top.

Nettle Broth
with Scallops
and Horseradish

People in the restaurant always seem to love this. It's quite a talking point, because there is something amazing about the textures and the way the slices of raw scallop cook as you eat the soup.

Serves 4

2 litres water

25g butter

1 large onion, chopped

4 cloves garlic, chopped

500g young nettles

250g crème fraîche

a knob of fresh
   horseradish (about
   100g), finely grated

lemon juice, to taste

8 medium scallops (no
   corals)

Put the water in a large pan, add a pinch of salt and bring to the boil.

Put the butter into a pan, add the onion and garlic and cook until soft.

Blanch the nettles very briefly, about 30 seconds, in the boiling water, then lift out and add to the pan containing the onions, along with 500ml of the nettle cooking water, which even after the brief blanching will be strongly nettle-flavoured. Take the pan straight off the heat.

Whiz in a blender, adding a little more of the nettle water to loosen it up if necessary. It should be bright green and still a little lumpy, as this is quite a rustic soup.

Season and return to the hob to heat through. Mix the crème fraîche and horseradish and whisk until creamy. Season with a little salt and lemon juice. Keep on one side.

With a sharp knife, slice the scallops thinly. Ladle the soup into bowls and arrange a ring of raw scallops on top. Sprinkle with sea salt and pepper. The salt will start to cure them from the top, as the soup cooks them from underneath. Spoon a small dollop of crème fraîche into the centre of the ring of scallops and serve immediately.

Seared Scallops with Quince, Black Pudding and Sage

Black pudding and quince, which is one of my favourite fruits: two quite old-fashioned ingredients, given a little bit of an exotic treatment with the sticky, sweet-sour caramel and vinegar dressing. And they look stunning: black rounds of pudding next to white rounds of scallop.

Bring the ingredients for the poaching liquor to the boil.

Meanwhile, peel the quinces, cut into quarters and remove the cores. Add to the pan of poaching liquor and simmer for 15 minutes or until tender. Remove from the heat and allow to cool in the liquor.

To make the dressing, put the sugar and water into a heavy-based pan and cook over a moderate heat until you have a light caramel. Keep cooking gently until it reduces enough to coat the back of a spoon – the texture of runny honey. Add the sherry vinegar and leave to cool, then taste, and if you think it needs a little more sharpness, add an extra splash of sherry vinegar and stir in well.

Heat some oil in a pan – no more than one-third full – and deep fry the sage leaves for 20–30 seconds until crisp. Drain well on kitchen paper and season with salt.

Cut the black pudding into slices the same size as the scallops.

Heat a frying pan until very hot. Add a film of oil, then put in the slices of black pudding and the quarters of quince. Cook everything quite fiercely for 2 minutes on each side, until brown and crisp and caramelised, then remove from the pan and keep warm.

Wipe out the pan, add a little more oil, and when it is very hot season the scallops and put them in. Again cook over a fierce heat for 2 minutes on each side until caramelised. Squeeze a little lemon juice over the scallops.

Arrange the scallops, quince and black pudding on plates and drizzle with some of the sherry vinegar caramel dressing. Top each plate with 3 deep-fried sage leaves and serve immediately.

Serves 4
2 quinces
a little vegetable oil,
   for deep frying
12 sage leaves
1 black pudding
12 scallops
a squeeze of lemon juice

Quince poaching liquor:
500ml water
125g sugar
50g runny honey
1 star anise
1 clove
¼ cinnamon stick

**Sherry vinegar caramel
   dressing:**
3 tablespoons sugar
1 tablespoon water
4 tablespoons sherry
   vinegar

Portaferry Clam Chowder

The story behind this soup, based on Boston clam chowder, is that for years in Portaferry in County Down the people thought they were catching clams, but all the time they were queenie scallops; so this isn't actually a clam chowder at all. You could, of course, make the same thing with real cherrystone clams if you like (all our Japanese and Chinese customers rate cherrystone clams, freshly opened for them at the bar, more highly even than native oysters).

Serves 4

30 queen scallops

100ml white wine

a knob of butter

1 large onion,
    finely diced

2 cloves garlic, sliced

500g potatoes, peeled
    and diced

150ml double cream

600ml milk

4 American-style cream
    crackers

a handful of chopped
    parsley

Scrub the scallop shells well under cold running water. Make sure they are all closed and discard any that aren't, and won't close when tapped. Put into a saucepan with the white wine, cover with a lid and steam open over a high heat. If any don't open, discard them. Strain through a sieve and keep the cooking liquor. Remove the scallops from their shells and keep on one side.

Heat a little butter in a separate pan, add the onion and garlic and sweat until soft. Add the potatoes and season. Add the strained clam liquor, cream and milk. The liquid should cover the potatoes by a few centimetres. If not, add a little more milk.

Bring to the boil and simmer until the potatoes are tender. Adjust the seasoning to taste.

Add the shelled scallops to the soup and heat gently.

Break up the crackers and add to the bowls. Pour the hot soup over the top. Finish with chopped parsley and fresh black pepper.

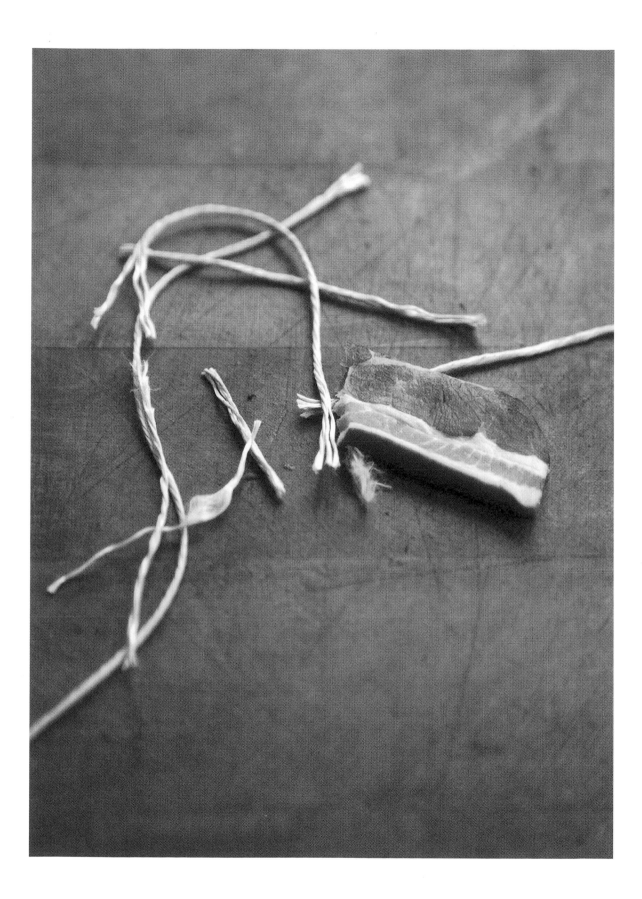

Meat
and
Game

When my kids were younger and I used to talk about real meat, my memories of the bacon, the boiling fowl, the beef and hams I grew up with, they used to look at me as if I was born in the Victorian era, because they grew up in a world where so much meat comes ready packed. Now, they get it. With meat it's all very simple. If animals are happy and well looked after with kindness, if they are fed naturally and allowed to grow to maturity slowly, rather than being plumped up as fast as possible, the meat will be special. Factory farming doesn't care about anything but the bottom line, whereas passionate individuals will always rear the best meat. End of story.

There may be cynicism about organic and biodynamic production, and not everything that's produced that way will taste fantastic, but it isn't all about taste, it's about removing as many chemicals as possible from the whole cycle of farming, which has to be a good thing. These movements are based on the simple truth that you can't go on pillaging the earth. Come on, what makes more sense to you, really? Farming naturally, without chemicals, according to the phases of the moon, or pumping brine and preservatives into industrially produced hams to cure them quickly and make them weigh more?

The Pig

The love of the pig is deeply ingrained in the British and the Irish people, and in fact in most countries of Europe. In Italy, Spain, France and Poland, especially, pork plays an incredibly important part in the meat portion of the national diet. Nothing quite gets the imagination going like a beautifully cured rasher of bacon sizzling in a pan with the fat turning crispy-salty, or a piece of pork from a traditional indigenous breed of pig that tastes the way meat used to before the march of intensive farming.

There's a respect for the pig that goes back hundreds of years, because if you lived in the countryside that pig would keep a family going for a year in fresh meat, bacon, cured ham, lardo or salami, depending on your culture. A beautiful piece of hand-carved Spanish pata negra or Italian Parma ham is a delicacy in itself with a perfectly ripe piece of melon, a piece of crusty bread, some olive oil and a bottle of light red. You just know that is wonderful food. There is a chef I admire a great deal, Fulvio Pierangelini, who has a tiny, two-Michelin-starred place, Gambero Rosso, in San Vincenzo on the Tuscan coast. He has the same love of cooking from the hip as myself, no recipe set in stone, and the same kind

of reverence for the pig, to the point of raising his own rare breed Cinta Senese animals, which are native to Tuscany, for lardo, salami, culatello and pancetta. He gives talks on 'an egg and a pig', both country foods at the heart of his cooking. Fulvio is as close to a genius as they come. He has sprightly women cooking with him in his kitchen, but he rarely lets other chefs in, so I was privileged to be one of the few. I was there once for one of his special twelve-course dinners with every dish dedicated to the pig. Such an inspiration.

When I was growing up in Meath, the pig was a very important part of the cycle of food preparation in our house. To this day it is still the legal right of every Irish household to own their own pig and have it killed and butchered in their own yard. Each year we'd go off in the car to buy a piglet, and we'd keep it for around eight months until 'killing the pig day' in late October. It was always when you cut the wood that you killed the pig; the farming mentality was all about stocking up and filling the larder for winter.

The feeding of the pig was my job. I liked looking after the animals. There were seven of us children, and I was third from the top, so while my older brothers would be doing heavier work, I'd be weeding the vegetable garden and feeding the ducks, chickens and the pig. We had loads of mangolds (roots for fodder) growing in the top field, and we'd boil them up in a big vat on the fire, then mash them and mix them with loads of corn or barley and maybe potato peelings, to make pig's feed. As a treat, I used to go to the orchards to pick up the unripe apples and put them into the pigsty. They used to love me bringing them, but we were farmer's kids, we knew that pigs were for food and we weren't about to get too sentimental or give them names (more likely we'd call them 'lunch' or 'dinner') – but they're very warm, funny, friendly animals and over the months we'd develop a real fond attachment to each one.

These were big country pigs, so for the day of dispatch our neighbours and cousins would be notified to come and help, because it was a whole day's job, and it was always a big celebration. There'd be bottles of Guinness and McArdle's ale put into the river to cool for later, then the pig would be led outside the dairy and shot with a heavyweight lead bullet. Dad would do the dispatching, a neighbour, Jimmy McKeon, would catch the blood, and my job was to bring the blood straight away to Jimmy's sister, Kathy, who would put her Marigold gloves on and make the black pudding. My mother never made the black pudding because she came from Irish-speaking Connemara, where the culture was more about fish (especially the local razor clams, which she used to call *scian mhara*), and not about killing pigs.

The first time I saw the pig killed I was probably only seven, and I remember an immense sadness seeing it shot, but we forgot about it quickly in the excitement of the event. Jimmy would take away the innards cleanly and then the men would haul up the carcass on to the rafters. They'd put a switch of hazel inside the animal to hold it open and aerate it while it dried. After four days the pig would be taken down, and you'd take off the shoulder or the leg to roast, then the rest would be portioned up and given to the people who'd helped to kill it, or a friend or an auntie who was housebound might be sent a little share. Then the sacks of salt would be brought in, and the rest would be salted for bacon.

The excess fat collected by the men during the butchering was always rendered down. You'd boil it with water and skim it off, so it was absolutely clear, and we'd have jars of it in the kitchen to fry with. When I hear people going on and on about goose fat, which is considered so fashionable, I think, 'Give me a break', because pig fat is absolutely gorgeous, too.

The black pudding, and the tenderloin, which we called grishkeens, would all be eaten quickly; often the grishkeens would be eaten on the killing day. They'd be cut up into little pieces while still warm and soft, then fried in a pan and served on top of country bread as a snack. When you cook pork fillet *that* fresh, browning it slowly in a pan, you feel like you are in gastro-heaven. It's hard to explain the intensity of the deliciousness. Grishkeens and brown bread is a delicacy I carry in my head from childhood, but which can never be repeated because I've never since seen pork fillet quite that fresh, or quite that big, from such a huge country pig.

It's heartening to discover artisan pig farmers making a name for themselves now in Ireland. T. J. Crowe's organic pig farm near Dundrum in County Tipperary, where they have their own abattoir, cure their own meat, and do their own butchery, is a very impressive operation, and when I put some of their bacon under the grill, I knew even before I tasted it that it would be as good as the stuff I ate as a child. You get none of the oozing of white liquid into the pan that results from industrial fast-curing and plumping up with water or phosphates, which leach out during cooking.

And I like Black Bacon from O'Doherty's in Enniskillen, County Fermanagh. Pat O'Doherty, whose father, James, started work as a butcher when he was thirteen, keeps his own old-fashioned breed of pigs on an island in the middle of Lough Erne. They're left there to forage for themselves, and they're nearly wild. You see forty of them coming over the hill towards you and you run! Pat dry-cures his pork using a 'secret' (salt and treacle) recipe, then matures it slowly for three months. One time when I was in his shop, there were two women there who had driven up all the way from Mullingar, in the midlands, which must be three and a half hours away, to buy their bacon because it reminded them of how bacon tasted in bygone days. I like that. Let's fight for bacon like that. Chickens are being championed now, at last, so how about standing up for pigs and real pork and bacon?

There is a pig farm in Caherbeg, in Rosscarbery down in West Cork, which always reminds me of the place I grew up. Willie and Avril Allshire have built up a lovely cottage industry, Caherbeg Free-Range Pork, dry-curing their own bacon and making sausage and white and black pudding from their own saddleback-cross pigs supplemented with pork from local farmers – they even have an orchard and they've planted trees, as we did. I see their two little boys sitting up on the tractor, mucking in and helping run the place, and they remind me of myself as a child. Their whole little business, developing and growing around the ethos of family farming and the God-given bounty they have on their acreage, is just wonderful. Behind any food worth talking about there are always passionate people like the Allshires, who believe in stress-free pigs running around, rooting and enjoying themselves, along with their small herd of Irish Angus cattle, until their time has come and they are taken to the small, local abattoir. When anyone believes, really believes in what they are doing, but in such a small way, you're always worried they are going to disappear tomorrow, that big business is going to swamp them, so I have profound respect for these families who can keep going and make a living consistently producing great food.

Maybe it's childhood memories that also endear me to another breed of pig, the English Middle White, which is so traditional and seems such a perfect breed for the British Isles, yet was on the endangered list of rare breeds not so long ago. The natural flavour of the Middle White is maybe the closest I can get to that country pig I tasted as a child. I just don't get the same flavour from some of the other popular traditional breeds, like the Gloucester Old Spot – and the fat/meat ratio is just perfect. Fat is very important: you need good fat on a pig, to keep the meat moist and tender when it cooks.

Middle White Pork Chops with Apricots, Honey and Sherry Vinegar

Pork and fruit go brilliantly well together. I like my pork chops untrimmed, with a piece of fat running along the back so you get crispy crackling, and there might be a little eye-of-the-needle bit of meat at the tail that you can suck on at the end of the meal.

I'd serve this with mashed potato and maybe a little salad of rocket or sprigs of watercress. The combination of potato and pork is just gorgeous. As kids, when we were working hard on the farm we'd come in and have a bowl of boiled potatoes for lunch with some cold pork belly on top, or a couple of grilled rashers of bacon on top of mashed potato, maybe with a bit of swede mixed in and lots of black pepper. I can nearly taste the fat of the bacon sinking into the potato now.

Serves 4

6 fresh, ripe apricots

a little olive oil

4 thick pork chops, preferably Middle White, bone in and untrimmed

a knob of butter

8 sage leaves

1 tablespoon runny honey

a dash of sherry vinegar

Preheat the oven to 200°C/Gas 6. Cut the apricots in half and remove the stones, then cut into quarters.

Put a heavy frying pan over a high heat and, when hot, pour in a film of olive oil. Put in the chops, colour well on both sides, then sit them on to their back edge so the fat can colour and crisp up. Transfer them to the oven for about 10 minutes, until the meat is cooked through and tender, or to the point you want it. If you feel like cooking the chops longer, do it: cooking is about what you want, all I'm asking is that you don't cook every bit of moisture out so the meat is stringy and dry.

Strain the pan juices and reserve them, then allow the meat to rest in the pan in a warm place for about 5 minutes – it doesn't need the same resting time as a piece of beef, and also I like my pork to be served really piping hot and crispy.

While the pork is cooking and resting, quickly sauté the apricots: put the knob of butter into a large frying pan over a medium heat and, when it is hot, add the sage and apricots and sauté briefly until the apricots take on a tiny hint of colour.

Drizzle over the honey and sprinkle with the sherry vinegar, just a drip at a time. Taste it to check the balance of sweet and sour as you go: the vinegar is there just to give the apricots an aromatic edge, not to make them aggressively sour. Don't be afraid to put in a spoonful of water to dilute it, or another spoonful of sugar if you need to sweeten it up to the taste you want. Add some salt and pepper if needed. Toss together and continue to cook for 2–3 minutes. Place a chop on each of 4 warmed plates, spoon the apricots alongside and drizzle over the juices from the pork.

Mr Colman Must Have Liked Ham

When I think of ham I also think of new potatoes pulled up straight from the fields or gardens, and what I especially adore is ham, hot or cold, with Colman's mustard. The two were made for each other. Gammon, Colman's, some beautiful leaves from the garden, good brown bread: it's one of the greatest things you can eat. Mr Colman, you must have been a ham lover.

When I say Colman's, I mean the original pure mustard flour, which you mix with a little cold water. Often mustards have sugar added to them, so they don't have the sharpness of old-fashioned English mustard powder.

Colman's mustard is a great answer to a lot of my questions. This is how my head works, the way the Corrigan thinking process goes: I love swede, so one night I was thinking about ham and swedes with a little bit of black pepper and cinnamon with loads of Italian mostarda, rather than mustard. Off I went to the library, looking for an old-fashioned recipe for mostarda… now, that is something hard to find. Mostarda – fruits such as apples, pears, quince and cherries, candied in a honey and mustard syrup – is made all over Italy to different recipes in each region, but the most famous is mostarda di Cremona. Everyone seems to buy it and when you do find a recipe, it uses mustard essence, which no one stocks outside Italy.

Then, on the internet, I saw something suggesting using mustard powder. So I tried it, and it was magnificent. Instead of fresh fruits, I used dried fruit: raisins, apricots, some mixed peel… I soaked the fruit overnight first, to plump it up, then I boiled up some sugar syrup, quite weak, about one-third sugar to two-thirds water, and added a bit of vinegar and some mustard powder – you need quite a bit. I always think with mustard, you just have to add it and keep tasting till you squeak, then you know you have enough. I took it off the heat, before it could go murky, poured half of it over the dried fruits and let them absorb it, put them into a sterilised jar, then topped up with the rest of the syrup. It wasn't rocket science, but it was just beautiful with a piece of boiled ham or a nice grilled Middle White pork chop.

A Lot
of Bull

When it opened in London in Blandford Street in 1989, Stephen Bull was the first minimalist, architect-designed restaurant in London. Stephen, a Cambridge graduate and self-taught cook, had come out of his previous restaurant, Lichfield's in Richmond, which was one of the first Michelin-starred restaurants in the country, and was turning his back on 'fine dining' in favour of serious, bistro food, very different, ground-breaking stuff. I had been cooking some serious food at the Oak Room, and in the Netherlands, and when I took over as head chef I was ready for some freewheeling food that felt new, new, new, but was like going back to the beginning in terms of simplicity.

I remember arriving and seeing all these tins of flageolet beans on the shelves and saying to him, 'What are you doing with all those tins of beans?' He said, 'Finest beans in the whole world. Take them out of the tin, wash them, and simmer them with a bit of cream, some grated garlic and chopped parsley.' And he was right. I still think that is one of the finest accompaniments to a piece of chargrilled or roast lamb today. And you can't say, 'I don't like tinned food,' because there's room for tinned food. Think of the Italians and their tomatoes, which have always been considered indispensable for sauces when the fresh tomatoes were finished.

It was a tour of the Mediterranean that we were on: cumin, cinnamon, cracked wheat, couscous, lentils, chickpeas, simple grills, lovely things like a piece of cod with hazelnut butter and rocket; white gazpacho. No one was making their own pesto and tapenade at that time; but we were. Italy, Spain, we walked through their repertoires. I tell you we were at the cutting edge in a way I haven't seen to the same extent since. All those cumin-ey, chickpea, chorizo flavours that I love today are legacies of my cooking with Stephen. When a spate of tapas bars opened in London a few years back I walked in and thought: we were cooking this kind of stuff years ago.

Stephen was a very smart intellectual and his attitude was a breath of fresh air. He was a part of that Rowley Leigh, Alastair Little fraternity of groundbreaking, university-educated cooks of the 1980s, but he didn't have the sense of structure and organisation to cook for a lot of people, so he needed someone to head up his kitchen, and we worked well together. He enjoyed the way I cooked, and I enjoyed his company.

One of his first dishes was a salad of crisp duck skin and oranges, which was so tasty and also, for the times, slightly mad; and I would make my own black pudding and serve it on a sharp purée of apple with a little orange rind through it. I'd cut ox heart into slices as thin as carpaccio and then dip them into gremolata before flashing them for a few seconds in a very hot pan.

Instead of cheffy gossip in the kitchen we'd be mulling over the writings and quiverings of Jane Grigson and Elizabeth David or questioning the roots of a recipe: was it Algerian, or Moroccan? I loved the free-wheeling discussion. Stephen would say, 'I want to do a rump steak burger,' and I'd say, 'Let's add some bone marrow,' and he'd say, 'What about marjoram?' And so it went on.

His girlfriend, now wife, Annie, was a Mahler fan, and there would be pretty heavy-going conversations on music and politics and a great camaraderie. The wine list was stonking: one hundred bottles all chosen according to Stephen's palate, and I was brought into the wine tastings with his equally interesting buddies.

I stayed at Blandford Street for two years and really enjoyed myself. That experience made me totally unafraid of any ingredient and ready to put my hand to anything. Most cooks have the feeling of being pigeon-holed at some time in their careers, but since then I never have. I have no fear of tackling any region or country's cuisine, and feel that I understand how to get to the root and essence and flavour of it. Blandford Street did that for me.

But eventually I had learned, studied and explored the food of the Mediterranean enough. I had mastered it and I appreciated it, and now I wanted to chase the starch of the spud again. For all its sunshine bent, the cooking at Blandford Street had elements of British food running through it, which was unusual in those days, and that was where I felt most comfortable. A spoonful of tapenade with a wonderful grilled red mullet and maybe a raw vegetable salad is a delicious thing. Bagna cauda, perfect. Don't get me wrong, I appreciate those influences to this day, and they are still there in the way I cook. But when the opportunity came up to open an Irish Bar called Mulligan's in Cork Street, I took it. It was a bit mad and Stephen was horrified, but the idea of cooking Irish country food appealed. Though I have to admit that for the launch, my nerve failed me. A lot of the great and good were there and the official opening was conducted by the former Taoiseach, Jack Lynch. I compromised, if you can call it that, by wrapping duck confit in pastry and serving it with carrot and cabbage sautéed in duck fat. Myrtle Allen, who was at the launch, said to me very quietly, 'What part of Ireland is that from?'

It wasn't long, though, before I was confident enough to be simmering hams and brining ox tongues and serving pig's feet with beetroot and a bit of horseradish on the side. I enjoyed myself and we were a success. We showed that we could be rightly proud of British and Irish food, and I'd like to think we contributed a bit to the revival of interest in it. Mulligan's, partly because of its location, had a clubbiness about it, and we had a lot of powerful people at our tables: businessmen, gallery owners, a lot of Jewish magnates who came in for the salt beef. One of the businessmen who came in regularly was Denis Cassidy, the chairman of Boddington's, the Manchester brewery. How Boddington's had ended up owning Bentley's, the oyster bar and restaurant that was founded in 1916 just off Piccadilly, I don't know. But they did and they had a problem. It was not performing. So I found myself leaving Mulligan's to spend a year and a half at Bentley's trying to restore it to its straightforward, simple, seafood glory.

By now, though, Stephen Bull was setting his sights on an upmarket restaurant in Chelsea, and I went in as a partner. When Stephen opened Fulham Road Simon Hopkinson was at his zenith at Bibendum, St John's had opened and was a huge success, and Gordon Ramsay was at Aubergine. This time we went up a few notches; we had to come up with clearly defined dishes, hence things like tartare of veal with parsley salad. We were refining dishes I had seen before and working on them to make them more exciting. I remember broad bean mousse with marjoram and Serrano ham, from Spanish importers Brindisa (who are huge now, but were working out of a small place in Crouch End at the time), carved up for customers in the dining room. And a very light summer consommé of lobster, with lobster cream, that was like a clear bisque, lightly jellified until it was almost quivering, with pieces of lobster set in it like diamonds. You'd take it out of the fridge and when it hit room temperature, you couldn't really say whether it was jelly or liquid … oh, it was good.

But the magic Stephen and I had had a few years back in Blandford Street was missing. Sometimes it is best not to revisit relationships looking to relive good memories. I wasn't the little student any more, but Stephen was still the boss. I had a different head on my shoulders, so did he, and it wasn't the easiest of relationships. It was a bit touchy and edgy, and even though we got a Michelin star within the first year, it was as if we were on both sides of a revolving door. I was going one way and he was going the other. I hadn't fulfilled my ambitions yet. I wanted to go back to my *own* roots again and really explore British and Irish food, the northern hemisphere.

My family life and the need to spend more time with Maria and our kids also came into play (our second child, Jessica, had been born), along with the long hours, the six days a week, the two night buses home, and the fact that popular as Fulham Road was, we didn't make any money. It all took its toll. I was burnt out.

So burnt out, in fact, that when the offer came up of a consultancy at the Hackney Stadium, setting up a restaurant and café, the bright lights of the dog track twinkled invitingly. It was a crazy idea but I've never been afraid to make U-turns in my life.

Boiled Ham with Nettle and Potato Mash and Cabbage

A ham like this always evokes powerful memories for me of watching my mother cooking hams with root vegetables from the garden, chopped up in big chunks, the aroma filling the whole house. We talk about boiled ham all the time, but in fact it's very important not to actually *boil* a ham. Bring it up to the boil, then turn the heat down and simmer it gently, or you'll end up with the toughest piece of meat in the world.

Serves 8

1 ham, bone in, soaked overnight in plenty of cold water
2 onions, halved
6 sticks celery, halved
6 carrots, cut into chunks
3 leeks, split in half
2 cloves garlic, split
1 bay leaf
a bunch of thyme
½ teaspoon black peppercorns
a good knob of butter
1 teaspoon Dijon mustard
a handful of parsley, coarsely chopped

Nettle and potato mash:
1.25kg floury potatoes, in their skins
around 250g young nettle leaves
225ml full-fat milk
100g butter

Cabbage:
25g butter
1 onion, chopped
1 carrot, chopped
1 head of cabbage, chopped

When nettles aren't in season, just serve a plain mash, or champ (see page 203). Eat what you like of the ham for this recipe, and keep the rest to have cold with salad and new potatoes and English mustard.

Rinse the ham and put it into a large pot, cover completely with cold water, bring to the boil, and skim any scum from the surface. Turn down the heat, add the vegetables, garlic, herbs and peppercorns, put the lid on the pan and simmer gently for around 3–4 hours, depending on the size of the ham. It is ready when you can pull the bone easily from the centre of the ham.

Take out the ham and keep warm. Skim the fat from the top of the cooking stock and push enough to make a little sauce through a fine sieve into a clean pan, pressing down on the vegetables. Bubble up on the hob so that the liquid reduces a little and intensifies in flavour. Add a knob of butter, the mustard and parsley.

Meanwhile, cook the potatoes in their skins until tender. Drain in a colander and allow them to steam for a few minutes to dry them out slightly. Peel while still hot and then mash.

Blanch the nettles for a minute or so in boiling salted water, drain and refresh under cold water to stop them cooking any further. Squeeze out the excess water and chop roughly.

Heat together the milk and butter and mix into the mash. Stir in the nettles, season to taste and keep warm.

For the cabbage, melt the butter in a pan, add the onion and carrot and cook until softened but not coloured. Put in the cabbage with a splash of water to help it steam and cook for a few minutes until it visibly wilts – don't put a lid on the pan, as it will lose its bright green colour.

Carve the ham and serve with the mash and cabbage and a little of the sauce.

Collar of Bacon
with Cabbage
and Onion Sauce

It isn't that easy to find collar of bacon these days, because it is often considered a fatty cut: it is the cured fore-end of the pig that is attached to the shoulder joint, and less fatty than the belly (which gives streaky bacon), but more so than back bacon. But it's the cut that most Irish families used to slow cook: the extra bit of fat keeps it beautiful and moist.

Soak the collar in water for 2 days, then cook with vegetables, garlic, herbs and peppercorns, as for boiled ham (see page 170) for about 2½ hours, depending on its size. About an hour before it is ready, put 4 whole, peeled onions into the pan.

When the bacon is cooked lift it out. Take out the onions and keep to one side, then strain the cooking water into a bowl, pour back into the pan and bring to the boil. Have a cabbage sliced up and washed, then put it into the cooking water, boil for a couple of minutes and strain.

Roughly chop the reserved onions, then put them into a blender, blitz to a purée and season. Serve with the ham, cabbage, a big bowl of floury potatoes boiled in their jackets, plenty of good butter to eat with them, and a pot of English mustard.

Steamed Ham

Ham hocks, steamed in white wine or cider in the oven, over a bed of vegetables which form a kind of trivet for the ham, taste stunning. The vegetables are only aromats, there to infuse their flavour, and they end up too fatty to eat, but without them I think the meat tastes too hammy-and-bony; they are very important in bringing a kind of subtlety to the ham.

I would serve the ham with colcannon (see page 270). Any ham left over can be used in the recipe for crubeens (see page 174).

If you like, once they are cooked, you can rub the knuckles with mustard, sprinkle them with breadcrumbs and bake at 180°C/Gas 4 for about an hour until they are golden. The mustard will cut through the sticky gelatinous richness of the meat.

Serves 4

a little vegetable oil

2 onions, roughly chopped

6 sticks celery, chopped

4 carrots, chopped

3 leeks, chopped

1 head of garlic, cut in half crossways

2 star anise

1 teaspoon crushed cardamom pods

½ teaspoon black peppercorns

4 knuckles of ham, soaked overnight in plenty of cold water

1 bottle white wine or cider

Preheat the oven to 160°C/Gas 3.

Heat a little vegetable oil in a large casserole (which has a lid), put in the vegetables and garlic and sauté very briefly just to give a little colour to the vegetables and bring out their sweetness.

Add the star anise, cardamom and peppercorns. Rinse the ham knuckles and place on top.

Pour in the white wine or cider and bring to a simmer.

Put the lid on the casserole and transfer to the oven. Cook for 2–2½ hours. The meat should be falling off the bone. Discard the vegetables.

Croquette of Pig's Trotter (Crubeens) with Beetroot, Horseradish and Sorrel

I like pig's trotters, but I'm not too fond of them in the manner that became the custom in restaurant kitchens in the 1990s, stuffed with chicken mousse and morels. It doesn't say pig's trotter to me. I much prefer to get my jowls round a crispy croquette of trotter, or a whole trotter, coated with mustard, dusted with breadcrumbs and slowly grilled, in the French style.

This is an old Lindsay House favourite. It's a time-consuming business, but well worth boiling up the trotters for several hours, picking the meat over and mixing it with some braised and shredded ham knuckles to make a delicious little pâté, crumbing it and shallow-frying it, then serving it with some beetroot and maybe a little mayonnaise with Colman's mustard mixed in. There isn't a huge amount of meat on a trotter, so the ham knuckle helps to give it more substance.

Usually we brine the trotters first. You don't have to, but I think it's important, as much for good looks as for flavour. Without brining, the meat of a trotter can be a bit grey looking. And I think brining works well with pork as a general rule. It brings out its flavour. At Lindsay House we would always have a pot of brine which we'd put a pork belly or best end into overnight, or we'd even dry salt them with a little crumbled sage and orange rind, so that they would become a little more like bacon. Then we'd wash off the salt or brine, and dry them, before cooking.

If you want to make up a brine, put 900g of sea salt into a large saucepan with 3 litres of cold water, 450g of light or soft brown sugar, 1 tablespoon of saltpetre (if you like), 1 whole clove, 10 black peppercorns, 6 juniper berries, 4 garlic cloves, peeled and split in half, 1 bay leaf and 3 sprigs of thyme. Bring to the boil, stirring until the sugar dissolves and skimming off the foam with a slotted spoon, then turn down the heat and simmer for 10 minutes. Remove from the heat and leave to cool.

If you are brining the trotters, put them in a big bowl, pour over the cold brine, put a plate over the top to keep the trotters submerged, and leave in the fridge for 24 hours.

You need 2 large saucepans. Heat a little vegetable oil in each, and divide the vegetables and garlic between the pans. Sweat until softened. Put the trotters into one of the pans (if you have brined them, rinse and drain them first), with 1 bay leaf and 2 sprigs of thyme, cover with cold water, bring to the boil, then turn down the heat and simmer gently for 3 hours. Take the pan off the heat and leave the trotters to cool down.

Serves 4

4 pig's trotters, cleaned and hairs removed (brined, if you wish; see method)
vegetable oil, for frying
1 carrot, finely chopped
2 sticks celery, finely chopped
1 leek, finely chopped
1 onion, finely chopped
4 cloves garlic, finely chopped
2 bay leaves
4 sprigs of thyme
½ bottle dry white wine
2 knuckles of ham
½ bunch of parsley, chopped
Dijon mustard
2 large cooked beetroot
a knob of fresh horseradish
a handful of sorrel leaves
20ml white wine vinegar
200ml olive oil
4 eggs
75g flour
150g breadcrumbs

Pour the white wine into the other pan and bubble up until reduced by half. Put in the ham knuckles with the remaining bay leaf and thyme sprigs. Cover with a tight lid and cook on a low heat, also for around 3 hours. Test by inserting the tip of a small knife into the knuckles – there should be no resistance. Leave to cool in the liquor.

When the ham knuckle is cool, take off the exterior fat, remove the bones and shred the meat. Add the chopped parsley, a little Dijon mustard and season to taste.

Take the trotters from the liquor, and with a sharp knife score through the skin and split them in half lengthways. Carefully take out the meat, discarding the bones and gristle but keeping the fat with the meat. Reserve the skins. Shred the trotter meat and fat and add to the ham.

Lay 2 large sheets of clingfilm on top of each other and smooth out any wrinkles. Lay the first trotter skin on the clingfilm, opening it out flat so that it forms a square. Lay another one next to it, overlapping slightly.

Spoon half of the ham mixture into the middle of the skin and form it into a long sausage shape. Use the double layer of clingfilm to roll it up inside the skin, then tie the clingfilm at each end. Repeat with the other two skins and ham mixture and chill in the fridge overnight.

Just before you are ready to serve, slice the beetroot into rounds and then cut thinly into strips. Peel and finely grate the horseradish. Add to the beetroot, along with the sorrel leaves. Season with salt and pepper and dress with the vinegar and olive oil.

To finish off the croquettes, take the 'sausages' from the fridge, remove the clingfilm and cut each one into rounds 6cm thick. Then cut each round into quarters.

Beat the eggs. Have the flour in one bowl, the beaten egg in another and the breadcrumbs in a third. Toss each piece of 'sausage' first in the flour, then in the egg and then, finally, encrust in the breadcrumbs.

Heat some vegetable oil in a large frying pan and shallow-fry for 3–4 minutes until crisp and golden brown. Serve with the beetroot, horseradish and sorrel.

The Salami Maker
of Schull

I have been down the bumpy lane in Schull where Frank Krawczyk makes his wonderful salami, next door to the cheesemaker Bill Hogan (see page 296), many, many times, but every time I visit this part of West Cork and get a few of the inimitable local directions I find myself calling up to ask, 'Which way do I go again?'

Eventually, past the acres of fields and yellow and white painted houses dotted here and there, you find the place where Frank cures and brines and smokes his extraordinary Eastern European-style charcuterie, which I rate right up there with anything the Italians do. Frank's salami is strong and real, often peppery and spicy, not numbed down for the modern palate. The first time I tasted it, I took a bite and thought, 'I'm not sure about this,' and then the flavour kicked in and my palate said, 'More.' When you find yourself longing for another slice of something, you know you are eating good food.

Frank is another of the spirited band of colourful émigrés who are helping to give Ireland the food badge I want it to wear. He was born to Polish refugees in a camp in Uganda, eventually moved to London, worked in all kinds of places from a drawing office to a building site, tried his hand living as a painter in Spain and eventually in 1974 moved to Ireland. 'My family history is chequered with resistance fighters and rebels … and Cork was historically a rebel county, so maybe that is why I ended up here,' he says. 'I have a sense of belonging to this part of Ireland. The locals often tell me I'm more Irish than they are.'

Now, he has a cause of his own, to make the kind of individualistic charcuterie that he sees as 'a form of art, an expression of my inner creativity' in the face of the authorities' demand that he spends hundreds of thousands of euros on a sanitised factory-style production operation. Coming from a smallholding environment myself, my natural instincts are always to stand up for the little people like Frank whose attitude is that you should be allowed to do your own thing. 'One doesn't give birth to children to have them all exactly the same; or write pieces of music and poetry, or paint pictures, for each one to be a replication of the other,' he says, 'so why does making charcuterie have to be part of a homogenised, mass production?'

He started making sausages in his kitchen, because, living in Ireland, the kind that he grew up on and could find easily in the Polish delis of London just weren't available. His mother had some recipes 'from the old land, and a handbook written for collectives by the communist government on how to make fresh sausages and salami, which detailed the process and science. People

said it was impossible to make salami in this country because of the humidity, but I was pigheaded enough to go ahead anyway,' he says. 'I'm sure in parts of the Po valley they have humidity to rival anything we have in Ireland, and yet they are able to produce Parma ham.'

In the beginning he wanted to replicate the flavours he remembered from his childhood, then he started thinking, 'I wonder what would happen if I do this…' As a result, he believes his charcuterie has an identity that is pure Frank Krawczyk, but at the same time is synonymous with Ireland and the particular land and climatic conditions, hence the name West Cork Salamis.

He has built his own little smokery, where whole hams hang and where the wood chips come from local furniture makers – it could be oak, juniper, eucalyptus, apple wood. 'I like to respond to whatever is around; likewise, the herbs. My recipes change according to what is in season.'

In the little maturing room, with its drawing of a pig on the door, he has created a cave-like atmosphere with unique natural cultures that make the salamis what they are. 'It's the same as producing Roquefort cheese. You can make something similar somewhere else, but you can't make Roquefort, because its character depends on ageing in the cellars of the caves at Combalou, which have their own particular microclimate. When I go to France or Italy, I see the local shops, restaurants, bars and markets celebrating with great pride local food that has been produced in pretty similar conditions to mine, and you feel that the food inspectors have been inculcated in the culture of food that has been passed down through the generations. Here, the inspector turns up in a hard hat, wellingtons, goggles, white coat, gloves… as though I was creating some germ warfare, and wants me to mature my salamis in a plastic-lined, temperature controlled unit. But the way I see it, sterility only leads to extinction.

'I am a responsible human being, I don't need the state to make decisions for me. I smell, I taste, I test … if I am unhappy with anything, it goes in the bin. I'm not in the business of poisoning anybody. I'm just an individual, transforming local pigs into a variety of produce to sell to local people and at farmers' markets,' he says. 'I make the food that I want to eat, and if I am prevented from doing what I do, then it isn't just me who is being deprived of the joy of making and eating it, but the individual who wants to share that pleasure.'

I agree with Frank, and I disagree. I agree with his championing of individuality over bland uniformity, but I disagree with his understandable pessimism that the little producer is in danger of being pushed out. I believe that times are changing, and that something good comes out of all the trials Frank and artisans like him go through, because people who love good food will always be on their side, and the more we hear about their struggles, the more we will support and rally behind such talented, stubborn, utterly brilliant individuals.

Ham and Chicken Stock

Ham Stock

I'd say I'm unusual among chefs in that I have ham stock on the go all the time. I think a ham on the bone cooked in water with a little bouquet garni of aromatic herbs, a bay leaf and some peppercorns, put in twenty minutes before the meat is cooked, makes the best jelly-like stock in the world: essence of magic. Seriously, I rate it right up there with the cheffiest *jus de veau*.

Years ago, when I was cooking at Mulligan's bar in Cork Street in London, we'd have a gammon on the simmer every day, and I just couldn't throw away the stock – it's the farming mentality: save everything, you'll find a use for it. There's never waste in my kitchen.

The reason chefs aren't often enamoured of ham stock is that they think it's too salty, so they thin it down, and then it doesn't taste of much. The secret is always to wash the ham really well first. Even if you buy a piece that says it doesn't need soaking, some hams will always be a bit saltier than others, so if you want to use the stock, always leave the ham in a pot of water overnight, then drain off the water and cook it fresh. I do the same thing with smoked haddock, incidentally.

Chicken Stock

The best way to make chicken stock is to follow the recipe for poached chicken on page 186. That way, you get a meal out of the chicken and even after you have spooned some of the stock over the bird and the dumplings you will have some left over, which you can freeze. Otherwise, you just need the carcass left after a roast chicken, or to buy some chicken wings. For a light, fresh, chickeny stock you only need to simmer the bones for about 45 minutes, not several hours.

Makes about 1.5 litres
1kg fresh chicken
   carcasses or wings, or a
   mixture
1 onion, halved
1 leek, white part only,
   cut into chunks
1 stick celery, cut into
   chunks
1 carrot, cut into chunks
1 clove garlic
4 white peppercorns
2 litres water
1 bay leaf
2 sprigs of thyme
4 parsley stalks

Put the carcasses and/or wings with the vegetables, garlic and peppercorns into a large pot and cover with the water.

Make a bouquet garni, using the outside layer of the leek (washed well). Wrap it around the bay leaf, thyme and parsley stalks, tie with string, then lower into the water and tie the string to the handle of the pot.

Bring to the boil, skim any scum from the surface, then turn down the heat and simmer for about 45 minutes. Pour through a fine sieve.

Chicken and Goose

People used to know that it was a rare thing to put a chicken on the table. It was on our farm table at home maybe once a month or on special occasions. The chickens we kept were really boiling fowl – they were the same chickens that gave us our eggs, but after about two years they'd stop laying.

When we were very small and still a bit squeamish, when Mum said, 'We're going to have boiled chicken,' we'd be screaming, because she'd be feeding the chickens one minute, and the next she'd grab one of them and have pulled its neck by the time she got to the kitchen door, then it would be hung for a day or so behind an outhouse door. Then next time we saw it, it would be on her knee being plucked and she would have it cleaned and washed and straight in the pot. She'd put whatever she had – leeks, carrots, onions – in the pot, too, and poach the chicken, which we'd eat with a big bowl of potatoes or mash, and then you'd be left with a gorgeous rich broth: the taste of it is still on my palate. I have a huge passion for deeply comforting food that takes your mind away from the stresses of everyday life, and a boiled chicken does that for me better than almost anything else. When my mother was ill – she finally succumbed to the cancer she had fought off since she was in her forties – I would boil up a big chicken with loads of vegetables in the old way, and put plenty of garlic in, and carve it up for her with a garlic mayonnaise on the side, which she loved. Sometimes when I do it today I'll put some belly pork in the pot with the chicken, add a little chilli to lift the stock, and at the last minute put in some little potatoes that I have part-cooked. That's great family food.

Those chickens from our farm were strong-tasting but delicious, and it was because they had run around all their lives, foraging in the woods and eating grain and developing proper, strong, mature bones full of marrow that they made beautiful, gelatinous broth. It's impossible to make a good stock with a cheap, poorly raised chicken slaughtered after a few weeks because of the brittleness of their immature bones. It's quite shocking: blow on them and they disintegrate. We kids would dry out the wishbones of farm chickens by the fire – and then pull them to make a wish – but you'd have to tug hard to break them.

Chickens are smelly old things. I know because when I was older I had to clean out the chicken sheds. I can't say they inspire the same fondness as a pig, but that is no reason to treat them as just another product, with no respect, stacking them into sheds, feeding them antibiotics and hormones and giving them no quality of life over the miserable few weeks of their existence.

In 2005 I caused a tidal wave in the Irish chicken industry when I said on television that industrially farmed chickens were crap. I really did get in trouble. Loads of trouble. They still talk about it in Ireland now. All the

intensive chicken farmers banded together over my 'vulgar outburst' and slapped a writ on me on behalf of the Irish chicken industry. It wasn't exactly planned. My wife, Maria, had always passed comment that she could never find a good chicken in Ireland. She'd go into the most gorgeous-looking butcher, but the chicken would always be the cheap old thing to be thrown on to the shopping list, and it rankled with me. But I'm very glad I did have my vulgar outburst, because the uproar brought home to people what they were eating in a way that years of more genteel discussion never would have. My big mistake was that I only mentioned Irish chickens, when I really wanted to highlight the plight of all industrial farmed chickens, wherever they might be.

I told the bosses of the industry I'd have my day in court; I'd turn up with two chickens, one under each arm, and represent myself and they'd really have a 'fowl day'. I was a bit nervous, I tell you, taking on a £100 million business, but I never got my big moment. I think they must have thought: we can't defeat this. It'll backfire. It was a shame in a way. To bring a bit of humour to a serious situation, I was thinking of opening a little organic chicken bar – Corrigan's Organic Chicken – outside the court for all the journalists. Joking aside, I'll tell you something: after that comment, chicken buying in Ireland changed. You could hardly find an organic chicken before, apart from in a really smart store. There wasn't the choice. Now all the cooks I know are buying organic or high quality free-range chicken, so we changed perceptions.

The chickens we buy for Lindsay House are produced by Reggie Johnson and Bud Swarbrick at their farm in the village of Goosnargh in the Ribble Valley. They are allowed to grow slowly, wandering round the fields, and only come into barns for shelter away from the foxes at night-time. Like their famous Goosnargh ducklings and geese (see the Christmas chapter for a recipe for marmalade goose), they are finished with special feed that is mixed up in their own mills. No additives or antibiotics, just well-looked-after chickens. I'm sure that Reggie and Bud could easily claim organic status for their poultry, but they choose not to. I come across many such farmers, whose practice is organic in everything but the rubber stamp, who don't feel they need the hassle of forms and tick-boxes to convince people that they are producing food of the finest quality.

Warm Chicken Salad with Fat Hen, Wet Walnuts and Verjuice

Fat hen is an old-fashioned wild plant with edible leaves; it's often thought of as a weed these days. If you can't find it, use any other salad leaves you like. When walnuts are harvested in October, if they are eaten immediately they are known as 'wet', as opposed to the ones you buy in the run-up to Christmas, which have been allowed to dry out and their shells to turn hard so they will keep. Wet walnuts are available only for a short time, because warmth and moisture make them go rancid quickly, but they are creamy and sweet-tasting because they haven't yet developed that intense, slightly tannic flavour, and you can crack their shells easily in your hands. I just love them. They're also great mixed into some crushed up potatoes, with some walnut oil, served with confit of duck or goose. Walnuts have been grown in Britain for thousands of years without crops ever being consistent, but changing weather patterns, with warmer springs and summers, are prompting some farmers in Britain to plant walnut orchards, so wet walnuts might become much easier to find.

Serves 4

1 lemon, halved

1 good free-range chicken, about 1.5kg

½ head of garlic

a few sprigs of thyme

a little softened butter

250ml verjuice (see page 49) or white wine vinegar

1 tablespoon chopped tarragon

200g fat hen or other leaves, such as rocket or watercress

200g shelled wet walnuts

200g peeled seedless grapes

Preheat the oven to 220°C/Gas 7.

Squeeze the lemon over the chicken and put the squeezed halves in the cavity along with the garlic and thyme. Spread softened butter all over the chicken. Season with salt and pepper.

Roast in the oven for 20 minutes then turn down the oven to 180°C/Gas 4 and cook for 1–1½ hours, basting occasionally, until the juices run clear when you pierce one of the thighs with a knife.

Remove the chicken from the pan and rest in a warm place.

Skim the fat from the roasting tin and pour in the verjuice or vinegar. Put the pan on the hob over a moderate heat, bring to the boil and stir to deglaze, scraping up the bits of caramelised meat from the bottom of the pan. Add the tarragon and strain into a jug.

Carve the chicken. Toss the fat hen or other leaves with the walnuts and grapes and dress with the verjuice and pan juices.

Arrange the chicken on top of the salad.

Poached Chicken with Herb Dumplings

This is such a stress-free meal to make, and so comforting to eat. It's the kind of thing I cook for my wife if she has been away somewhere and is arriving home tired. It's especially good with salsa verde. The dumplings are a cross between traditional ones and potato gnocchi, and full of herbs, so they are really speckly green, and lift the look of the dish, which is quite pale. You could also serve it with some steamed leeks.

Serves 4
1 leek
some thyme, parsley stalks and 2 bay leaves for a bouquet garni
1 free-range chicken
1 carrot
1 stick celery
4 cloves garlic, peeled
1 onion
salsa verde, to serve (see page 188)

Herb dumplings:
a little butter
½ onion, very finely chopped
1 clove garlic, very finely chopped
50g plain flour
50g semolina
4 egg yolks
450g plain mashed potatoes
2 tablespoons each tarragon and parsley, very finely chopped
a pinch of salt

First make the dumplings. Heat the butter in a pan and sweat the onion and garlic until soft.

In a bowl, mix the flour and semolina, make a well in the centre and mix in the egg yolks, then the mashed potato and herbs. Season with salt.

Flour your hands well, take pieces of the mixture (it will be quite sticky) and roll into balls, about the size of a golf ball. The trick to keeping the dumplings in one piece is to twice-cook them, otherwise they are liable to break up. So bring a pan of salted water to the boil, put in the dumplings and cook until they rise to the top. Drain carefully, refresh gently under the cold tap, then put them on a tray or plate and leave in the fridge until the chicken is done.

Use part of one of the outer layers of the leek (washed well) to wrap around the herbs and make a bouquet garni. Tie with string and then tie the string to the handle of a large pot.

Put the chicken in the pot with the whole vegetables, bouquet garni and enough water to cover, then bring to the boil, skim and turn down the heat. Simmer gently for an hour, then check that the juices of the chicken run clear when you pierce one of the thighs with a fork. Discard the vegetables, as all their flavour will have been sapped into the broth.

Lift the chicken out of the broth and put it on a warm platter. Take the dumplings from the fridge and drop them into the broth. Simmer for about 3 minutes, until heated through. Lift out with a slotted spoon and arrange around the chicken. Spoon a little of the broth over the chicken and dumplings and serve the rest separately in a jug.

Serve with the salsa verde.

Salsa Verde

Makes enough for 6

2 tablespoons flat-leaf
  parsley
1 tablespoon mint
1 tablespoon basil
1 clove garlic
3 anchovy fillets
1 tablespoon Dijon
  mustard
½ tablespoon white wine
  vinegar
1 tablespoon capers
olive oil

This is the classic accompaniment to boiled meats in Italy, and it is great with steamed fish.

Chop the parsley, mint and basil.

Crush the garlic and chop the anchovies.

Mix together with the mustard and vinegar and add the capers. Stir in the olive oil and season to taste.

Goose Confit,
Black Pudding
and Red Cabbage

I grew up having no fear about cooking with any part of an animal, from black pudding to cow heels (delicious cooked slowly, then shaved into a dandelion salad) to ox tongue, brined overnight, poached in stock, peeled and cut into thin slices, with a bitter green salad, some beetroot and mustard. This is majestic stuff.

Black pudding has a special place in my food memory bank, because as a child I used to watch it being made every year by our neighbour Kathy McKeon, on the day we dispatched our pig. She'd have a big copper pan on the range, with some rendered pig fat in there, the finely chopped onions ready, and garlic if there was any. Much later on I talked to Kathy in the years before she died about the way she made those puddings and she told me that she didn't like cooking with onions and garlic in the same pot. I never heard anyone else say that until one year, in Italy, I was talking to the Italian chef Fulvio Pierangelini at his restaurant Gambero Rosso in Tuscany about onions and garlic, and he said to me that in his opinion in Italian food you really shouldn't cook onions and garlic in the same pot. It was like déjà vu!

Kathy would sweat the onions down, put in some breadcrumbs and oatmeal as a filler, to bring everything together, take the pot off the stove to cool everything down a bit, and then the blood would be brought in to her. She would put in some vinegar to stop it coagulating, then pour it into the pot, stirring all the time until it turned a deep bishop's purple. Maybe there'd be a bit of mace in there, but we liked our pudding piggy rather than spicy, the way they prefer it in the north of England. Maybe the story there is that you wanted a bit of warmth if you were taking your pudding to eat down the mines or at the mills. But in our house, we were of the opinion that spicy black pudding and fried eggs for breakfast don't go together. You want pig and eggs; not spice and eggs.

You can't rush a black pudding. When the mixture was ready Kathy would stuff it through a funnel into sausage skins, which she'd get from the butcher, and tie them with string. Then they'd go into a big pot of barely simmering water, skins pricked a little to stop them bursting, and when they floated to the top they were ready. After that they'd be hung up in the cold dairy to dry out. Terry Wogan loves this combination of confit and black pudding and red cabbage so much he asked if we would send him fifteen portions one year for Christmas. That's a nice compliment for a chef.

I would use rock salt, rather than sea salt for curing the goose, as it is harder and doesn't melt in the same way. If you don't want to use the confit goose legs straight away, once they are cooled you can transfer them to a sterilised jar and pour all the fat from cooking over the top so that they are completely covered. Then you can keep them for a month or so in the fridge.

Serves 4

4 goose legs

100g rock salt

a small bunch of thyme

4 cloves garlic, halved

1 teaspoon black peppercorns

zest of ½ orange

1kg goose fat

1 black pudding, about 200g

a little vegetable oil

Red cabbage:

½ red cabbage

1½ tablespoons sea salt

2 red onions

a little olive oil

juice and zest of 1 orange

1 Bramley apple

4 tablespoons Demerara sugar

125ml port

2 tablespoons quince jelly or redcurrant jelly

Rub the goose legs with rock salt and put into a bowl. Add the thyme, garlic, peppercorns and orange zest. Leave to cure for at least 24 hours.

Core and thinly slice the red cabbage, toss with the sea salt and leave overnight.

When ready to cook, preheat the oven to 160°C/Gas 3, melt the goose fat in a heavy casserole on the hob. Brush the excess salt from the goose legs and pat them dry. When the fat is warm, put in the goose legs, bring to a simmer, cover with a tight lid and transfer to the oven. Cook gently for around 2 hours, until the meat comes easily away from the bone. Leave to cool.

While the goose legs are cooking, rinse the salt well from the red cabbage and drain. Thinly slice the onions. Peel and grate the apple.

Heat a little olive oil in a heavy-based pan with a lid, put in the onions and sweat until softened. Add the rest of the red cabbage ingredients, together with the drained cabbage, and stir to mix everything well. Put the lid on the pan and cook over a gentle heat, stirring occasionally, for 1–1½ hours, until the cabbage is tender. Taste and adjust the seasoning if necessary.

Towards the end of the cooking time for the cabbage, turn up the oven to 220°C/Gas 7 ready to finish off the goose. Remove the goose legs from their fat. Lay them on a rack over a roasting tray and put into the oven for 10–15 minutes, until crisp and golden.

Slice the black pudding. Heat a little vegetable oil in a frying pan and sauté on both sides. Serve the goose with a generous spoonful of red cabbage and slices of black pudding.

A Doorbell
in Soho

When I opened Lindsay House in Soho in 1997 it was a monster success from the word go. We were about as anti-formula as you could get. It was a crazy location in retrospect. Four stories of a narrow eighteenth-century townhouse shouldn't really work as a restaurant, but it did.

I think there was a feeling about town of, 'Yeah, we know the guy can cook; but can he sustain his own place?'

I was fresh from my adventures cooking at the Hackney Stadium, and then at the Barbican. Most cooks who take the kind of U-turns I had taken after leaving Fulham Road are lost for ever – a dog and motorbike track isn't the obvious career path – but I just saw it all as another interesting window of opportunity, and the deviation did me no harm whatsoever. On my first menu at Hackney I had Simon Hopkinson's hare and lentil soup and a roast chicken and fennel terrine, with loads of tarragon (based on a recipe from the great French chef Freddy Girardet). The journalists followed me down to Hackney, most probably to see what a shambles the crazy Corrigan had made of his career, but then discovered they liked it. It was just a mad, fun time.

Next, like a gun for hire, I was drafted in to the Barbican, where I saw catering on a scale I had never witnessed before. My arrival there coincided with Sir John Tusa taking over as managing director. He and the artistic director, Graham Sheffield, were making huge changes and I rode on the wave of it. I think they liked what I was doing because they allowed me to carry on and turn around the brasserie, make it somewhere people wanted to eat, because before that it was shocking. Graham Sheffield called me the Herbert von Karajan of the kitchen. We put a bakery and butchery in the kitchen and refurbished everything.

I have a tough streak in me. I don't think you can get to the top of a cock of hay without it, and any other institution would probably have sacked me within twenty-four hours for the way I went about things – the Corporation of London's city solicitor told me he had an easy life for twenty years, until I came along! But I put together a good team and we turned the place around, because I believe you can always make things better on any level and on any scale. And I loved the cultural environment of this amazing place that had been put together for the people of Britain, but up to that time wasn't used nearly enough: the library, the concerts, the theatre going on around us. It was brilliant, a welcome change from the life that we often live as chefs, immersed in food and cooking for six days a week, eighteen hours a day, with no time for anything else. There was a great library beside the kitchen, which I used to go into all the time. I got the idea for the fig tart and tobacco syrup that I put on the menu at Lindsay House, from reading about ingredients in that library.

But the farmer in me wanted to be my own boss. At this stage of my life I'd have made bacon butties in a caff, just to be self-employed. What kills most cooks is getting the money together to buy their own restaurant, and when I had left Fulham Road I was quite broke, but with the proceeds from the consultancies and the help of a couple of shareholders, I was able to buy Lindsay House. Talk about a shoestring, though. Someone said we probably gave £3 to a designer and got £2.90 back. We wrote quotations from the likes of James Joyce and Brendan Behan on a wall, and the Soho writer, broadcaster and photographer Daniel Farson gave me twelve of his pictures for the walls, for a small exchange of money and a deal to throw his farewell to Soho party. When people heard, they said, 'He'll bankrupt you; the party will run for a week,' because he was a serious alcoholic at the time. But sadly he died two days before the party.

At Lindsay House you had to ring the bell on the front door to get in – an idea I have always loved. You feel you are in on a special secret when someone comes to the door and says, 'How are you? Come on in!' It was like saying, 'Welcome to my place.' I wanted to serve stonking, fresh, local food; a bit Bohemian, old Soho, but a bit restrained, too, with all the experiences I had been through from Irish farm to Mediterranean food drawn together. I didn't want to be pigeon-holed, I just wanted integrity, happy punters, and a full house.

A. A. Gill was the guy who gave us the real leg up. I was probably down to my last few pounds when he came down to review Lindsay House. I remember Tom Colicchio, the head chef from the Gramercy Tavern in New York, was sitting in the restaurant. One of the staff had run down to Piccadilly Circus and picked up an early copy of the *Sunday Times*, and we read the review, and Tom said, 'You're a success.' We drank a few bottles and went home at three or four in the morning.

You don't memorise your reviews, really you don't, but when they are that significant, you find you still talk about them years later. If I recall rightly Gill had saddle of hare spiked with cloves, and some Chinese greens that we had run over to Chinatown to get for the evening's service, then fig tart with tobacco syrup; and a big lump of Keen's Cheddar afterwards. He asked for biscuits, but we didn't have any, we had only our own-made bread, so we went round the corner to the French House to get him some biscuits. Gill said afterwards he was in shock: 'What the f… was going down here?' But I think he likes a bit of madness, and he wrote in his column, 'Don't walk – to get down there – run.' And they ran.

There was a great crowd of revolutionaries cooking around the time: Alastair Little, Rowley Leigh, Fergus Henderson, Henry Harris, Mark Hix, Stephen Terry… we were all producing spontaneous food, with a bit of a flourish, a bit of craziness, and when we closed the kitchens after service, some serious partying went on, I can tell you. How my wife Maria put up with me, I'll never know; let's say there were always a lot of roses in our house!

Lindsay House has been a fabulous experience over the years, but Bentley's has allowed me to take a much simpler approach to cooking. A businessman I know in Ireland made a great comment to me that when chefs send him out amusettes, amuses-gueules, amuses-bouches, pre-desserts… he sends them straight back, saying he's chosen what he wants to eat and he doesn't want anyone interfering.

I think more and more people are coming round to that way of thinking now; the whole haute cuisine thing as we knew it is changing. My new restaurant, Corrigan's, is on Upper Grosvenor Street, in Mayfair, in the space that was once Chez Nico. Nico was one of the greatest chefs of his generation, and, I can honestly say, even more opinionated than me! I don't know what it is about this site, but it attracts some strong-minded people. It's a grand location, right enough, but it will still have the British and Irish spirit singing from every door and window.

Lamb

Sheep farming is an ancient tradition among the Celtic peoples. Their sheep are animals that have adapted and can thrive on poor mountain land, growing strongly and slowly on the wild plants that grow there, which give flavour to their meat. Around some of the more extreme wild and rocky West Cork, Kerry and Connemara coastlines you'll see them up on the cliffs or in a ditch, with nothing for miles around but tiny old abandoned stone houses, or they'll appear suddenly and crowd onto the road. Around Connemara, too, people are now raising saltmarsh lamb, which has long been a speciality in France, where they call it *pré-salé*. Saltmarsh lamb, which is grazed on salt-tolerant grasses, herbs and plants like samphire, has a very special flavour all of its own.

In London our lamb actually comes from Wales, from Daphne and William Tilley and their sons, John and David, in the Elwy Valley. The Tilleys are a passionate, committed bunch whose farm overlooks an amazing expanse of green fields in front of the Snowdonia mountain range. Daphne's grandmother was apparently a great friend of Escoffier and she knows her food. She's a real Welsh warrior, galloping around the hills on her horse and championing the very best-quality meat; no compromise. Her family have been farming up in the hills for about a thousand years, and they have spent the last twenty-five years carefully cross-breeding traditional speckly faced Welsh Beulah Hill sheep, which are quite lanky, athletic, mountaineering animals, with other breeds, so that you end up with meat that has extra muscle and a high ratio of lean meat to bone and fat, but still keeps the flavour and texture of the original breed. The animals graze up to 1,000 feet up on grass (they get hay in the winter), and about six weeks before slaughter they are brought down from the hills and fed valley grassland, which gives a real burst of muscle and flavour on top of the mountain herbs. They are slaughtered locally so they're not stressed. With lamb this is particularly important, the Tilleys say, because if the animals are roughly handled or panicky, blood clots can appear in the meat, which affect the flavour and it will be tougher. The meat is hung for 10–15 days to let it mature a little, which is the way it would always have been done in slower, less money-grubbing times, so it has a very different character to most supermarket lamb, which is slaughtered, cut up and in the shops as quickly as possible.

People talk about spring lamb, but the best time to eat lamb is actually in the summer through to the autumn, because this is when you get true spring lamb, which means the animals were actually *born* in the spring and raised on lush summer grass in the lowlands, or natural vegetation and herbs up in the mountains, so their meat becomes sweet and tasty and has that nice layer of fat you always want to keep it juicy and tender when you cook it.

That ridiculously expensive Easter lamb we've all got used to will actually have been born indoors around Christmas and January and then grazed on lowland winter grasses, with a supplement of other feed to bring it on, so the meat is quite light, not only in colour but in flavour, too. What I do like in spring is lamb's sweetbreads, just cleaned, steeped in cold water, patted dry and peeled, then dusted in flour, beaten egg and finally breadcrumbs, shallow-fried for a couple of minutes on each side until crisp and golden brown. Cheap, delicious food.

Likewise around Easter I love lamb's kidneys, lightly cooked in a pan with some Madeira splashed in, then set to rest so the juices mingle together … such a fantastic flavour. Or pan-fried lamb's liver – seared quickly in a hot pan, then rested (you have to treat it more delicately than calf's liver), sprinkled with some sea salt and balsamic vinegar and served with crispy salad leaves – culinary heaven. Or fried up for breakfast with a few pieces of bacon: it's one of the best things you can eat.

Anyone can cook prime cuts of lamb, but when the meat is as good as that of the Tilleys' you can make good use of the shoulder, which when you cook it slowly becomes meltingly tender – one recipe we do involves cooking it slowly for eight hours.

The cook and writer Richard Olney once said that the Irish stew was closer to the Frenchman's heart than the Irish, which could be seen as a bit of a bitter and twisted statement, but I knew what he was saying, because not only in Ireland, but throughout the British Isles, we aren't nearly as proud of our wonderful slow-cooking processes as we should be. A stew or anything slow-braised is still not considered refined cooking here – maybe in Ireland it still has connotations of famine and emigration – whereas a French person is rightly proud of their daubes and navarins. It is hard for me to convince customers to eat an Irish stew, but in Bentley's in Dublin, I hope to revive it.

If I put in some tomatoes, peppers and olives and call it a daube, on the other hand, people love it. There is a part of me, though, that agrees that lamb takes more kindly to the Provençal-style treatment, because the fat on a shoulder of lamb can be quite harsh and can come through on the palate strongly. The classic Irish stew, to my mind, is pretty pure, plain and white, with the meat not being browned first. It isn't thickened with roux or creams, or made with gigot chops. Myrtle Allen, however, browns her meat for Irish stew and thickens it with flour, too. And you know what, we can debate it all night, and we frequently do, but it's best to have such discussions over a bottle of wine and enjoy yourselves.

The way I get over the fat factor is to bring the lamb to the boil first in salted water with some thyme, then simmer it gently for a short time and just skim off any excess fat. I let it cool down, so any remaining fat sets, and you can scoop it off. Then I put the water through a sieve, to get the little bits of impurities out, put it back over the lamb in the pot and get a good stock going, with some large pieces of carrot and onion, a bouquet garni, some sea salt and water. About fifteen to twenty minutes before it is fully cooked, I take out the meat and pass the stock through a fine sieve again, pushing all the vegetables through, then put everything back in the pan with one part carrots, one part onions and two parts potatoes, cut into chunks, and some thyme. Some of the potatoes I cut into smaller dice, so they break up and become the thickening agent.

Pearl barley is used in different parts of Ireland, which I don't mind, and of course the traditional Irish stew was more likely to have been made with mutton, not lamb, but the scarcity of Irish mutton over the years has often meant a scarcity of such Irish stew on menus.

There's been a huge resurgence in the popularity of mutton, which, incidentally, is defined as meat from an animal that is over two years old, but could be as mature as four or five years. Under a year old it is lamb, and over one year, before it gets to be mutton, it is a hogget. Mutton is in season from October to March, and I like a wintry Irish stew made with it on frosty days, or mutton chops in a Lancashire hotpot-style dish, browned off first, but in truth I think mutton can be a bit overrated. I've seen chefs cooking mutton dishes all day, doing this process and that process, and I'm thinking, 'What are you waiting for: a miracle?' It's mutton. Good and tasty, yes, but just mutton.

Eight-hour Lamb

Serves 6

1 shoulder of lamb,
  boned and rolled

5 sprigs of rosemary

2 cloves garlic, sliced

200ml olive oil

1kg goose fat

The lamb is marinated for 3–5 days before cooking, so it's a long, slow process that will leave you with meltingly tender meat and the flavour of the garlic and rosemary really coming through.

Make a series of small incisions in the shoulder with the tip of a sharp knife and stud with rosemary and slices of garlic. Pour over the olive oil and leave to marinate in the fridge for 3–5 days.

Preheat the oven to 150°C/Gas 2.

Put the lamb into a large casserole. Melt the goose fat in a pan and pour it over the lamb.

Put a circle of greaseproof paper on top to make a 'cartouche', which will keep all the moisture and juices inside, put into the oven and leave to cook slowly for 8 hours.

Remove the casserole from the oven and take the lamb from the goose fat. Season liberally with salt and pepper. Allow to rest for an hour in a warm place before carving.

Spiced Lamb with Chickpeas and Roasted Peppers

Serves 6–8

3 tablespoons coriander
    seeds
1 tablespoon cumin
    seeds
200g natural yoghurt
1 shoulder of lamb,
    boned and flattened
2 cloves garlic, sliced
2 small chillies, deseeded
    and sliced

**Chickpeas and roasted
    peppers:**
1kg dried chickpeas
4 red peppers
olive oil

Soak the chickpeas in cold water for 24 hours. Long soaking really helps them to soften properly when you cook them later.

Heat the coriander and cumin seeds in a dry frying pan, until they release their aroma. Crush in a pestle and mortar or blender and put through a fine sieve. The fine powder is what you're looking for. Mix most of this into the yoghurt and rub all over the inside of the lamb (keep a little back for the chickpeas). Leave to marinate overnight.

Drain and rinse the chickpeas, put them in a large saucepan, and cover with about twice their volume of water (don't salt it, as salt will toughen the skins of the chickpeas and make them wrinkly). Bring to the boil, then turn down the heat and simmer for around 2 hours until tender, topping up with water if necessary.

Towards the end of the cooking time for the chickpeas, preheat the grill. Preheat the oven to 200°C/Gas 6. Halve and deseed the peppers, coat them in olive oil and grill them until the skins begin to blister. Place in a bowl, cover with clingfilm and allow to cool. Once cooled, peel away the skin, roughly chop and cover with more olive oil until you need them.

Scatter the garlic and chilli over the lamb, roll it up and secure with string. Wrap it in greaseproof paper and then in foil. The double layer will keep all the juices inside and the greaseproof will stay strong, whereas foil on its own has a tendency to split. Put into a roasting tin in the oven and roast for about 20–30 minutes, until it is melting. Allow the meat to rest for 35 minutes in a warm oven while you finish off the chickpeas.

When the chickpeas are cooked, drain them and mix with the peppers and olive oil and add the reserved powdered coriander and cumin. Season to taste.

Unwrap and slice the lamb and serve with the chickpeas.

Steamed Lamb Pudding

This is a dish that was made first by Chris McGowan, my head chef at Lindsay House, and has become a big favourite. You need a 3-pint/1.75-litre pudding bowl. You can make the suet paste the day before, if you like; wrap it in clingfilm and leave in the fridge.

Serves 6–8

500g diced lamb
  shoulder

olive oil

1 onion, diced

2 carrots, diced

4 sticks celery, diced

2 cloves garlic, crushed

½ bunch of thyme

1 tablespoon tomato
  paste

2 tablespoons flour

¼ bottle red wine

¾ litre chicken stock

100ml water

a little butter, for
  greasing

Suet paste:

300g self-raising flour

1 tablespoon baking
  powder

a pinch of salt

150g suet

up to 140ml chilled
  water

Preheat the oven to 150°C/Gas 2.

First make the filling: season the lamb and brown it in a little olive oil in a large flameproof casserole. Add the vegetables, garlic and thyme and cook for 4–5 minutes. Add the tomato paste and flour and stir well. Pour in the wine and let it bubble up and reduce by half. Cover with the chicken stock and water, transfer to the oven and allow to braise for around 1½–2 hours until tender, then take off the heat and leave to cool down in the casserole.

To make the pastry, sift the flour, baking powder and salt into a bowl. Mix in the suet and stir in just enough water to make a soft and pliable dough.

Turn the dough out on to a floured surface and knead it quickly and lightly, then roll it out. Cut out a circle about 30–35cm in diameter. Gather up the remaining dough, roll out again, and cut out a second circle the same size as the circumference of the bowl. This will be the lid.

Grease the pudding basin with butter and lift the larger circle of dough into it, pressing it into the base and around the sides. Brush the top edge with water.

Spoon in the braised lamb with a slotted spoon, then pour over the sauce, checking first that it is good and thick. If it isn't looking thick enough, put it into a pan and boil it hard to reduce, before pouring it in.

Lay the dough 'lid' over the top, seal and pinch the edges of the dough together, and then cover with a buttered disc of baking parchment.

Wrap the entire pudding in foil, then place the bowl on a steamer rack in a large saucepan and pour in enough boiling water to come three-quarters of the way up the basin. Cover the pan and steam for 2 hours, adding more boiling water when the level goes down.

Alternatively, steam in a pressure cooker.

Lamb's Liver with Red Onions, Sage and Champ

A bowl of champ on the side is beautiful with this. When I make champ these days I don't like to mash the potatoes completely any more. The only time you will ever hear Richard Corrigan talking about crushing spuds – oh so fashionable in restaurants for a while – is when I'm making champ. I just like to break them up with the back of a fork. I don't let my scallions soften up either, because I want them to crunch a bit and I want that sharp oniony flavour singing at the back of my mouth and around my ears.

When fresh figs are around, you could halve them and toss them into the pan of liver at the end, along with the sherry vinegar and a handful of chives.

Sometimes, instead of serving the liver with champ, I toss some pieces of bread through the onions after they've finished soaking, to make a little salad, with lots of soft, mixed herbs.

Serves 4

4 large red onions
a bunch of sage leaves
800g lamb's liver, cut
  into slices about 1cm
  thick
vegetable oil, for frying
  and deep-frying
100ml sherry vinegar

Champ:

500g medium-size floury
  potatoes, in their skins
75ml milk
4–5 spring onions,
  chopped
60g butter

Slice the red onions very thinly and pour boiling salted water over them. Leave to stand for 45 minutes. This softens and rounds off their flavour (in the same way as roasting garlic cloves).

Meanwhile, cook the potatoes in their skins in a pan of boiling, salted water for about 20 minutes until just tender – you want a bit of resistance still in there.

Drain in a colander and then put the colander over the pan in which you have just cooked them (off the heat) to dry them out a bit. Peel while still warm. Crush them roughly with the back of a fork.

Put the milk in a clean pan with the spring onions and bring to a simmer for about a minute, no longer, because you want to keep the crunch in the onion. Add the potatoes and mix in, then put in the butter, let it melt, stir it through the potatoes and season. Keep warm.

Press 4 sage leaves on top of each slice of liver. Put a film of oil in a pan, and when it is very hot put in the liver, sage-side down, and cook for about 1½–2 minutes, then turn over and cook for a further 1½ minutes, until medium rare.

In a separate pan, heat a little vegetable oil (make sure it comes no more than one-third the way up the pan) and fry the rest of the sage leaves very briefly until they are crisp. Drain on kitchen paper.

Take out the liver and keep warm. Pour the sherry vinegar into the pan.

Let it bubble up while you stir to deglaze the pan, scraping up any caramelised bits of meat that have stuck to the bottom.

Drain the onions, pile them up on to your serving plates, top with liver and pour the pan juices over the top.

Garnish with the deep-fried sage leaves and serve with the champ.

Lamb's Kidneys on a Rosemary Skewer

I love offal, but I think you have to be at one with it to enjoy cooking it. I also think that you need a strong flavour to go with something like kidneys: in this case some homemade harissa. Mixed with the juices from the kidneys, with a bowl of tabbouleh or couscous, I think this is one of the best things in the world. This is the way I want to eat.

If you like you can cube some lamb fillet, add it to the marinade and alternate it with the kidneys on the skewers. Or even add some sweetbreads. Soak them in cold water for several hours (overnight is ideal), changing the water a couple of times first, then put them into a pan of clean water with a pinch of salt. Bring to the boil and simmer gently for a minute or two, then plunge the sweetbreads into a bowl of iced water and peel them when cool. Dry them and then add them to the marinade.

We make the harissa with piquillo peppers – slightly spicy, roasted red peppers from Spain, which you can buy in jars – but if they are too costly or you can't find any, just grill two red peppers until blackened, then peel, deseed and chop them.

If you like, you could also serve this with some raita, made with chopped cucumber, mint and a little crushed garlic, mixed into Greek yoghurt and seasoned with salt. And if you don't want to make harissa, you could add a splash of sherry vinegar to the kidneys, just before serving – but I wouldn't do both.

Cut the kidneys in half and remove the core; a pair of sharp scissors will do the job. Put in a bowl with the olive oil. Strip the rosemary branches of their leaves – keep the branches to act as skewers – and add the leaves to the kidneys along with the garlic and some pepper, then marinate for a minimum of 2 hours in the fridge.

To make the harissa, put the spices into a dry frying pan and roast until they release their fragrance – take care not to let them burn. Crush in a pestle and mortar or spice grinder, and put through a fine sieve.

Put the chillies, garlic and peppers into a food processor with the ground spices, a pinch of salt and the olive oil, and blend to a paste.

To make the tabbouleh, rinse the bulghur wheat under cold water to remove some of the starch, drain and tip into a bowl. Drizzle a little olive oil over the

Serves 4
12 lamb's kidneys

50ml olive oil

4 strong branches of rosemary

2 cloves garlic, sliced

a pinch of salt

Tabbouleh:
100g bulghur wheat

olive oil

200ml boiling water

4 spring onions, chopped

1 tablespoon chopped parsley

1 tablespoon chopped mint

1 tablespoon chopped coriander

lemon juice, to taste

Harissa:
2 teaspoons coriander seeds

2 teaspoons caraway seeds

1 teaspoon cumin seeds

4 large red chillies, deseeded and chopped

4 cloves garlic, chopped

½ jar piquillo peppers (or red peppers, see above)

2 tablespoons good olive oil

wheat, add a good pinch of salt and stir well. Pour over the boiling water, cover the bowl tightly with clingfilm and leave for 20 minutes.

Drain the bulghur wheat through a sieve, pressing with a spoon to remove the liquid. Tip into a clean bowl. Add the spring onions to the wheat. Mix in the chopped herbs, dress with lemon juice and olive oil to taste and season well with salt.

Remove the kidneys from their marinade and thread on to the rosemary branch skewers. Season with salt and grill over hot charcoal for 2–3 minutes on each side or until cooked to your liking. Alternatively, use a ridged griddle pan.

Serve with the harissa and tabbouleh.

Beef

My first taste of 24-month-old Hereford grass-fed beef from the countryside around Tipperary was a few years back at Peter and Mary Ward's well-known little coffee shop and deli, Country Choice, in Nenagh, which is always packed with local produce and homemade dishes. On a table outside there'll be big bowls of hen's eggs in different colours and sizes, and inside there are farmhouse butters and soda breads on the counter, pig's trotters and carrageen moss. I'd been invited for lunch one day, but I got there an hour and a half late, so the beef that Peter had been roasting for lunch was 'over', as my mother would have said. And yet when he carved it up it was still gorgeous, like nothing I'd tasted in London. That said it all to me. I was flabbergasted by the quality. Peter is a man after my own heart, from Dunderry near Dublin, completely dedicated to supporting local farmers and producers. He gets as lyrical about proper butter and milk as I do, and he even used to cut peat when he was a boy, too! The reporter from the local paper dropped by and we had a bottle of wine or two and the funniest Irish story-telling lunch. I had to keep asking myself, is this real, or are we in a Flann O'Brien novel?

It was the first time I had been excited about beef in so long. I had barely had it on the menu at Lindsay House because I'd lost interest. I wasn't excited by kobe beef being fed beer and given massages either, even if it was appearing on smart menus. Give us a break: are we that bored with our food that it takes stories like this to get us interested? Especially as our own native grass-fed beef was considered the best in the world until the BSE crisis dented our reputation.

But the pride and the passion is beginning to come back, and there are serious, thoughtful farmers now in Britain and Ireland who are really getting beef production right, who want to deal directly with their customers and are happy to talk to you and answer questions, because they really care about what they do.

People talk about traceability, but I want the real thing, not lip service. I want to be able to talk to a butcher and ask him which farm my meat came from, and for him to know everything about it, almost down to the name of the cow.

Good meat isn't just about good practice but genetics, too. You want smaller, old-fashioned breeds that have adapted themselves to their native terrain and pasture, and are allowed to grow slowly to maturity on grass, as opposed to modern breeds of bigger animals that can be fattened up quickly, are often kept inside in sheds, and are slaughtered early. We are incredibly privileged in Britain and Ireland to have cattle that can be out grazing on grass for ten months of the year. It's a unique scenario, which, at its best, produces the greatest beef in the world. In the case of the Irish Hereford and Angus cattle, good practice and grazing on grass results in a marbling of fat evenly throughout the meat, which is what will keep it succulent and tender when you cook it, especially harshly on the grill or in a pan.

Beef has to be aged. Traditionally, every butcher would have hung their beef as a matter of course, for at least three weeks and sometimes up to five, but these days you'll be lucky if it is hung for a fortnight. In supermarkets it often isn't aged at all: you can tell, because it is bright red, whereas aged meat turns a darker burgundy colour. It will often just be butchered in massive cutting plants, put in 'modified atmosphere' packs and sent straight into the chill counters. Hanging is a skill. You have to understand the meat and the way it matures, controlling the conditions so that the natural enzymes work on the proteins, breaking them down and tenderising the flesh and making it more tasty. But from a supermarket's point of view it is a time- and space-consuming business. Also, the longer you age your beef, the more it loses moisture and therefore weight, at a rate that must be quite shocking to a businessman thinking how much money he is losing with every kilo.

Braised Short Rib of Beef with Thai Spices

I ate something similar to this in New York, thought it was absolutely delicious, came back and told Brendan about it, and he came up with this dish, which I love. Serve it with some steamed jasmine rice.

Serves 4

about 3cm piece fresh ginger, roughly chopped

3 sticks lemongrass

2 cloves garlic

2 shallots, chopped

a bunch of coriander with stalks and roots

3 green chillies, deseeded

2 tins coconut milk

a little vegetable oil

20 short ribs of beef

a small knob of fresh galangal, roughly chopped

1 teaspoon palm sugar

Preheat the oven to 150°C/Gas 2.

Put three-quarters of the ginger into a blender with 2 of the lemongrass sticks, the garlic, shallots, coriander stalks and roots and 2 of the chillies and blend to a paste.

Carefully open the tins of coconut milk (do not shake them, and keep them the right way up). Spoon the cream from the top of the tins into a wok or large saucepan. Add the spicy paste and cook gently for a couple of minutes until the spices release their aromas, taking care that the mixture doesn't catch and burn (if you are worried you can add a touch of vegetable oil). Pour in the rest of the coconut water from the tins, stir well, cook for a couple of minutes, then take off the heat.

Heat a little vegetable oil in a large flameproof casserole dish. Season the short ribs and put them into the pan. Brown them quickly on all sides, then pour in the spicy sauce. Put into the oven for about 1½–2 hours, until the meat comes easily away from the bone.

Chop the remaining ginger, lemongrass and chilli.

Take the ribs out of the sauce, put them on a serving plate and keep them warm. Put the casserole on the hob and bring the sauce to the boil. Add the ginger, lemongrass, chilli, galangal and palm sugar, bring back to the boil for about 30 seconds, then pass the sauce through a fine sieve over the top of the ribs. Scatter with the chopped coriander leaves.

Hand-chopped Rump Steak Burger with Peppered Bone Marrow

I think our burgers, made with bone marrow, the way we used to do them at Stephen Bull's restaurant in Blandford Street, are the best in the world; lovely chargrilled on a summer's day, eaten in your hand – you don't want them on a plate. I just think beef for burgers has to be hand cut; has to be. When you get ultra-fine minced meat, it's not meat you're eating any more; it's baby food. I really think you have to respect the composition of good beef, and you can't ever grind it down mechanically as well as you can hand-cut it. I really believe that.

The burgers I made with Stephen always had a little grated bone marrow in there, to give them some extra juiciness, but I like the idea of encrusting some more little rounds of bone marrow in crushed peppercorns and sitting them on top.

The other 'must-have' is marjoram, plenty of it. Beef needs marjoram! Sit the burgers on some grilled sourdough with garlic béarnaise (see page 214) – the boys in my kitchen are all mad for garlic béarnaise; they'd eat it on anything. Or some salsa rossa, just some red onions, red peppers, garlic, tomatoes and chilli all chopped together, with some grated horseradish mixed in at the end. Just great grub.

Serves 4

125g bone marrow

25g butter, plus a little extra

1 medium onion, finely chopped

1 tablespoon picked marjoram leaves

400g rump steak, trimmed of any excess fat and sinew

a handful of black peppercorns

a little vegetable oil

a little olive oil

4 slices of sourdough bread and garlic béarnaise (see page 214), to serve

Keep the bone marrow, wrapped, in the freezer until you are ready to use it – hardening it up will make it easier to cut and grate.

Heat the butter in a small pan and sauté the onion for 2–3 minutes, until soft but not coloured. Add the marjoram, stir, take off the heat and leave to cool.

With a very sharp knife, chop the steak finely until it looks like coarse minced meat. Cut four rounds from the bone marrow (use about three-quarters of it) and put them back into the freezer, then grate the rest of the bone marrow on top of the steak. Mix in the cooled onion and season well.

Shape the mixture gently, without squashing, into four 9 x 2cm patties, and put on a plate in the fridge for about an hour to firm up.

Meanwhile, crush the black peppercorns in a pestle and mortar or wrap them in a clean cloth and bash them with a rolling pin.

Heat the vegetable oil in a large frying pan and cook the burgers over a medium heat for 3 minutes each side for medium rare (cook for longer if you prefer your burgers more well done). Remove the burgers from the pan, cover and allow to rest.

Take the rounds of bone marrow from the fridge and dust them on both sides with the peppercorns. Add a knob of butter and a little olive oil to the pan, get it good and hot, and put in the peppered bone marrow. Fry quickly on each side until caramelised. Put one round on top of each burger.

Put the slices of bread into the pan and toast for a minute on each side until they soak up all the lovely juices and turn crisp and golden. Lay a burger (topped with peppered bone marrow) on top of each slice and eat immediately with a little garlic béarnaise on top.

Garlic Béarnaise

Makes enough for 10
450g butter
2 tablespoons white wine
4 tablespoons white wine
  vinegar
4 egg yolks
1 teaspoon chopped
  parsley
2 cloves garlic, crushed
salt and cayenne pepper
lemon juice, to taste

To clarify the butter, melt it in a small pan then carefully tip out the golden oil, leaving behind the milky residue, which you can throw away.

Put the white wine and wine vinegar in a non-reactive pan. Bring to the boil, then turn down the heat and reduce until only a tablespoon is left in the pan. Take off the heat.

Stir in the egg yolks, then slowly pour in the clarified butter, whisking all the time, until all the butter is absorbed and the sauce starts to thicken.

Stir in the parsley and garlic. Season with salt and a little cayenne. Taste, and if you want a little more acidity, add some lemon juice.

Osso Bucco-style Braised Veal with Capers

Serves 4

4 shanks of veal

500ml red wine

olive oil

a knob of butter

1 onion, roughly chopped

4 sticks celery, roughly chopped

4 cloves garlic, chopped

6 plum tomatoes, roughly chopped

a handful of marjoram

a handful of capers, drained

Gremolata:

equal quantities of grated lemon zest, chopped parsley and garlic

Put the veal shanks into a bowl, pour the red wine over and leave in the fridge to marinate for 24 hours.

Heat a little olive oil and butter in a large pan. Take the veal shanks out of the marinade (reserving it) and pat dry. Season the shanks and brown them on all sides, then take out of the pan and set aside.

Put the onion, celery and garlic into the same pan and sweat until softened, then return the shanks to the pan. Add the chopped tomatoes and reserved marinade and bring to the boil to burn off the alcohol. Turn down the heat and simmer gently for 2½–3 hours, until the meat starts to come away from the bone.

Take out the meat and keep warm. Pass the cooking liquid through a sieve into a bowl, pushing down on the vegetables with the back of a spoon to extract as much flavour as possible, then return both liquid and shanks to the pan, heat through again gently and add the marjoram and capers.

Mix together the ingredients for the gremolata, sprinkle over the top, and serve with buttered pappardelle or tagliatelle.

Rump of Beef
with Sauce Nivernaise

Fillet steak? No thanks, it's very overrated except served raw as carpaccio. It's the marbling of fat that drives the flavour of a piece of beef, and fillet, which is taken from the inside of the loin, is a bit of a lazy muscle. That is why it is the most tender steak you can have, but it is too bland for my liking. When you cook any steak, make sure you take it out of the fridge and bring it to room temperature before cooking, otherwise it will be too cold, and will take longer to cook. Season it with black pepper and sea salt immediately before cooking, no earlier – otherwise the salt will draw out the moisture and juices that you want to keep inside the steak.

This is an old favourite recipe that I've been cooking for a long time. It is based on a recipe of Elizabeth David's in *French Provincial Cooking* for Sauce Nivernaise, in which you first make a snail butter with parsley, garlic, lemon juice, salt and pepper and then add it to a sauce made with white wine. However we make a sauce in the same way as the garlic béarnaise (see page 214). As well as absorbing the flavours of the sauce, the snails give back their own earthy, distinctive flavour. We think of eating snails as something very French, but there is a tradition of collecting and eating them in Britain that goes back to the Romans; and at one time they were a wild, cheap food that everyone in the countryside would have made use of.

For a long time there weren't many snails other than tinned to be had in Britain, unless you went hunting for them yourself, but now there are one or two snail farmers around the country who are breeding them commercially, feeding them on a mixture of cereal and herbs, preparing and cooking them and sending them out by mail order or supplying specialist shops. If you can find some, they are a cut above the canned ones, which tend to soak up the brine they are kept in, affecting their flavour.

This is good served quite classically with some chunky chips (see page 88) and bunches of watercress.

First, make the sauce. To clarify the butter, melt it in a small pan then carefully tip out the golden oil, leaving behind the milky residue, which you can throw away.

Put the white wine and wine vinegar in a non-reactive pan. Bring to the boil, then turn down the heat and reduce until only a tablespoon is left in the pan. Take off the heat.

Serves 4
vegetable oil
4 x 225g rump steaks

Sauce Nivernaise:
225g butter
1 tablespoon white wine
2 tablespoons white wine
   vinegar
2 egg yolks
100g cooked snails,
   chopped (if canned,
   drain them first and
   rinse)
1 teaspoon chopped
   parsley
2 cloves garlic, crushed
salt and cayenne pepper
lemon juice, to taste

Stir in the egg yolks, then slowly pour in the clarified butter, whisking all the time, until all the butter is absorbed and the sauce starts to thicken. Stir in the snails, parsley and garlic and season with salt and a little cayenne. Taste, and if you want a little more acidity, add some lemon juice.

To cook the steaks, pour a thin film of vegetable oil into a heavy-based pan and when it is really hot season the steaks and add to the pan, cooking in batches if necessary. Sear them without disturbing them for around 2–3 minutes, depending on their thickness, and how rare you like your meat, then turn over and cook the other side. You can test how well done the steak is by pressing it with your finger or the back of the fork. It will still be very springy when it is rare; for medium rare there will still be a little bit of spring; and for well done there will be no give at all.

Take out the steaks and rest them for 5 minutes before serving with the sauce.

Beef and Oyster Pie

You can make this up the day before, if you like, and keep it in the fridge until you are ready to bake it. Sometimes instead of covering the pie in pastry, we make a cottage pie. Just use 1kg of floury potatoes. Towards the end of the beef cooking time, peel the potatoes and cook in boiling salted water until tender. Drain in a colander, allow the potatoes to steam for a couple of minutes to rid them of excess moisture, then mash and season with salt and pepper. Pipe the potato over the pie – or spoon it, and go over it with the prongs of a fork – then sprinkle with a couple of tablespoons of fresh breadcrumbs mixed with a tablespoon of grated Parmesan and bake for half an hour until golden brown.

Serves 8

8 rock oysters
500g braising beef
   (flank, blade or chuck)
1 x 330ml bottle
   Guinness or oyster
   stout
a little vegetable oil
1 small onion, diced
1 carrot, diced
1 stick celery, diced
1 clove garlic, crushed
a few sprigs of thyme
1 tablespoon flour
500g puff pastry
1 egg, beaten

Shuck the oysters (see page 122) and reserve the liquor.

Trim the beef of excess fat and gristle and cut into cubes. Pour the stout over and allow to marinate for 24 hours.

Preheat the oven to 160°C/Gas 3. Remove the meat from the marinade (keep this on one side), pat dry and season with salt and pepper. Heat a little vegetable oil in a large flameproof casserole, put in the beef and brown on all sides. Remove from the casserole and reserve. Add the vegetables, garlic and thyme and cook until the vegetables are golden, then return the beef to the casserole, sprinkle with the flour and stir well.

Pour the marinade over the beef and vegetables, and bring to the boil. Add the oyster liquor and enough water to cover.

Put a lid on the casserole and transfer to the oven. Cook for 2–3 hours, until the beef is meltingly tender. Allow to cool and set, so that when you lay the oysters on top they won't fall through too much.

Meanwhile, roll out the pastry into a shape large enough to cover the top of your casserole and overhang slightly.

Turn the oven temperature up to 180°C/Gas 4. Lay the oysters on top of the beef.

Moisten the edges of the casserole with water, drape the pastry over the top, seal the edges and brush with beaten egg. Bake in the oven for around 30 minutes, until golden brown.

Muscle
Man

There aren't many butchers I know who look like they're dressed by Savile Row, speak fluent French, have a string of gorgeous South American women as customers and get the opening of their butcher's shop in *Hello!* magazine. But the very suave, softly spoken Jack O'Shea from County Tipperary, with his gentleman's long coats and his revolutionary attitude to cutting meat, is a one-off. When Jack talks about meat, and especially beef, it's like listening to poetry.

He grew up into the family butchery business in Templemore, which had been handed down through the generations since 1805. His father had a small mixed beef herd: Herefords, Angus, Limousins, Charolais; and they had their own slaughterhouse. 'We were only small scale, but my father was a genius with cattle, and his father, and his father before him,' he says. 'We had the full package. He could tell you the weight of a carcass just by looking at it, and he taught me things like the way stress in an animal at slaughter will show up in a muscle: the meat will look dark in places, and it can taste metallic. He also used to say any fool can sell sirloin, the real art is selling the rest.'

Even so, as a young man he was more interested in training horses than in butchery, so he went off working with showjumpers in Brussels. Then his mother fell ill and he came home to help out in the family business. By the time she was better and he was ready to go back to Brussels, he had decided to open a butcher's shop there. 'I had to fight every step of the way with red tape and bank managers,' he says, but ten years on, Jack O'Shea's on the corner of rue le Titien, presided over by his sister Grainne, is the most famous butcher's in Brussels; and Irish beef is the speciality.

Working in Brussels changed Jack's attitude to butchery totally. He learned to seam out a carcass the way a French butcher would do it, to produce more interesting cuts and steaks like *onglet* and *bavette* which you see in every French bistro, but which in our islands would be more likely to be minced up, or put into something like Cornish pasties. *Bavette* is what we know as flank; it comes from the diaphragm, and *onglet*, which the Americans call hanger steak, comes from what we call the skirt; it's the bit that hangs below the ribs, and when you carefully take out the connective tissue, tidy it up and, cut it across the grain, it makes a great steak. Another thing he likes to do, instead of taking the fillet off the bone, is to take the sirloin off, and leave the fillet on the bone, which makes what can be an uninteresting cut much, much better.

The butchery might have been a revelation, but the Belgian beef didn't match up to Jack's expectations. 'Brussels is full of excellent chefs and thousands of

great gourmets, but apparently in the fifties every Belgian doctor was saying you'll die of a heart attack if you don't eat lean meat,' he says, 'so they are all allergic to fat. You'd go into a restaurant and order a steak, which would come with a beautiful Bordelaise sauce with marrowbone, red wine and shallots, but the actual muscle would be nothing like a steak from an Irish Angus or Hereford. The Belgian Blue cattle have a double muscle in the back; they look like pumped-up bodybuilders. They are slaughtered relatively young and the meat has no fat and is completely tender. To me, they just can't match an animal that has been growing slowly on pasture for most of the year like a fine-tuned, grass-eating machine, putting on natural marbled muscle. Our steaks are all dry-aged for between twenty-eight and sixty-five days, but you can't dry-age a piece of meat that is completely lean; you need a certain marbling of fat to protect it or it will rot.'

'People don't understand the importance of the marbling of fat on a piece of beef,' he says. 'It is unsaturated, "olive oil" fat, which is crucial for cooking. It's what melts into the meat and keeps it moist. It's like the difference in taste and texture between two bowls of mashed potato, one all by itself and the other with butter.' Our only point of difference is that Jack believes the Angus is the ultimate animal for marbled meat, whereas, personally, I prefer the Hereford.

What he realised was that if you could combine our beef with continental cutting techniques, you'd be on to something really special; so he started bringing out Irish Angus beef to Brussels, reared by a network of trusted farmers around the south-west of Ireland, who knew what he was looking for in cattle. Ten years on, he decided to open up in London, on another corner, in Knightsbridge; he called in to Bentley's and we had a whiskey downstairs in the bar. Jack knows how fussy we are about our meat, and the way he tells it, I was very cautious, until I was sure he knew what he was talking about! But we've been buying meat from him ever since. He'll come in and watch us cook steaks, and see how we use his cuts; and always he'll have a story about how he's just braised a shin of beef with capers and anchovies, or barbecued short ribs on his Argentinian grill, or shredded and mixed meat from different cuts in search of the most stunning burger. It's not all beef of course, and it's not all Irish. He just sources the best meat, from Scottish, Welsh or Yorkshire lamb to organic and free-range pork; and he makes his own sausages and fresh marinades.

The point is we both know that great meat is about a chain of knowledge and expertise from the field to the plate. Every link is important, but at any stage a link could break. As he says, 'You can have a great animal, but it can be hung badly. It's not about putting a hook up, setting the clock and saying, "Right boys, we'll come back in a month." You have to control the temperature and the humidity, and be aware of the composition of the piece of meat. Then again, you can have a great piece of beef, everything done right, but give it to the wrong chef and they'll wreck it. As the butcher you're the last line of defence. If someone eats a tough piece of meat they're going to blame you. You can be the best or worst butcher in the world in a matter of minutes.'

It isn't just French styles of cut that he specialises in, he's gone off on his travels to see how the rest of the world raises their beef, butchers it and cooks it. Another of his favourite cuts is the *picanha*, which is the triangular cap muscle from a rump of beef, which he learnt about in Rio. 'The Brazilians prize it above fillet,' he says. And he's mad about *asado*, barbecuing Argentine-style on a grill over the embers of a very hard wood, traditionally *quebracho*, because you can sear the meat hard, then move it to cooler areas and slow cook it. British or Irish beef, cut French or Brazilian fashion, and Argentinian cooking techniques, are a killer combination in Jack's book.

Ever since he opened up his shop he had customers coming in and saying the best beef they ever ate was in Argentina. 'The Argentinians eat more meat than anyone on the planet, and they wax lyrical about the cattle roaming the pampas plains which go on for ever, but a cow can only eat so much grass,' he says. 'It can sustain itself quite happily on an acre a year; it won't be any better for having a hundred acres… why check into a four-star hotel, when what you really need is a campsite? For me, their style of meat is too young, bright, fresh and lean. It's like drinking Beaujolais, when what you want is an aged Bordeaux.'

Talking of campsites, he tells a good story about travelling in Argentina. 'When I went out there,' he says, 'we drove about a hundred miles to a campsite in Patagonia in a South American version of a Volkswagen Golf, made in Brazil, which was lightened up and made for the local market. Effectively it had anything of any value taken out of it, so there was no stereo, nothing. Finally we got to the campsite – in Argentina virtually every campsite has grills, and when you arrive you buy some meat and some wood, and in this case, a bag of rock salt; because you don't marinate the meat, just salt it.

'I went in and introduced myself as a butcher to the woman running the campsite, and she said, as I knew she would: "Oh, Argentinan beef is the best." She was going on and on about it, and I couldn't help saying to her, "Do you realize where it comes from in the first place? You brought the very best pedigree Angus bulls over from Ireland." She looked at me and said, "Yes, but we improved it." "Just like you improved the Volkswagen Golf," I told her. I was lucky I wasn't thrown out!

'Of course I grilled the meat over the hot cinders and it was gorgeous, but you're on holiday, you're relaxed and all the endorphins are flowing. If you were to cook that same steak in a Teflon frying pan back home over an electric ring with horizontal rain outside, it would taste completely different. Each to their own, though. As my mother would say, "Everyone thinks their own geese are swans."

'The Argentinians don't want meat that has been hung for a long time; whereas some of my aristocratic British customers, who have been raised in households where pheasants have been hung by the neck until they fell off the hook, are quite obsessive about aged beef. I like people who are that serious about their meat. Especially for one customer I aged a loin of beef for sixty-five days; not something most butchers would be inclined to do, because there's a huge amount of waste, but he and I knew that once you cut away the black, virtually rotting flesh from the outside and got into the nugget in the middle, it would be sublime. This man came back after he'd cooked it, almost misty-eyed, and said, "Jack, that beef: it was a near religious experience."'

Game

There wasn't much that ran wild that we didn't shoot for the pot when I was growing up. Squirrel was about the only thing that never made it on to the table. But you have to understand that hunting for food, rather than just for sport, goes hand in hand with a deep love of nature. We had a wonderful wildfowl lake in the middle of the bog, and as children, we used to go and hide in the rushes and see the wild ducks fly in. There was something quite magical and fairy-like about the place: the stillness, the birdsong, the distant call of the curlew. I love to eat wild duck, especially mallard. There's a special little window of opportunity at the end of its season, when the first of the Seville oranges come in, and for about a week and a half only there is the chance to have a beautiful Seville orange sauce with the mallard. But I believe in only taking what you need from the wild, not going after it in excess. You don't have to be a green, badge-wearing leftie to see that we all need to take a step back for a moment and accept that there should be a balance between what you take, what you give back and what you should leave alone.

My dad was a great hunter and a poacher for most of his life, but he was a generous old spirit who loved nature and would never see an animal treated badly or suffering needlessly. He was a decent, old-fashioned poacher, in the cherished tradition in rural Ireland, the kind, like all our neighbours, who believed poaching for profit was anti-social, but poaching for the pot was a right. Not a legal right maybe, but there was always a sense that at one time the 'big house' families had stolen the land from the ordinary people, and that having the odd pheasant or salmon was a kind of compensation. And most of the time, as I've said before, the law turned a blind eye.

I'd go out deer stalking with him as a child, at five-thirty in the morning, and if we caught a lovely roe we'd shoot and skin it, and it would be wonderful to eat. Wild venison is the only kind I want to eat; farmed venison doesn't come near. Then there were the wild rabbits; we'd only ever shoot the young, summer ones that tasted of sunshine and grass; never older rabbits. We'd sauté them with garlic and eat them in our fingers, almost like tapas. That would be a lunchtime meal for us. What a memory; they were quite delicious. We loved food like that in our household.

As far as game birds are concerned, they need some human management and intervention to help them survive when the natural habitat and the eco-systems they depend on come under threat. If you drain all the lovely wet holes in the bog, as eventually happened in rural Ireland, all the wild ducks disappear; if you don't look after the grouse moors and the heather, there will be no grouse. Of all the game birds, grouse are the only ones that are always completely wild; you can help them, by protecting them and their environment, but no one has been able to reproduce their lifestyle and breed them in the way of pheasant and partridge. Some years, no matter how well managed grouse estates are, weather conditions, disease and predators will mean there are very few red grouse to be had; and black grouse, which used to be common in Britain, but need a particular scenario of moor, bog, pine and birch trees, are now so rare they are on the endangered list.

At one time on the farm we used to breed pheasants in coops for the Forestry Commission as part of their plan to put game back into the wild. They'd come in as hatchlings and we'd feed them in the run up to the shooting season, then release them. Some would be shot, some would be taken by nature, some would live on. At night sometimes we would go out lamping the pheasants that had been released into the woods; you'd shine a light on them in the trees so they'd fly up and you could shoot one or two; and no one can say, 'Oh, that's not jolly fair'… we were hungry. The pheasants would be hung up on the back of the door to the dairy just for a few days to relax and rest a bit, and then they'd make a meal for the family. I'm not one for the traditional practice of the gentry of hanging pheasants until they are high to the point of nearly being rancid. I want to enjoy my meat, not eat it with a turned stomach.

I like a pheasant just coloured in a roasting pan then put into a hot oven, 220°C/Gas 7, for about 20 minutes, with some rashers of bacon around it. After that, turn down the heat to 180°C/Gas 4 for about 15 minutes. When it's done you have to let it rest and relax. While it's cooking, I like to make a little vegetable stew out of some nice big pieces of swede, carrots and onions cooked in a bit of stock, thickened up with some cornflour if you want. I cut up the rashers of bacon after roasting, add them to the root vegetables with some chopped chives and parsley, and serve the roast pheasant on top: delicious.

I like some of the smaller birds like snipe and woodcock, too, but they are getting so rare. I don't want to be the last guy having them on the menu. It's like the cod syndrome: don't cook them for the sake of it, if they are that scarce. Stop taking, taking, and let them alone for a few years to replenish themselves.

Of all the game birds, though, I think grouse is king, roasted simply, maybe even cut into strips and served in a salad, or in a pie. Pastry and game work well together. However, I was invited on a shoot in Yorkshire a few years ago, and the idea of a lot of rich folk bagging birds for a bit of fun doesn't sit squarely with me, or with what I think is the English sense of fair play. I do think on the whole the English are lovers of nature, and yes, it's a lovely day out. If you keep your kill, take it home and enjoy a great meal from it, fair enough, but the greedy, grabby nature of shooting for sport is a long way away from the wandering-in-the-wild kind of shooting that I grew up with. A few years ago, I heard about people shooting small ducks, just taking the breasts off, and leaving all the carcasses behind. To me that sort of shooting is outrageous.

Towards the end of his life, when we kids had grown up and there was no longer the necessity to shoot for the pot, my dad didn't want to shoot anything any more. He put away his guns and he was so reluctant to disturb nature that I remember one year he didn't even want to remove a wasps' nest from the tree just outside the house. He still enjoyed fishing, but it was the sense of being at one with his surroundings, the camaraderie of being by the lake, maybe taking along a little stove, that was what he enjoyed most; and I think the older I get the more I understand how he felt.

Game recipes can sound a bit complicated, because most of the traditional ones, at least, with their various accompaniments, have their roots in the big country houses with their butlers and the cook with her brigade of minions preparing lavish food for the shooting party getting sozzled in the drawing room. We've simplified them down, though, and even where there is a bit of time involved, with the feathered game, especially, it's worth it to make the most of the short time of the year when game is there to be enjoyed.

What I really like the idea of is a big family game roast to celebrate the season: maybe some teal, grouse, pheasant… eight people, eight birds, all roasted and carved up on big platters in the middle of the table, so everyone can just serve themselves. No fancy jus or game sauces, but maybe some apple sauce, spiced up with a little orange rind and cloves, or a damson compote, since damsons are in season along with most game (see recipe below), and/or bread sauce and a big bowl of game chips (wafer thin slices of potato, deep fried for a couple of minutes until crisp and golden).

Damson Compote to Serve with Roast Game

To make around 4 large jars, stone 2kg of damsons, peel and grate 500g of Bramley apples, then put the fruit into a non-reactive pan with 400g of sugar and 200ml of cider vinegar. Make a muslin spice bag: take a square of muslin, put about 10 cloves, half a stick of cinnamon, 3 star anise and the zest of a lemon in the centre, then bring up the corners and tie together. Pop it into the pan, bring to the boil, then turn down the heat and simmer until most of the liquid has evaporated, and you have a nice moist compote. Cool and seal in sterilised jars and it will keep for up to 3 months in the fridge.

Game Bird
and Lentil Soup
with Juniper Cream

This is based on another of Simon 'Hoppy' Hopkinson's recipes, for grouse soup, which is in *Roast Chicken and Other Stories*. I just love his books, especially the early ones. There is magic in those pages. Whenever you've enjoyed a couple of pheasants, or other feathered game, keep the carcasses for this soup. The whole flavour depends on the carcasses – so if you have a butcher who supplies game, ask him to collect some for you. If you have roasted some game birds yourself and have any meat left over, shred it finely and add it to the soup just before serving. If you like, you can scatter some pieces of toasted bread over the soup, or perhaps some chopped roasted chestnuts.

Serves 4

about 3 tablespoons
    olive oil
about 1.5kg game bird
    carcasses and/or legs
2 carrots, roughly
    chopped
2 sticks celery, roughly
    chopped
1 medium onion,
    roughly chopped
1 clove garlic
6 juniper berries
½ teaspoon black
    peppercorns
1 bay leaf
1 large sprig each parsley
    and thyme
150ml port
150ml Madeira
2 litres fresh chicken
    stock (see page 181)
125g Puy or green lentils

Juniper cream:
6 juniper berries
1 small shallot, finely
    diced
100ml sweet white wine
3–4 tablespoons double
    cream

Heat the olive oil in a large saucepan or stockpot and brown the game bird bones and/or legs. Add the vegetables and garlic to the pan and continue to cook until nicely coloured and caramelised. Add the juniper berries along with the peppercorns and herbs and cook for a minute or so.

Pour in the port and Madeira and bring up to the boil. Bubble away to reduce by half, then pour in the stock and bring back to the boil. Cover the pan, turn down the heat and simmer for about 1½ hours, skimming the surface from time to time to remove any impurities.

When you have a nice rich stock, strain it into a bowl, discard the vegetables, herbs, etc. and pour the strained liquid back into the saucepan. You should have about 1.5 litres left. Return it to the heat and stir in the lentils. Bring to the boil, then turn down the heat and simmer, uncovered, for about 20 minutes, until the lentils are soft and creamy.

Meanwhile, make the juniper cream. Crush the juniper berries in a pestle and mortar or chop as finely as you can. Put the shallot, crushed berries and white wine into a small pan, bring to the boil, then turn down the heat and simmer for about 5 minutes, until the shallots are softened and the wine has evaporated. Leave to cool.

Whip the cream until it forms soft peaks and stir in the cooled shallots. Season lightly and keep on one side.

When the lentils are ready, take the soup off the heat. Whiz it in a food processor, then pass it through a sieve into a warm bowl, rubbing it through with the back of a ladle. It should be velvety smooth. Taste and adjust the seasoning if necessary. Serve the soup piping hot, with a spoonful of juniper cream slowly melting in the centre.

Roast
Wild Duck
with Beetroot

Serves 8

3 raw beetroots

2 teal (wild duck), prepared and legs removed

25g butter, softened

1 clove garlic, split in half

2 sprigs of thyme

olive oil

beetroot or red chard leaves, to garnish

a pinch each of sugar and salt

a squeeze of lemon juice

Preheat the oven to 180°C/Gas 4.

Scrub the beetroots gently with a scrubbing brush. Wrap in aluminium foil and place on a baking tray. Bake for 1½–2 hours until tender. Unwrap the beetroots and leave until they are cool enough to handle, then peel and coarsely chop them – you can use gloves to prevent your hands from getting stained.

Turn the oven up to 200°C/Gas 6.

Rub the teal breasts with butter and season with salt and pepper. Stuff each bird with half a clove of garlic and a sprig of thyme.

Heat a little olive oil in an ovenproof frying pan until hot. Add the teal and brown for 1 minute on each side. Transfer to the oven and roast for 3 minutes, or until cooked through. Remove and allow to rest for at least 5 minutes. Dissolve the sugar and salt in a little lemon juice and drizzle over.

Carve the teal breasts off the bone and slice thinly. Place spoonfuls of the beetroot on to plates, and top with slices of teal breast and beetroot or chard leaves.

Roast Wood Pigeon with Figs and Sherry

Serves 4

100ml sherry

4 wood pigeon crowns

a little olive oil

4 ripe figs

4 bunches of watercress

Sherry vinegar caramel dressing:

3 tablespoons sugar

1 tablespoon water

4 tablespoons sherry vinegar

Pouring some sherry over the pigeon to marinate it overnight takes away any bitterness in the flesh and tenderises it. The next day you can make this little salad or starter very quickly.

Pour the sherry over the pigeon crowns and leave overnight.

Preheat the oven to 200°C/Gas 6.

Season the pigeons, then heat a little olive oil in a heavy-based pan that will transfer to the oven. Put the pigeons in the pan, skin-side down, and sear for 1½–2 minutes or until browned. Turn the birds over and brown the other side. Finally, turn back on to the skin side, and put into the oven to roast for 5 minutes. The meat should be rosy pink.

Remove from the oven and set aside in a warm place to rest.

To make the dressing, put the sugar and water into a heavy-based pan and cook over a moderate heat until you have a light caramel. Keep cooking gently until it reduces enough to coat the back of a spoon – the texture of runny honey. Add the sherry vinegar and leave to cool, then taste, and if you think it needs a little more sharpness, add an extra splash of sherry vinegar and stir in well.

Cut the figs into four.

Remove the pigeon breasts from the bone and slice. Serve on the watercress, scatter the figs around and drizzle with the sherry vinegar caramel dressing.

Grouse and Foie Gras in Pastry

A dash of herby green Chartreuse is amazing in a game sauce.

In the restaurant, we would add some veal jus, because we have the luxury of having such things on the go. It gives the sauce a deeper colour and a little extra depth of flavour, but at home, water is fine.

Serves 4

butter, for frying

1 onion, finely chopped

500g button mushrooms, finely chopped

a pinch of thyme

4 young grouse

1 small lobe of fresh foie gras

4 large Savoy cabbage leaves

1kg puff pastry

4 eggs, beaten, to glaze

watercress, to serve

Sauce:

a little vegetable oil

grouse legs and carcass (from above)

1 small onion, chopped

1 carrot, chopped

1 stick celery, chopped

2 cloves garlic, chopped

¼ bottle red wine

splash of green Chartreuse (optional)

Heat a little butter in a pan, add the onion and sweat until softened. Add the mushrooms and thyme, and cook over a medium heat until the liquid has evaporated and the mixture is dry – 10–15 minutes. Season to taste and leave to get cold.

Carefully remove the breasts from the grouse, remove the skin and keep the carcass. Season the breasts. Heat a little more butter in a hot pan, put the breasts in and sear for 10 seconds on each side. Remove from the pan.

With a hot knife, slice the foie gras into four – each slice should be about 2.5cm thick. Season and put into the hot pan in which you have seared the grouse breasts. Sear the outside of the foie gras for 20 seconds on each side, and remove immediately. Keep on one side.

Blanch the cabbage leaves for about a minute in boiling salted water, refresh under the cold tap, drain and pat dry.

Cut 4 large squares of clingfilm. Lay a cabbage leaf on each. Put a spoonful of the mushroom mixture (you are going to need to divide it into 8 spoonfuls in all) in the centre of each cabbage leaf. Lay a grouse breast on top, then a slice of foie gras, and finish with the other breast. Put a spoonful of the remaining mushroom mixture on top.

Pick up the four corners of the clingfilm and twist them together, so that the cabbage leaf encloses the grouse and foie gras. Keep twisting the clingfilm so that you end up with a tight cabbage ball. Tie in a knot to secure.

Put the cabbage balls into the fridge, to set the foie gras and firm everything up while you roll out the pastry.

Cut off a third of the pastry, roll out, then using a saucer (about 14cm diameter) as a guide to cut around, cut out 4 discs and put them into the fridge.

Roll out the rest of the pastry, and this time, cut out 4 circles of around 20cm diameter (use a suitable plate again, to cut around). As you cut out each one put it into the fridge – it is good to keep pastry cool at all times.

Lay the smaller discs out on a clean work surface and brush with beaten egg. Unwrap the clingfilm from the cabbage parcels and put one in the middle of each disc. Cover with the larger disc, and pinch together and seal the edges. Brush each round parcel well with beaten egg. Put back into the fridge until ready to cook.

Preheat the oven to 225°C/Gas 7.

To make the sauce, heat a little vegetable oil in a pan, put in the grouse legs and carcass, together with the vegetables and garlic, and cook until the vegetables have softened. Pour in the red wine and a little water and bring to the boil. Skim off any impurities, turn the heat down and simmer to reduce rapidly until you have a nice light sauce – not too thick. Stir in the Chartreuse at the end.

Put the parcels into the oven for 15 minutes until the pastry is golden. To check that the grouse is done, insert a skewer into the middle. It should come out warm. Serve with the sauce and a little watercress.

Roast Partridge with Pears and Parsnips

Serves 4

2 bay leaves

4 sprigs of thyme

2 cloves garlic

4 partridges, prepared

8 thin rashers streaky
  bacon

olive oil

butter

2 pears

a little sugar

watercress, to serve

Parsnips:

500g parsnips

olive oil

50g butter

1 clove garlic, chopped

a sprig of thyme

100g clear honey

1 tablespoon sherry
  vinegar

Bread sauce:

250ml milk

1 small onion, studded
  with cloves

1 clove garlic

1 bay leaf

6 slices stale bread, crusts
  removed

Place half a bay leaf, a sprig of thyme and half a clove of garlic into the cavity of each bird. Place 2 rashers of bacon over the breasts. Tie the birds with butchers' string.

Preheat the oven to 200°C/Gas 6.

Cut the parsnips into quarters, then cut out the woody root at the base with a sharp knife. Put a little olive oil into an oven tray on the hob and when hot, put in the parsnips with about 50g of butter, the garlic and thyme. Cook until lightly golden, then add the honey and sherry vinegar, toss and transfer to the oven to finish cooking.

To start the bread sauce, put all the ingredients apart from the bread in a pan, season to taste with salt and bring to a simmer. Take off the heat and leave to infuse for about half an hour.

Meanwhile, to cook the partridges, heat a film of olive oil in an ovenproof frying pan. Brush the birds with butter, season, and brown all over for about 3–5 minutes. Transfer to the oven and cook for a further 6 minutes.

Take out of the oven, remove the string and leave to rest, upside down, in a warm place.

While the partridges are resting, finish off the bread sauce. Strain the milk into a clean pan and bring back to a simmer. Add the bread and mash with a fork until the sauce thickens, but keep it quite rough and rustic.

Peel and quarter the pears. Sprinkle a little sugar into a pan and when it starts to colour, put in the pears. Leave them to caramelise without touching for about 3 minutes, then turn over and caramelise on the other side for another 3 minutes.

Serve the partridges on a big platter, surrounded by the parsnips, pears and some bunches of watercress, and carve at the table. Serve the sauce separately in a bowl.

Roe Venison Wellington

Serves 4

1kg puff pastry

4 outer leaves from a Savoy cabbage, central stalks removed

1 half loin of roe venison, about 30cm long, boned and trimmed

a little vegetable oil

2 eggs, beaten

Mushrooms:

a little butter

1 onion, finely diced

1 clove garlic, crushed

500g button mushrooms (or half button mushrooms and half ceps), finely chopped

a pinch of thyme leaves

Herb pancakes:

100g plain flour

2 eggs

350ml milk

50g melted butter

a pinch of salt

1 teaspoon chopped herbs, such as parsley and chervil

This might take a bit of time, but if you can feed four people and they have a happy time eating it, that's time well spent. The idea of wrapping the pancakes around the meat is traditionally to absorb the moisture and stop the pastry from becoming too soggy, but some of the juices always seep through to the pastry, and I think that is the pleasure of this dish: slightly soggy, gamey pastry has to be one of the most divine things you can put in your mouth.

First make the pancake batter. Sift the flour into a mixing bowl, add the eggs, milk, butter and salt and whisk until smooth. Stir in the herbs and set aside to rest in the fridge.

Roll out the puff pastry into a rectangle 45cm long and 30cm wide, the thickness of a £1 coin (about 3mm). Lay the pastry on a sheet of parchment paper and put into the fridge.

For the mushrooms, heat a little butter in a pan, add the onion and garlic and sweat to soften.

Add the mushrooms and thyme and cook for about 10–15 minutes, until all the juices have evaporated and the mixture is dry. Season and leave to cool.

Blanch the cabbage leaves for about a minute in boiling salted water, refresh under the cold tap, drain and pat dry.

Season the venison. Heat the vegetable oil in a roasting tin and put in the venison. Sear quickly on all sides until nicely browned all over. Remove from the pan and place on a clean tea towel to cool.

Cook the pancakes: you need four. Lightly oil a 20cm non-stick frying pan and heat until very hot. Pour in a small ladleful of batter and rotate the pan so that it covers the whole surface. When it is golden underneath, flip over. Lift out and lay on a piece of parchment paper. Continue until you have made three more, layering up the pancakes between parchment paper until you are ready to use them.

To assemble, lay a piece of clingfilm twice the size of the pastry on your work surface. Lay the pancakes on top, slightly overlapping so that there are no gaps.

Lay the cabbage leaves over the top, overlapping again, and then spoon on the mushroom mixture and spread over the cabbage.

Lay the venison on top. Now you need to roll everything up, as if you were making a swiss roll. Lift up the edge of the clingfilm running parallel to the venison, and roll the pancakes with their cabbage lining over the top. Tuck in, and then use the clingfilm to help you continue to roll up tightly so that you have a long cylinder. Twist the ends of the clingfilm to tighten, then tie them in a knot. If you don't feel that the cylinder is tight enough, repeat again with an extra sheet of clingfilm. Put into the fridge for about an hour to firm up.

Preheat the oven to 200°C/Gas 6. Put a baking tray in the oven to get hot.

Take out your rectangle of pastry from the fridge, lay it on your work surface and brush the uppermost side with beaten egg. Remove the clingfilm from the wrapped venison and place on top of the pastry, parallel to the long side. Roll up in the pastry and seal the edges. Brush the whole thing generously with more beaten egg.

Lay the wrapped venison on the hot baking tray and bake in the oven for 20 minutes, until golden brown. To test the meat is cooked, insert a metal skewer into the centre. It should come out warm, for medium rare meat. If you want the venison to be cooked a bit more, when you next test the skewer should be hot.

Rabbit
Pie

If you like, you can make up the filling the day before and have it ready in your pie dish in the fridge.

Serves 4
10ml olive oil
a little flour
4 rabbit legs
1 large onion, roughly
   chopped
1 clove garlic
a small bunch of thyme
½ bunch of tarragon
1 litre chicken stock (see
   page 181) or water
100ml double cream
1 leek, roughly chopped
a small handful of
   morels, (optional)

Pastry:
300g plain flour
a pinch of salt
150g butter
2 egg yolks plus 1 egg,
   beaten for glazing

First make the pastry. Put the flour and salt into a bowl and rub in the butter until you have fine crumbs. Add the egg yolks and a turn of black pepper and mix to a smooth dough (you can do all this using a food processor if you prefer). Roll into a ball, cover and chill in the fridge for 15 minutes.

Heat the olive oil in a large saucepan. Flour the rabbit legs, season well and colour lightly on all sides. Remove the legs from the pan.

In the same pan, sweat the onion, without colouring, for 4–5 minutes. Add the garlic and thyme, then the browned rabbit legs. Cover with stock or water, bring to the boil and simmer gently for no more than 40 minutes. Remove the rabbit legs and set aside to cool.

Pass the liquid through a fine sieve into a clean pan and bubble up to reduce by half. Add the cream and simmer for 15 minutes until you have a smooth sauce. Check the seasoning.

Blanch the leeks for a minute in boiling salted water and drain.

Take the meat from the rabbit legs and mix with the morels, if using, the leek and tarragon. Put this mixture into an ovenproof dish. Pour the sauce over and allow to cool, then chill in the fridge for an hour or so just to firm everything up ready to take the pastry.

Dampen the edge of the dish with water. Put something like an upturned egg cup in the middle of the filling to help prop up the pastry. Roll out the pastry and drape over the top. Crimp the edge, brush with beaten egg and leave to rest in the fridge for 1 hour, to firm up the pastry and prevent it shrinking when you bake it.

Preheat the oven to 180°C/Gas 4.

Bake for about 40 minutes, or until the pastry is golden brown. If you insert a skewer through the pastry into the filling it should come out hot.

Vegetables
and Salads

I have an Irishman's love of meat, but more and more I find myself thinking about vegetables. Especially with the nastiness of so much industrially produced meat, I'm coming to believe more and more that it is best to pay for great quality meat, ethically produced, just once or twice a week, and the rest of the time to let vegetables, along with beans and pulses, command the bigger part of main courses, as they do in other European countries where there is much more of a tradition of respect for the vegetable course. In our islands we have yet to really get over the idea that a vegetable is something on the side of a plate of meat. The closest most of us come to revering a vegetable is celebrating English asparagus, and even then there is always the temptation to put a bit of cured ham with it.

A plate of steamed leeks, served with a vinaigrette and maybe with some chopped tarragon sprinkled over it is delicious. Tarragon and leeks have a great affinity. Or a bowl of globe artichokes and fresh peas: lovely. A dish in its own right. But if you put it in front of many an English or Irish person, they would say, 'Is that it?'

One of the things I remember so strongly about living in the country is just going out into the garden to get your vegetables or a salad for tea, and the older I get the more I value those old-fashioned salads: just leaves, some boiled eggs cut in half, scallions (spring onions), maybe some beetroot. Spending time at the Irish Seed Savers deep in the countryside of County Clare (see page 250) has done that for me: re-awakened that love of everything that is garden fresh. When I see just-harvested asparagus, tender spinach, fresh peas and scallions sitting on a table, I sing like a bird and the ideas just start flowing.

Whether you want to eat vegetables as an accompaniment or in their own right, it takes so little, maybe a herb or a spice, a bit of good butter and some crunchy sea salt, or a dressing, to transform a plain vegetable that is a bit too puritan in its nakedness into something that makes you say, 'Mmm. More, please.'

Too much exposure to water when you're cooking vegetables, I think, just flows the flavour away. You'd be surprised how quickly you can blanch a vegetable if you just want to soften the crunch from it. Have a big pot of boiling water, with some salt in it, and as you drop the pieces of vegetable in, count to ten and then take them out. That even applies to carrots, if you cut them thinly enough. But I prefer them, like most vegetables, cooked in just a spoonful or so of water in a heavy-based pan with some butter and a pinch of sugar and salt, and scattered with a herb at the end.

Summer or winter, if you have some good ham or chicken stock handy, you can have a gorgeous vegetable soup made in minutes. There's a recipe for nettle broth on page 152 (you can leave out the scallops if you like), and one for colcannon soup here, but I'm inclined to think soups don't need specific recipes. They are the produce of your garden or vegetable rack and what you have in the fridge. Swede, sweated in some butter with a little bit of onion and garlic, ham stock poured in, simmered briefly and then blitzed in a blender, with some cinnamon sprinkled on at the end, will turn what can sometimes be a bit of a boring tuber into a great soup. You could do a similar thing with parsnip and nutmeg. Kohlrabi, peeled, sliced really thinly, dropped into boiling ham stock and served with just a handful of sorrel: dynamite. Courgettes, again, lightly sweated in butter, stock added, blitzed and served chilled with some slightly sharp, bitter sorrel and a sprinkling of paprika, makes a lovely summer soup, as do peas, done the same way, but finished with mint and chilli.

Seed
Savers

Everything that I believe in, the way I feel about the land and about growing food, is embodied in the Irish Seed Saver Association in Scariff in County Clare. The first time I went down there I thought I had discovered Nirvana.

The organisation is dedicated to finding, conserving, researching and distributing Ireland's disappearing native, heritage varieties of fruit, vegetables and grains, though they also have rare seeds sent to them by people from all over the world. They have the Native Irish Apple Collection (some were given from the UK and Irish collection held at Brogdale), including unusual self-rooting trees; there is a brilliant collection of heritage potatoes and tomatoes, and they have been building a bank of Irish seeds. Ireland was the only Western country not to have a native grain collection, so they have spent ten years tracking down traditional varieties of oats, wheat, barley and rye. Some of the seeds have been discovered as far away as Russia, Germany and Norway.

Seed Savers was founded by an American woman Anita Hayes, in 1991, from her own garden, expanded to include a group of locals and now thrives, though in a very frugal way, with the help of donations and government grants.

On one level it is just a beautiful place, with a wonderful ethos about it; on another, what they are doing there is serious, serious work with a powerful, political message, which we all should be aware of, because without Irish Seed Savers and their sister organisations around the world, the biodiversity of the world's crops would be disappearing at an even more alarming rate than it already is, and we could be looking at a potential situation in which, in the face of global poverty and hunger, the control of the seeds of the world's food could be concentrated in the hands of a few multinational companies.

Everyone worries about who is controlling the world's oil or water supplies, but most of us never think about seeds, which are at the heart of our food security and sovereignty – the most natural human right is surely to decide for yourself what to sow, harvest and eat.

There are seed banks all over the world held in case of a nation's crops being wiped out, but they themselves are vulnerable, and have been lost or looted in uprisings and wars, or destroyed by natural disasters. 'As far back as Roman times, when a nation invaded another country, one of the first things they'd do would be to secure the seed bank', says Seed Savers' Dermot McKinney. The biggest in the world is the underground Svalbard Global Seed Vault in Norway, which has been built to withstand everything from missile attacks

to earthquakes. Every country in the world has been invited to put duplicates of seeds from their collections into the so-called Doomsday Vault, and they remain their property, sealed inside 'black boxes'. Assurances have been given that there will be no access to plant-breeders, but, says Dermot, 'you have to remember that the backers include big seed companies.'

I came across the guys at Seed Savers five or six years ago when I read an article about them, and I was always looking for an opportunity to link up with them in some way. I think as a chef, sometimes, you have to use your profile, to help try to change things. Then I had the chance to do some filming down there for my series on RTÉ, and I was so inspired.

They have around eight hectares of vegetable gardens, orchards, natural woodlands and nurseries, all farmed organically and biodynamically. Now, I'm not interested in buying bio or organic produce for the sake of the label, or image shopping with private-jet foodies in marble halls, but at Seed Savers when they talk about farming according to the natural rhythm of nature, it is a very real, deep and meaningful thing.

The place is full of intelligent human beings with all kinds of academic qualifications behind them, and God bless them for going out and digging the fields and not going into some branch of food science. They have created the most stress-free, refreshing environment you could imagine. You go down to County Clare and you think, 'Are your values all skewed?' Here you have a completely alternative lifestyle where finance and making a buck isn't even in the equation. There are people who have worked there since the beginning, when they were little more than a group of locals growing their own food from seed, and new people who have joined more recently, but there are no puppets and no strings, there's a commune feel to it all. They even have a geodesic dome like the ones the hippies used to live in in California in the sixties, which they throw a tent over and use for activities for kids when they have events going on – they are forever running projects for schools and workshops on everything from beekeeping to dry-stone wall building, and they bring in guests who run courses on things like making farmhouse cheese or country wine.

All the bullshit of city life just rolls off you when you spend time down there. You've come to meet your maker, basically, and it's not what you've brought, it's who you are. And if all of this sounds a bit hippy, leftie-foodie, I'm sorry, but I just love these people.

On that first visit we caught sea trout in the lake, cooked it in a cast-iron pan on a woodburning stove, and ate it with salad leaves from the garden and a warm German-style potato salad I made with Red Duke of Yorks, just pulled from the earth (see page 68). What amazed me was they were growing all this wonderful produce for its seed, but they never used to sit down and eat it themselves –

I think I changed that. We had great fun, one of the maddest, magic, spontaneous days ever. Once the cameras had stopped rolling, we opened some of the wine that is made locally in Killaloe from apples, berries and elderflowers, and ended with a bunch of them doing the 'GM rap' for me. Now, they all sit down together every lunchtime around a big table, kids and all in the holidays, and share food from the gardens, with local breads and cheeses.

You walk through the orchards, with their apple, pear, cherry, damson and plum trees, and you come across little seats that someone has carved out of wood, and there are trees and benches that local people have dedicated to children that have been born, and family and friends who have died. It's quite a touching place to be, and it reminds me so much of where I grew up: the silence, except for the birds, the wind through the trees, and just running free, picking an apple from the orchard on a sunny day on holiday from school. What is interesting is that they have found that the old Irish varieties of apple, which were grown before pesticides came on the scene, are more resistant to scab, mildew and canker, because the trees had naturally adapted themselves to the local weather conditions. And if you taste an apple there is an intense burst of flavour that you just don't get from the handful of varieties that are grown commercially on a big scale.

I especially love the drills of heritage potato plants, with their names written on wooden markers at the end of each line, and I see the pea pods forming and remember picking them from the garden at teatime when I was a kid. There was something so deeply satisfying about running your finger through the pod and eating the sweet little peas there and then.

Up at the top beyond the apple trees there is a meadow that especially puts me in mind of a similar field at home that I used to throw myself into and look up at the sky and the trails that the jets made, and let my imagination run wild. They have a hut made out of cob and now a clay oven which they built when we were filming down there on another occasion. A few weeks later I went back and we cooked in it for the first time. I had been thinking about baking bread and doing something utterly pretentious like roasted beetroot and vegetables with goats cheese, but when I arrived I got talking to one of the workers, an Italian guy called Matteo, and he and I went to the local shop and bought some flour and yeast and some lovely cheeses and he made a pizza dough. He kneaded it for exactly twelve minutes, and then made one of the best Roman pizzas I have ever eaten. Afterwards he just melted some really good chocolate on some dough, as a little sweet snack, which was beautiful. The whole experience of watching them build the oven, and then eating the food we baked in it will stay with me for the rest of my life.

Even though everything in the gardens will be allowed to go beyond the eating stage in order to collect the seed, the salad leaves are so good, you just

want to eat them as they are, naked, no dressing whatoever. It's the first time I have ever felt like that about leaves, which is why we are paying for a polytunnel there, where they will trial and grow more salad leaves and herbs, and also grow some for us in Bentley's in Dublin. I want different leaves, salads that aren't commercially available, a mix with the right weight and flavour: spicy, peppery, soft, subtle… which is what you need for a great leaf salad. I walk around picking leaves, putting them all together and rolling them up like a cigar, so you get a taste of each leaf when you bite into it… that's when the alchemy happens and you know straight away when you have a great combination.

The seeds, around 600 different varieties, are all catalogued and kept chilled, to stop them germinating, in the painted seed house, which looks like an overgrown beach hut, except for its 'GMO Free Zone' sign outside. Some of the seeds are beautiful, like shiny beads in amazing colours and shapes.

The head gardner is Peter Bourke, who discovered Seed Savers on a field trip during his agricultural course at college in Kinsale and joined them as soon as he had graduated. Like most of us, he had had no real idea of the global importance of saving seed until then.

As he explains, for centuries people around the world have grown fruit and vegetables and saved their naturally open-pollinated seed for the next year. You'd often swap seeds with other families, to try out different varieties. It's what we did with our seed potatoes, too. My dad would always be on the lookout for good varieties. Without really thinking too much about it, it was how you kept a healthy biodiversity going, because over time different varieties adapt to regional conditions and develop resistance to local pests. The importance of biodiversity, they stress at Seed Savers, is a lesson Ireland learnt the hard way back in 1845, the year the potato famine began. The Irish had been growing potatoes for hundreds of years, but at that time most poor families had come to rely on one high-yielding variety. When the blight swept through the fields, around a million people starved. The question you have to ask is, had there been a wider diversity of varieties planted, with different resistances to the rot, might the scale of the famine, and the whole of Irish history since, been completely different?

Up until a few generations ago you would have had small family-owned seed companies with their own breeding programmes, supplying local farmers with heritage or 'heirloom' seeds, but gradually the little people got swallowed up by bigger companies who began breeding hybrid seeds known as F1s, first-generation seeds specifically bred from two parents, for special characteristics, such as bumper yield, special colour, flavour, or good disease resistance, that can be worth a lot of money to the seed companies, who formulate and then patent them. In the case of companies like Monsanto, not only did they own the rights to the seed, but they also manufactured the chemicals needed to fertilise and kill the weeds on them.

But according to Seed Savers, what really hit biodiversity hardest was the European Union deciding in 1980 to amalgamate the national seed lists of its member states. Up until then, each country had a national seed directory of sorts, but when they were amalgamated about 1,500 varieties were lost because they were deemed duplicates, even though they might have had different names and properties.

Since then, you can only sell seeds legally if they are registered on the European directory, and before you can register a seed it has to satisfy criteria of distinctness, uniformity and stability. So the old heritage, open-pollinated varieties that weren't owned by anyone, they were just seeds of the people, suitable to local conditions, wouldn't comply with the uniformity and stability that was required for commercial sales. And even if a small company was still selling traditional seeds that could satisfy the criteria, the chances are they wouldn't be able to afford the high fees you now had to pay to register a new seed and have the right to sell it each year.

The next killer blow is that F1s are designed to be used once only. If you save the seeds, the next crop won't be identical.

So the world relies more and more on buying new F1 seeds (and what the big companies would really like us to move on to is their patented GM seeds). Usually the crops that are grown for these universal seeds are planted in hot-climate countries, and so they aren't as adaptable to local conditions as the old traditional varieties.

The message that Seed Saver organisations around the world is trying to give us is that you could have an entire hybrid crop fail, say, in a developing country, and the farmers would have nothing to sell and not enough money to buy more seed for the next year. Meanwhile, if the gene bank of old varieties their ancestors planted, among which could be a resistant strain, has been lost, it would be like the potato famine of 1845 over again.

Dermot points out that there was a huge seed bank in Iraq, which is in the region considered to be the cradle of all agriculture, and where seed saving among farmers had been traditional for centuries. They also had a seed bank but it was at Abu Ghraib, and during the war the seeds disappeared or were destroyed (though some say a selection was previously deposited for safekeeping in a seed bank in Syria). 'One of the last things done by the administrator for the Provisional Coalition Authority in Iraq, Paul J. Bremer,' says Dermot, 'was to bring in Order 81, preventing farmers in Iraq from saving seeds from any "new" variety registered by a company who had developed it, i.e. the big American companies, who can now demand payment for the use of their seed every year.'

Things get more disturbing when you consider the possibility of what is called the terminator gene being used in the future by the big companies promoting GM seeds. The technology exists to produce GM seeds that sterilise themselves as they develop, so that anyone tempted to illegally distribute patented seeds won't be able to – it's like putting anti-copying devices into DVDs. The idea is so controversial that in 2000 the United Nations Convention on Biological Diversity imposed a moratorium on sterile seed technologies, but if that changes, it would be impossible for a farmer to save patented seeds to replant for the next harvest even if he wanted to, so no matter how poor he is, he would have to keep paying out.

The idea of a sterile seed, believes Peter Bourke, is 'morally completely wrong. Quite apart from the inherent capitalism of it all, and the fact that the control of food could extend to the point where the small grower has no choice, logistically it is madness, very short-sighted, and biologically potentially quite dangerous. No matter how much the producers of these seeds claim that the crops would be controlled, with no danger of cross-contamination, nature always finds a way,' he says. 'What happens if a bee finds its way into a polytunnel? You would be sending out the seeds of sterility into the wider biosphere.'

The role of a seed-saving organisation isn't just to preserve the seeds for future generations; it is to get the seeds back out there into gardens and smallholdings. They're not allowed to sell them commercially, so they give them away free to people who become members of the association. 'Anita Hayes, our founder, always said the safest way to save seeds is not to hoard them, but to give them away,' says Peter. 'Get people growing food for themselves locally, using seeds that are perfectly adapted to small local production, then saving their own seeds so they are in charge of their own food security. It's about not being beholden to some big company to decide what you can grow, and being less dependent on fruit and vegetables grown on a vast scale in other countries. It all fits in with fears about climate change, carbon emissions, food miles and really gives a lot of hope to individuals again in these uncertain times. Everyone is looking for large solutions to global problems, but it is small democratic solutions that can inspire people.'

I know how inspiring it can be. Even in my London garden, I have grown salads from seed in a Belfast sink and for two months of the summer we just picked the leaves as we needed them, letting the rest grow; it's a deeply satisfying thing to do.

'Because the European legislators allow each member state to interpret the law as they see fit,' says Dermot, sometimes, as in the case of Irish Seed Savers, they are allowed to sell a few seeds in tiny quantities in their shop. 'As long as we stay small we are OK,' he says, 'but because the open-pollinated seeds we give out can be planted and then the seeds saved again and again, we could potentially be a challenge to the business of the big companies. In France, a sister seed saving organisation, Association Kokopelli, were taken to court by a big seed company, Baumaux, and fined thousands of euros for selling traditional seed varieties that weren't on the EU list.'

I just think without organisations like Seed Savers the world would be a weaker, more hollow place. 'But,' as Dermot says, 'you can get too bogged down with the enormity of it all. What Anita said when she founded Seed Savers was, we're just a whisper in the wind . . . we just have to do what we do and don't be complaining about what other people are doing. What the big boys want is for you to be fighting them, because it distracts you from what you should be doing. That way you're too busy puffing against their wind, instead of blowing your own.'

Peas

Picking peas is one of my best memories. Mum would send me out with a bowl, but I wouldn't be able to resist popping the pods and eating the little peas inside, so by the time I got back to the house there would be barely any left. I have to contradict the commonly held view that there is no difference between a fresh pea and a frozen pea. Clarence Birdseye might have done the world a big favour by proving you could freeze a vegetable, and, to be fair, peas frozen within an hour of picking are fine and they see you through the winter, but when you are brought up on freshly picked peas, nothing matches them for sweetness and starchiness, crunchiness and flavour, or that perfume that is there for a moment, then gone. In a frozen pea the starch has turned itself to sugar, so it has a slightly more sugary sweetness. It's enough of a difference to make it worth taking the family out to a farm for the day and picking them yourself.

Fresh peas don't need much cooking. My mother would put them into a cast-iron pot, with a dash of water (they were never thrown into masses of boiling water), salt and a bit of butter, just to take the crunchiness off them. I like to add a pinch of sugar, too, and then throw in lots of chopped scallions at the last minute.

Peas are one of the most versatile of vegetables – I think of Russian salad (see page 53), or peas and baby gem lettuces, with some chopped spring onions, lightly cooked together in a bit of water and butter with a dash of cream stirred in at the end. Courgettes and peas are lovely together, the courgette shredded on a mandoline and salted very gently, then rinsed and drained. Just blanch the peas, really quickly, in boiling salted water. Heat a little olive oil in a big sauté pan, put in the courgettes and peas and stir-fry them until the courgettes take a bit of colour, then throw in masses of chopped basil. Fantastic served with chicken.

Pea, Asparagus and Spinach Salad with Crème Fraîche Dressing

Serves 4
roughly equal quantities
of:
fresh peas, podded
asparagus, peeled and cut
into batons
baby spinach, washed

Crème fraîche dressing:
250g crème fraîche
100ml extra virgin olive
oil
juice of 1 lemon
a bunch of mint, finely
chopped

This has some of my favourite vegetables in it. Young spinach has that iron-ey, cabbag-ey, kale green deliciousness that makes me want to eat more and more of it. I like it just wilted in a pan with no water in it, and a little butter added, because you have to be able to taste it in its earthy, raw naturalness. Here it is literally dropped into boiling water for seconds, just to soften it. This salad is lovely and fresh by itself, but you could easily serve it with a piece of steamed fish.

Put the peas into a pan of boiling salted water and cook for 3 minutes. Take them out with a slotted spoon and put them into a bowl. Put the asparagus into the same cooking water for a minute, lift out, and add to the peas.

Finally, put in the spinach for just 3 seconds, and drain. Combine with the peas and asparagus. Spoon everything on to plates or into bowls.

Mix all the dressing ingredients together and drizzle over.

Fresh Pea Beignets

These are brilliant just with some of the aioli on page 90 or the scorthalia on page 49 – you could chop a little bit of mint in, too. They are also fantastic alongside some pan-fried scallops.

Use the tempura batter on page 126. All you have to do is cook about 500g of fresh peas in a pan of salted water until tender, then drain them. Soften a chopped onion and garlic clove in a little olive oil, add a chopped bunch of marjoram, then put this mixture into a blender with your drained peas. Whiz just for a couple of seconds to crush the peas, so they are very roughly puréed but still have nice pieces of pea in there. Cool and shape with your hands into little balls, a little smaller than a golf ball. Put them on a tray in the freezer for half an hour so they really firm up, then dip them first into some seasoned flour and then into your tempura batter and deep-fry very briefly until the batter is golden.

Potatoes

The potato was placed in high reverence in our house, and in all the houses around us. Good seed potatoes were always a hot topic for discussion, and I'm still passionate about the spud. One of my first memories is of helping my dad prepare the field for the potatoes. We had a horse and plough to turn the soil, because the tractor was never allowed into the vegetable gardens. Where we lived on the fringes of the bog, the soil was very soft, wet, black peaty clay, so you could never put a tractor in there, as it would just sink and compact the soil too much. We might have been living a simple lifestyle, but farmers back then, in all their glorious bliss and ignorance of modern technology, were so at one with the land that they knew all the magic little details about growing, and I think I was very privileged to have grown up where I did. It was a beautiful thing to see the soil being turned over so gracefully in the silence. Then came the hard work. All the seed potatoes, kept back from the previous year, had to be planted by hand, and it was a big field. But there is something lovely about drills of potatoes in all their flowering glory, and when you knew it was time for the first crop, it was an incredible thing to push the fork into the ground, loosen the earth, then pull up the stalk, shake off some of the soil and watch the potatoes, maybe still a bit undersized, appear like little truffles. It was always a huge treat to bring them in, wash, cook and eat them that evening with some cold meats from the larder.

Something that my mother never did, but which I love, is the German style of warm potato salad, made with hot vinegary onions poured over cooked potatoes. Served with a piece of gammon or with fish, such as brown trout (see the recipe on page 68), it is stunning.

At other times of the year there would be a big bowl of mash. I love mashed potato, but done the Irish or British way. I'm just not interested in chi-chi French-style purées; they do nothing for me. When the food critics used to come back from Joel Robuchon's Jamin in Paris back in the 1980s, waxing lyrical about his famous *pommes purée*, I used to put my nose in the air and say, 'You don't know what you're talking about.' Yes, I understand the philosophy of passing the hot potato twice, first through a mouli so it makes for a finer potato that will absorb more fat, and then through a fine sieve to make it really smooth, and yes, there are times when it is nice to have a fluffier mash, maybe with a whole baked fish. And yes, I occasionally turn a blind eye in the kitchen when some of my chefs, who are in love with the idea of *pommes purée*, can't resist it. You have to let young guys have a bit of rein sometimes, or you end up a dictator. But when I'm making mash, I really don't want equal quantities of potato and fat: deeply unhealthy stuff under the guise of haute cuisine and refinement. I want my potatoes to taste of potatoes, of starch, not milk or cream and butter. Potatoes with butter, please – not the other way round.

Colcannon

There's no such thing as a recipe for colcannon, really. It's something that is put together with love, not measurements. But for around 600g of good, floury potatoes, you need around half a head of kale, chopped finely, almost shredded; a few chopped scallions (spring onions), about 100ml of milk and 60g of butter. Bring the potatoes (unpeeled) to the boil in plenty of salted water and cook them until they are just soft. Drain them, return them to the pan, off the heat, and cover with a tea towel to let them steam and dry off for a few minutes, then uncover them to let them cool just enough to peel. While they steam, drop the kale into boiling salted water for a couple of minutes until it is just tender, but still retaining its bite, and drain. Heat the milk in a small pan with the butter until it has melted – don't let it boil – then add the scallions and take off the heat. Peel the potatoes, put them into a warm bowl and mash with the back of a fork, add the hot milk and butter and beat in, then add the kale and season with salt and pepper.

You can serve colcannon with anything, but when I think of potatoes and cabbage or kale, my mind automatically skips on to pork or bacon. Every food culture and farming community has its trilogy of ingredients that are just there, in and of the land around, and all over northern Europe you find combinations of pork, potatoes and vegetables. In parts of Holland you find a tradition of *stamppot boerenkool*: curly kale and potatoes, very similar to colcannon, with smoked sausage on top and a bit of gravy – just brilliant. Growing up on a farm, there was never any question of not having these ingredients, no having to go to the market for them. It was cuisine à la larder. There always seemed to be cabbage around, especially. When virtually everything else in the garden was gone, there would still be cabbage, which I love with a collar of bacon, floury potatoes in their jackets, with lots of good butter, or champ, which is very similar to colcannon but with only scallions (see page 203), and maybe an onion sauce with a bit of mustard in it. But for colcannon, I'd say go for kale when it is in season. I love its earthy, iron-ey flavour, which is less sweet than cabbage, and because of its coarseness it makes a lot more sense when you serve it with coarser cuts of meat.

There's long been a debate about kale versus cabbage for colcannon and I have to say I've done a complete U-turn. In my first book I argued against kale, maybe because I was stuffed full of it as a child and turned against it for a while. Now, maybe it's an age thing, but, you know what, I've come to love it, lightly blanched. I can eat a whole plate of it and feel like I'm taking in pure goodness. You crunch into it, and it's like detoxing. It really is great stuff. But when it isn't around, go for a dark, Savoy-type cabbage.

Colcannon Soup

Sometimes if we had leftover colcannon, my mother would add the stock from boiling a ham, to turn it into a soup. It's the kind of thing you want to eat when the frost is on the ground. I tend to think vegetable soups don't really need detailed recipes any more than colcannon does, but if you want to make something similar from scratch, this is how I'd do it. It makes a great supper, with some grilled rashers of dry-cured bacon on toasted soda bread (see page 312).

Serves 4

2 tablespoons butter

1 large onion, chopped

4 cloves garlic, crushed

250g potatoes, peeled and thinly sliced

enough ham stock (see page 180) or chicken stock (see page 181) to cover the vegetables

1 bouquet garni

1 head of kale or cabbage, shredded

300ml double cream

Heat the butter in a large saucepan, put in the onion, garlic and potato slices and cook gently for 5 minutes without colouring. Pour over enough stock to cover the vegetables, add the bouquet garni and season. Bring to the boil, cover and simmer for 15 minutes.

Add the kale or cabbage to the soup and bring back to the boil, then remove from the heat. Whiz everything up in a blender. Put back on the hob, add the cream and check the seasoning. Serve piping hot.

Mrs Smith's Temptation

This is our variation on a great Swedish snack. One story about how it got its real name, *Janssons frestelse* (Jansson's temptation), is that this was the food that tempted a religious zealot called Jansson to give in to earthly pleasures. Since in Sweden the surname Jansson is a bit like Smith in England, somewhere along the line we started calling it Mrs Smith's temptation in the kitchen, and the name has stuck.

Serves 4

600g starchy potatoes
600ml double cream
200ml chicken stock
2 cloves garlic, grated
1 bay leaf
2 sprigs of thyme
25g cheese, such as Bill Hogan's Desmond (see page 296), or Cheddar
10 salted anchovies, rinsed and patted dry

Peel the potatoes, but don't wash them, as you want them to retain their starch. Preferably using a mandoline, cut them into matchstick pieces.

Put the cream into a pan with the stock, garlic and herbs, season (go easy on the salt as you have both cheese and anchovies in the dish) and bring up to the boil. Turn down the heat and put in the potatoes, cheese and anchovies. Cook very gently for 10–15 minutes, until the potatoes are cooked but still retain their shape. As the potatoes release their starch the mixture will thicken. Taste and adjust the seasoning if necessary.

While the mixture is cooking, preheat the grill. Pour the mixture into a gratin dish and put under the grill until the cheese bubbles and browns on top.

Mushrooms

When I think of mushrooms, my mind doesn't immediately turn to the likes of ceps and girolles, but to field mushrooms. As kids, the minute they came up we'd literally be running out to the fields to pick them, they were so good. Cooked in a little bit of butter on top of the stove, they were a feast. You might have been eating a steak. The fields belonging to our neighbours the Douglases had the best for miles around. We took the Swedish view that you don't need permission to pick mushrooms, they are there for everyone, but you always had to watch for the bull that invariably lurked in Irish fields.

You had to keep an eye on the weather, too, because you would know that after a spell of light drizzle and a spot of humidity of an evening the mushrooms would 'grow for a night' as we used to say. The next morning they would have popped up all over the fields and off we'd go with our baskets because they were only good for a moment, or the worms would have them. Thinking back, there were puffballs, too, but at the time we were too scared to take anything we didn't know.

When we had a real glut, Dad used to make a field mushroom ketchup, boiling them up with a drop of vinegar, some peppercorns and salt, though the actual recipe was a bit of a secret.

Slow-cooked Field Mushrooms

When you cook field mushrooms really gently for several hours with garlic and thyme they become very soft, but still keep their shape, and the flavour is phenomenal. Serve them with a rocket salad, or for breakfast with fried eggs.

Serves 4

16 big field mushrooms
lots of olive oil
1 head of garlic, cloves
   sliced
a bunch of thyme or
   rosemary

Preheat the oven to 140°C/Gas 1. Peel the mushrooms but leave on the stalks. Lay them in a roasting tray, stalk-side up. Sprinkle over lashings of olive oil. It will get soaked up by the mushrooms. Sprinkle over the garlic, thyme leaves and some salt. Put into the oven and cook very slowly for a minimum of 4 hours, until really soft.

Puffball 'Pizzas'

We get extraordinary, enormous puffball mushrooms in the summer, brought to us by Miles Irving and his team of gatherers from Forager, who go out into the woods and countryside collecting wild fungi, roots, flowers, fruits and plants, from wood sorrel to Japanese knotweed, which they deliver to the kitchen door. You never quite know what they will bring, but that is half the fun.

You can find puffballs all over the country in disused fields, growing behind nettles. They're quite mad-looking when they grow to their full size, but they are fantastically earthy and meaty tasting. We took Rowley Leigh's way of slicing and blanching them, and then treated the slices like little 'pizza' bases.

Instead of baking them in the oven, you could also just brush the slices of puffball with olive oil, season them and put them under a hot grill for about 4 minutes on each side, then serve them underneath a piece of beef or a steak, with some garlic béarnaise sauce (see page 214) and watercress.

Serves 4

1 giant puffball
   mushroom, the
   diameter of a dinner
   plate
a little olive oil
8 tomatoes, sliced
a little dried oregano
whatever topping
   you like: taleggio or
   mozzarella cheese,
   olives, anchovies

Slice the top from the puffball and cut the rest crossways into 4 thick slices. Bring a pan of salted water to the boil, put in the mushroom slices, blanch for a minute, drain and pat dry.

Preheat the oven to 200°C/Gas 6. Brush each slice of puffball with a little olive oil, arrange some sliced tomatoes on top, sprinkle with a little oregano, and add any topping you like, from cheese to anchovies. Bake for about 15 minutes or until heated through.

Asparagus

I love English asparagus, which I'd put right up there with a fresh pea for intensity of flavour, but I also like white asparagus, the favourite in Europe, especially in France and the Netherlands, which is now being grown for the first time here. People tend to make comparisons between green and white asparagus, but I think that's wrong, because they are two different things; you can't compare one to the other. White asparagus has something in common with forced rhubarb, in that instead of the shoots coming up and developing chlorophyll in the sunlight so that they turn green, they are kept in the dark, covered in sandy soil so they stay white.

The first time you taste white asparagus, it can seem quite bitter, but the second or third time you start to understand and appreciate it. You can pickle it – in France you see it in jars in every delicatessen or *traiteur* – and it is beautiful served with a soft duck egg and some brown shrimp in the same way as the green asparagus in the recipe on page 280, or with smoked ham or bacon. But it is at its best with melted butter and nutmeg. It has a minerally quality which lends itself to those flavours. That's the way the Germans and Dutch serve it, and they have it right. In our islands we find nutmeg and vegetables a bit difficult to comprehend, but take it from me, when you get your head around it, it's the best way to enjoy white asparagus. The trimmings make a great soup, too, though you need to cook them for a while to really get the flavour out of them.

Something I do that is quite luxurious, but reminds me of my time in the Netherlands, is to make a Sauce Americaine (as in the recipe for royal fish pie on page 111), but using langoustines or crayfish instead of lobster (you need around 24 langoustines or crayfish). I cook the asparagus briefly, drain it, pour the sauce over the top, then blanch the langoustines or crayfish for about 2 minutes, peel them, and scatter them on top.

According to Greg Secrett, of Secrett's Farm in Surrey, who supplies us with asparagus and freshly picked peas, Britain has the perfect climate for growing green and purple asparagus, because in the first two years before you can begin harvesting, it needs the fern to grow through a summer which isn't too hot. Then it dies back to provide enough nutrients for the crown (the root system of the asparagus) to grow steadily, healthily and strong, so that in the third year it produces spears with that concentrated flavour that English asparagus is so famous for.

Like most vegetables, you can't beat asparagus freshly pulled from the ground, because once harvested the sugars in the spears start converting into starch very quickly and the flavour starts to fade. English asparagus is grown in different sizes, from thin (sprue) to fat (jumbo), and everyone has their favourite. Personally, I like spears around the thickness of your forefinger.

English Asparagus, Brown Shrimp and Crushed Duck Egg

Of course, you can use hen's eggs instead of duck eggs, but as they are smaller, allow 2 per person and reduce the boiling time to 4 minutes. Instead of brown shrimp you could stir ribbons of smoked salmon into the eggs, or, to be a bit decadent, a little caviar.

The asparagus needs to be cooked for just a minute, so the spears keep their bite and retain all their flavour.

Serves 4
4 duck eggs
20 asparagus spears, stalks peeled
50g of butter
200g peeled brown shrimps
some snipped chives, or finely sliced spring onion (just the green part)
juice of 1 lemon
quarters of buttered toast, to serve

Bring a pan of water to the boil, lower the duck eggs into the water and keep at a rolling boil for 5 minutes. Run under cold water for 1 minute, then peel the eggs (they will be very soft-boiled, just holding their shape).

Cook the asparagus spears in boiling salted water for approximately 1 minute.

Melt the butter in a small pan over a gentle heat. Add the eggs and crush with a fork until they are just beginning to set. Stir in the shrimps and chives and season with lemon juice and salt.

Serve the asparagus spears on warm plates with the toast, topped with the egg and shrimp, alongside.

Onions

An onion isn't just an onion ... a fresh white one will feel nice and firm and crispy and the moisture content will be high, so it will be oozy when you slice it up. If you sweat it really, really slowly and gently in butter or oil until it becomes transparent, the juices will take longer to evaporate and you will end up with a lovely soft onion, whereas a dry old onion will end up quite tough and leathery.

I find red onions, cooked slowly in the same way, a little too sweet and sugary, but they are beautiful in a bread salad, with capers, anchovies, cucumber, etc (see page 284). Many people find onions unpalatable if they are completely raw, so I like to pour boiling water over them and leave them for about 45 minutes, just to take the sharp edge off them.

All Irishmen love the scallion, in champ or colcannon. I like mine barely introduced to warm milk and butter so that you keep the crunch, and I love them chopped and thrown into a dish of peas and other green vegetables, right at the end.

A newer discovery is the calcot, the multi-headed onion from Tarragona in Spain that is a little like a cross between a scallion and a young leek, which is traditionally served with a spicy Romesco sauce (see page 286).

Onion
Tart

This is a substantial tart that will feed a family of eight. The onion is the star of the show, so use beautiful fresh ones.

The filling is a custard, with some quite pungent cheese – I like to use Bill Hogan's aged Desmond cheese (see page 296), or you could use an aged Cheddar, even one you have kept a bit too long and find a bit too powerful to eat on its own. I used to go down to Neal's Yard and get all the end bits of the cheese that would be left over when they had sold most of the truckle, and which would have otherwise gone in the bin, because they were just great for this tart. The smell when it comes out of the oven is beautiful, and after it has been cooked very slowly and gently and rested for a couple of hours it is brilliantly gooey, like fondue of onion.

With some nice piquant Spanish olives on the side, or even a spoonful of tapenade, and some crusty bread, it makes a great summer supper.

Makes one 21cm tart
Serves 6–8
4 large white onions
75g butter
2 tablespoons olive oil
a good handful of
  marjoram
6 eggs, plus 1 egg beaten,
  for eggwash
600ml double cream
250g aged Desmond
  cheese or similar,
  grated

Pastry:
175g plain flour
75g cornflour
½ teaspoon sea salt
120g butter
2 egg yolks

Peel and halve the onions, then slice thinly. Heat the butter and oil in a large cast-iron or heavy-based pot, put in the onions, season and cook gently for up to an hour. The onions should become very soft and transparent but not coloured. Add the marjoram about 5 minutes before the end of cooking – the heat will just extract all the beautiful flavour from the herb. Remove from the heat, drain the onions and allow to cool.

Make the pastry. Whiz the two flours, salt and butter to fine crumbs in a food processor (or rub the butter in by hand). Tip into a bowl, then mix in the egg yolks and about 2 tablespoons of ice-cold water until you have a smooth dough. You may need some extra trickles of water. Form into a ball, wrap in clingfilm and chill in the fridge for a minimum of 20 minutes.

Heat the oven to 160°C/Gas 3.

Roll out the pastry on a lightly floured board, into a circle large enough to fit a loose-based flan tin 21cm in diameter and 3cm deep. Roll it around your rolling pin, then lift it over the top of the tin and drape it over. Press gently into the tin, taking care not to stretch the pastry. If it cracks, just press it together again. Don't trim the edges, leave them overhanging. Line with foil and dried or ceramic beans and chill for 15 minutes in the fridge to firm it up and help stop it shrinking in the oven. It may still shrink a bit, but if you don't trim the edges until after baking you can compensate for this.

Put the flan case on a baking tray and bake for 45 minutes, then remove the foil and beans and bake for another 5 minutes, until the pastry is dry on the base. Brush the whole of the inside of the pastry with eggwash.

Turn the oven up to 180°C/Gas 4.

Beat the eggs and cream together, stir in the cheese and season well. Mix with the cooled onions and pour into the flan case. Return carefully to the oven and bake for 20 minutes, then turn down the heat to 160°C/Gas 3 for another 40 minutes, until the top is pale golden and the centre barely wobbles.

Remove from the oven and cool for about 2 hours before eating, so that the filling sets further.

When cool, trim the edges, push the tart up out of the flan tin and slide it on to a board or a flat platter.

Bread Salad
with Red Onions
and Anchovies

I'm not saying this is a traditional Italian panzanella (bread salad), because I'm not keen on my bread being soaked in vinegar so it is a bit mushy, which is traditional in Italy. I prefer to toast it. Italians tend to be amused by my version, but they also seem to like it.

Slice up some red onions, pour some boiling water over them, and leave for 45 minutes to soften them out and make them less aggressive. You want some baguette or other crusty bread that has gone a little hard and stale. Tear it up into bite-sized pieces, brush them with some olive oil and garlic and toast them.

Chop up some good tomatoes and cucumber and mix with some chopped anchovy fillets and capers. Drain the onions, mix everything together with some rocket or other leaves, and dress with vinaigrette (made with extra virgin olive oil and red wine vinegar, salt and pepper) and masses of chopped basil.

Calcots with Romesco Sauce

My interest in calcots was sparked off by a piece I read in the *Financial Times* weekend section about the festival in Valls, in Tarragona, where they celebrate the arrival of these special mild many-headed onions, which are roasted or barbecued and typically eaten with romesco sauce. All over Catalunya whole families invite friends to celebrate the calcot season, in the same way as asparagus, with grilled meats to follow, but in Valls, where calcots were first cultivated, there are huge celebrations in the town square. The calcots have their own protected geographical status, *Indicación Geográfica Protegida*, which means they must be grown within a specific area, to certain criteria. What is particular about them is that in summer the tops of the onion bulbs are sliced off and the rest planted in shallow ground so they 'can hear the church bells ring'. Once they start to sprout shoots they are covered in soil, a bit like white asparagus, to keep out the light and force the shoots, which stay white.

I had never cooked calcots, but I said to the boys in the kitchen: let's get some in and try them. We'll put them under the grill and try out a few sauces with them. They make a beautiful little starter, and the traditional spicy, peppery romesco sauce is perfect with them: a great combination. The sauce is often blended to a paste and loosened with sherry vinegar, so you can just hold the calcots by their tails and dip them into a bowl of it, but I quite like a chunkier sauce.

Calcots aren't easy to get hold of, but if you see them, snap them up; and if you don't, you could make something similar with young leeks, fat scallions, or even new season's garlic.

Serves 4

about 24 calcots (or
   alternatives, see above),
   cut lengthways
olive oil

Romesco sauce:
4 red peppers
olive oil
25g blanched almonds
25g blanched hazelnuts
1 onion, sliced
4 cloves garlic, sliced
2 red chillies, deseeded
   and chopped
sherry vinegar

Start the sauce. Preheat the oven to 200°C/Gas 6. Lay the peppers on a roasting tray, drizzle with olive oil, sprinkle with salt and put into the oven for 15–20 minutes until starting to blacken. Remove and allow to cool. Peel the peppers, deseed and chop.

Put the almonds and hazelnuts on a tray and put them into the oven very briefly (turning them over), until just beginning to colour.

Heat some more olive oil in a pan, add the onion, garlic and chillies and cook gently together to soften. Add the peppers and nuts, stir in a splash of sherry vinegar and adjust the seasoning to taste.

Get a griddle pan, grill or barbecue hot, brush the calcots with oil, season, and grill on both sides until they soften and begin to char. Serve with the sauce.

Celery and Celeriac

I love braised celery hearts, sautéed briefly with a little chopped carrot and garlic, then seasoned and transferred to the oven with a bay leaf and a little chicken stock poured over, covered in tin foil and cooked slowly for about an hour and a half at 180°C/Gas 4. When they are just soft, I turn the oven up to 200°C/Gas 6, drain some of the liquid from the celery, scatter some breadcrumbs and grated cheese over the top and put them back into the hotter oven for 5–6 minutes, until the cheese has melted and you have a nice golden brown topping.

I also like the combination of celery flavour and earthy root vegetable that you get in a celeriac just out of the ground, whizzed up into a soup with some stock, or roasted or mashed with potato or apple.

Celery Slaw

Serves 4
juice of 3 limes
1 dessertspoon sugar
1 head of celery
1 head of fennel
1 apple
about 100g seedless
   green grapes

This is something we have been doing for years. Serve it with whatever you like, but it is brilliant with shellfish, red mullet or cold poached fish, such as sea trout. The trick is to do everything at the last minute, so that the lime in the dressing keeps its zing, and the apple and fennel don't discolour. Don't add any seasoning, as salt, especially, destroys the freshness of the dressing.

Mix the lime juice and sugar together to make the dressing, then finely slice the celery and fennel. Peel and grate the apple, and halve the grapes. Finely chop any fennel fronds. Toss all together in the dressing.

Caponata

When I think of caponata, celery always comes to mind above anything else. I like lots of celery in there, and I like to cool the caponata down and pile it up on top of some toasted bread, rubbed with olive oil and a bit of garlic. It's also great on a summer table, like a chutney, to eat with cold ham or chicken.

Serves 4

a little olive oil

1 aubergine, diced

1 onion, finely diced

6 sticks celery, diced

2 cloves garlic, crushed

2 tablespoons sugar

2 tablespoons sherry
   vinegar

8 tomatoes, diced

12 black olives, stoned

1 tablespoon capers

1 tablespoon pine nuts,
   toasted

a bunch of flat-leaf
   parsley

Heat a little olive oil in a frying pan and add the aubergine. Fry until golden brown on all sides, season with a little salt and pepper and tip into a colander to drain.

Heat some more oil in a large saucepan, add the onion, celery and garlic and cook gently until softened.

Add the sugar and sherry vinegar to the pan and cook for a couple of minutes. Add the tomatoes and the cooked aubergine and simmer for another 20 minutes.

Add the olives, capers and pine nuts and cook for 5 minutes more.

Season to taste, finish with chopped parsley and serve at room temperature.

Celeriac and Apple Mash

This is a great mash to have with pork.

Serves 4

a little butter

1 head of celeriac, peeled and diced

a sprig of thyme

1 Bramley apple, peeled, cored and chopped

Heat the butter in a pan, add the celeriac and thyme and cook gently for a few minutes. Season with salt.

Add the apple, cover with a 'cartouche' (a circle of greaseproof paper) and cook very gently until both the celeriac and apple are soft. The juices will come out of the apple and the greaseproof 'cartouche' will help to stop them evaporating.

When tender, mash roughly with a potato masher, season with black pepper, mix in a little more butter and serve.

Cheese, Eggs, Bread and Butter

Where would we be without bread and cheese, bread and butter, cheese and eggs? As a child I watched my mother make bread every day in a bastible, a cast-iron pot oven, smothered in crushed coals from the turf fire. We had ducks and hens to give us eggs, and the whole idea of having cows to give fresh milk and homemade butter made a lasting impression on me. Although we never made our own cheese, I have always been compelled by the idea of the small artisan cheesemaker, and the tastes of the traditional dairy products from my childhood have left me searching for the real thing ever since.

Cheese

We have made historic strides forward in terms of cheesemaking in these islands over the last thirty years; it's been a golden time, it really has. And I believe that we should support our own cheesemakers as other European countries have supported theirs. Of course, the great European cheeses are beautiful. In season, a Bleu d'Auvergne or French mountain goat's cheese, Brie de Meaux or Beaufort can be immaculate; a Vacherin Mont d'Or from late autumn until Christmas is quite magical, and I can't imagine pasta without some proper Parmigiano Reggiano over the top.

Mozzarella, eaten within twenty-four hours of it being made, is sensational. On holiday we used to buy it from the guys who would drive up from Napoli to the richer parts of Italy, with the fresh, just made cheese, and park on the side of the motorway, selling it. When they ran out, they would drive back and pick up the next day's batch. A little olive oil over the top, some sea salt to crunch against the cheese – does it need anything else? I'm not so sure. With something that pure, I think you just say, 'No tomatoes, no basil, no Parma ham; this is perfect.'

The point is that a cheese should say something about the land where you are standing, and the people who made it. In Amsterdam there is a wonderful shop, De Kaaskamer (the Cheese Chamber), where they pull out little local cheeses and when you taste the individuality it is as if a flag flies above the produce, saying, 'Someone here made this, it didn't come out of a factory.' I remember a cheese called Cow Plot, which reminded me so much of Ireland, where you traditionally had cow plots, pieces of common land that local people could keep their animals on, which were to be kept for future generations of a community: you might build a school on them, or a garden. I thought what a brilliant name for a local cheese.

So when I am in Britain or in Ireland, my heart will always be with the British and Irish cheesemaker, and I am proud to have on my cheeseboard a piece of Keen's or Montgomery's Cheddar, Mrs Kirkham's Lancashire, Bill Hogan's aged Desmond from Schull down in West Cork, a goat's cheese made by Silke Croppe in Ulster, and a semi-soft washed rind cheese from the milk of local Friesian herds, made by Jeffa Gill of Durrus down on the Sheep's Head Peninsula near Bantry. Jeffa began making her cheese in a pan on her farm stove in the late seventies and was at the spearhead of the Irish farmhouse cheese movement.

From the day we opened Lindsay House, we have always treated British and Irish cheeses seriously. Randolph Hodgson at Neal's Yard introduced us to the best farmhouse cheeses, and he would tell you that though Lindsay House was small enough to fit into the porch of many a London restaurant, we sold more cheese, because we wanted everyone to try some, whenever they wanted: after the main course, after the puddings… for a small supplement everyone could have a plate of cheeses. Our Cheddars were so good; even my discerning Scottie dog could recognise the quality. I used to take the end bits home to him and he would wait for them: much tastier than any bone, thank you.

In the early days we would go down to the Neal's Yard shop every day to pick up our cheeses, and choose what was best. We must have driven them mad, especially in the run up to Christmas. Imagine, customers queuing out of the door and the Lindsay house chefs turning up wanting to pick cheeses for a hundred people. I was sad when they started supplying us directly from their cellars and the cheese arrived instead in their little chilled vans, because for the boys in the kitchen there is no substitute for the knowledge you gain by seeing the whole cheeses, tasting the differences from cheese to cheese, young to aged, season to season – the best cheeses, as Randolph would say, are often made in the late summer, otherwise the acidity in the grass can be too high.

In Ireland especially, I take my hat off to the small producers who are reviving traditions of cheesemaking that date back to ancient times, but that were lost over the centuries, bringing new skills to old ideas, and reinvigorating the craft. People like Maja Binder who is German, and her partner Olivier Beaujouan, a Frenchman who settled in Ireland nearly twenty years ago and started out smoking fish with Frank Hederman in Cobh. Maja makes Dingle Peninsula Cheese, stone-pressed cow's milk cheeses from local herds, including Dilliskus, which has seaweed running through it. The seaweed is Olivier's speciality. He runs his own business, On the Wild Side, making things like Sea Spaghetti, Japanese- style pickled seaweed, and Tapenade of Sea Vegetables along with fish pâtés and wild rabbit terrines.

Great cheese can't be mass-produced. Once you up the production, you lose the consistency and focus that comes from driven, obsessive individuals like Bill Hogan (see page 296) or Silke Croppe running the show. Like Olivier and

Maja, neither of these are native Irish, but they would be an important addition to any culture, and I'm so glad they chose to settle in Ireland. I tasted Silke's goat's cheese at a tasting before I met her, and I knew I had tasted greatness. I was standing there shouting, 'Who made this cheese? Where is she? I need to meet this woman.'

She's an amazing person: German, but the look of her, with her red hair, you'd think she hails from the hills of Cavan. A supporter of the Slow Food Movement, which really has cheesemaking as one of its bedrocks, she makes the most gorgeous goat's and cow's milk cheeses at Corleggy Farmhouse in Ulster on the banks of the River Erne, between Cavan and Fermanagh. The animals graze on local pasture and herbs around Corleggy and the goat's cheeses are made from pasteurised milk, while the cow's milk ones are made with raw milk.

Bill Hogan tells me that the way of the cheesemaker is one of the most seamless, genuine, almost spiritual lifestyles, but it also demands total dedication, particularly if you are making blue cheese, like Bellingham Blue (see page 301), which needs so much attention – there's no time off, no holidays. Get it wrong and it's a disaster, especially for those making unpasteurised cheese. You are forever battling against the grinding red tape, officials trying to shut you down, all the negatives the authorities pit against you because they don't want the nuisance of trying to regulate the little people and they don't want their big brands tarnished by some timewaster of a rogue cheesemaker. It's a minefield, and to come through shining, well, these guys are more than just producers, they have to be talked about, encouraged, supported, championed.

It isn't that they want to be difficult, or that they are trying to poison the world by refusing to pasteurise their cheeses; they just stand by their belief that the greatest cheese they can make is unpasteurised. People – especially the authorities – like to say that you can't tell the difference, tastewise, between a pasteurised and an unpasteurised cheese, but I promise you I can.

And yes, you have to have controls and incredibly high standards when it comes to food, and yes, I know that the authorities are terrified of *E.coli*, but hang on, I have been drinking raw milk since I was a child, like most people on working farms would have done, and your body builds up its own immunities – the only thing that makes me ill is processed food! If we ban everything that is unpasteurised, we will have a much bigger problem in fifty years' time, when no one has a proper immune system. Fine, put a label on the cheese that says 'Unpasteurised. Eat at your own risk', but give us a break and let individual choice rule.

Gabriel and Desmond

I'm hooked on the whole idea of the obsessive cheesemaker, the craftsman, working on a tiny scale. People have no idea of the energy these fine, passionate, fanatical individuals dispense into making their cheese, or, in some cases, the struggle they have to keep going. Bill Hogan, down in Schull in West Cork, is the epitome of the dedicated artisan, an amazing cheesemaker, a real intellectual and philosopher, who makes two cheeses, Gabriel, after Mount Gabriel, and Desmond, which comes from the Irish Deasmumhain, the old name for the tip of South Munster. His cheeses are semi-hard and beautiful when they are matured. Aged Desmond is a particular favourite of mine, a strong, mouth-puckeringly tangy cheese – Bill calls it 'foxy', and two-year-old Desmond is almost like Parmesan, absolutely beautiful. A cheese like that should be eaten all on its own; you don't need anything with it.

Bill lives down a little lane right next door to my favourite charcuterie maker in Ireland, Frank Krawczyk, another extreme individual (see page 176). When I eat these guys' cheeses and salami they open up such interesting flavours in the mouth and brain that tell your body, 'You have to eat this again.' Food should do that for you. It's not just stuff to stick in your mouth and swallow to fuel you up.

Most artisans making great food are pretty smart people. Spend an evening cooking and cracking a few bottles of wine with Bill and some deep thoughts will be expressed around the table, I can tell you. Samuel Beckett is bound to come up, as is the book of seminal photographs of him taken by his great friend, the photographer John Minihan, who often drops by to put the world to rights over a glass or two. Bill has a great history. He was born in New York and when he was eighteen he worked for Martin Luther King at the height of the civil rights movement. After both Dr King and Robert Kennedy were assassinated in 1968, he went to Costa Rica, finished off his university degree and lived on a farm in the mountains, where he learned to make local cheese. He had always had a leaning towards agriculture and had a feeling for cheese since he tasted his first great Cheddar made with raw milk in Canada. He told me the flavour sizzled in his mouth; it was a taste that haunted him.

Through the Swiss embassy he met the famous cheesemaster Joseph Dubach, who was helping countries like Costa Rica, with a diverse food culture and interest in European ideas, to learn about cheesemaking. Dubach, and later another Swiss cheesemaster, Josef Enz, taught him about traditional thermophilic Gruyère-Parmesan style cheesemaking, based on yoghurt, which uses unpasteurised milk but involves heating the curds to a high temperature.

Bill wound up in Ireland because he had visited it as a child, knew the milk was good and felt it would be a great place to make these cheeses. 'When I was in Costa Rica a friend brought me some Irish Cheddar and it was an inspiration,' he says. What he didn't know was that Ireland once had its own great tradition of thermophilic cheese, which had been lost, and now here he was about to restore it. 'Professor Regina Sexton of University College Cork has done a lot of work on Irish food pre-famine and earlier, and she has verified that hard thermophilic cheese and many other dairy products were made here from ancient times,' he says.

Bill makes his cheeses with a former student, Sean Ferry, and when they started up, Joseph Dubach came over to Ireland to help them. They call themselves the West Cork Natural Cheese Company, and the actual cheesemaking goes on only for four months of the year, in high summer, using milk from local farmers with small herds that graze on grasses, plants and heather up in the peaty hills between Mount Gabriel and the sea. The idea comes from the Alpine tradition of transhumance, which you still see in Switzerland, when the cows are taken high up into the mountains in summer to take advantage of the fresh pastures. Instead of forcing poor land in the other months or using milk from cows fed on silage, you work with the cycles of nature, make your cheese just once a year, and then you have something you can store away for winter.

According to Bill, the cheese might be made with unpasteurised milk but after maturing for three to four months it's bacteria-proof anyway. 'It's just not a good medium for bugs: it's too dry, too salty, too acidic. Bugs just don't like it,' he says. Which is what saved them when they had to take on the authorities back in 2002. The department of agriculture failed to test for TB one of the herds that supplied their milk, and then, after the batch of cheese had been made, a delayed test showed a positive reaction. A detention order was put on the cheese. 'We would have gone out of business,' says Bill. But he boned up on the science and the law, and was even represented in court by Helen Collins, the grand-niece of Michael Collins. Backed up by Irish cheese expert Dr Tim Coogan and Swiss research, they were able to prove scientifically that their cheese was fit to eat. It helped that the judge turned out to be a fan of his cheese.

'We won the battle, but we lost the war to an extent,' says Bill, 'because the authorities dragged everything out over more court cases, fighting our claims for compensation, and underneath it all, ever since the farmhouse cheesemaking movement got started twenty to thirty years ago, there has been a covert policy to eliminate raw milk. There's a terrible resistance to Sean and myself and others who are trying to bring diversity and distinctiveness to Irish food, because we don't fit into the centrist, one-size-fits-all policy. The authorities don't want the bother of trying to certify and regulate us, but they have missed the whole point, which is that in other European countries small producers receive great

acceptance and recognition by the state. We're just pipsqueaks, Sean and I, and the fight has taken a lot out of us, but we had to stand up for ourselves.'

Their one concession to the authorities is that they have moved their cheesemaking from their small place in Schull to a space dedicated to them at the Newmarket co-operative creamery in Cork – 'if anything comes up now they are there to protect us' – but it is still matured in racks in the cheese room next to his house. And Bill's fight for human rights goes on, not only to continue to make unpasteurised cheese, but against the bigger issue of what he calls the commodification of food. 'My argument,' he says, 'is that if we are not allowed to experiment and diversify, then the true voice and spirit of the land is being stifled. Commodified food can be very good, and produced to a high standard, but it is not romantic and it's not musical. Today, more than ever, with the world energy crisis, we have to support and bring back the small family farms and build strong, viable, diverse rural communities, which are the most basic link in the human life chain.

'You know, Dr. King was inspired by Mahatma Gandhi, and Ghandi believed that civilisation wasn't about the wealth and prosperity displayed in urban centres. He believed that civilisation began the moment we tamed the cows and domesticated other animals, and established viable systems of agriculture, making cheese, setting up markets, putting down arms and coming together to sell and buy goods. He also believed in lives led decently, based on right relationships; that "a non-violent revolution is not about a seizure of power ... but rather a transformation of relationships ..."'

When you sit and talk with Bill around the big wooden table in his great old room with its stove and its windows with no curtains so he can enjoy every bit of the West Cork light, with the wind outside whipping in from the sea, and he's talking about the struggles of Irish artisans and poets and playwrights, and you're eating this gorgeous cheese that he and Sean have made, you feel totally invigorated. Whenever I come away from Schull I am inspired, and more convinced than ever of our obligation to support these seminal individuals who are doing everything all by themselves, the way they want, against the odds.

Risotto with Bellingham Blue, Celery and Wet Walnuts

Peter and Anita Thomas make Bellingham Blue cheese in Castle Bellingham in County Louth. It's a fascinating, beautiful unpasteurised cheese, very different from the more famous Cashel Blue, more Italian-ey in style. Peter, who is a Glaswegian, used to be a printer and Anita comes from a local dairy family. More lucky imports! They started making cheese commercially in 2000, using the farm milk, and straight away were winning awards.

I spent some time making cheese with Peter a few years back. I'd made butter with my mother when I was a boy, but never cheese, and it was an absolute privilege. His little daughter had a day off school and was in there helping him in the spotless dairy, and the whole experience was oh, so special. But I had to ask him, 'How do you survive?' I doubt the man had had a holiday in years, and what's more his dairy was closed down during the foot and mouth outbreak of 2001 – imagine, the only part of Ireland that was affected was County Louth. He told me that Feargal Quinn, who runs the Superquinn supermarkets in Ireland, gave him a job on the cheese counter in one of his stores, just to see him through. Isn't that something?

You always need to be careful about adding salt to a risotto in the early stages, partly because the concentration of stock adds a saltiness, and partly because you are usually going to add a salty cheese at the end, so wait until you have added the cheese, then taste, and add salt if necessary. Because the cheese is creamy it's best not to put too much into the risotto, instead I like to have some crumbled on top to pop into your mouth with the rice and nuts.

When wet walnuts aren't available, you can use dried walnuts, but put them into a pan of milk, bring it to the boil, then drain and when cool enough to handle rub the skins and they will come off. Boiling in milk rather than water keeps the colour of the nuts.

Sometimes, instead of the walnuts, we make this with around 200g of purple sprouting broccoli spears, cooked in boiling water for around 2 minutes, so it is tender but still retains some bite, served on top of the risotto.

Have the stock hot in a pan on the hob.

Melt the butter in a heavy-based pan. Add the shallots and sweat until softened but not coloured.

Serves 4

500ml good-quality chicken (see page 181) or vegetable stock

50g butter

4 shallots, finely chopped

250g vialone nano or carnaroli rice

100ml dry white wine

2 sticks celery, finely chopped

100g Bellingham Blue cheese, or similar, crumbled

a handful of wet walnuts, in season, chopped (see page 301)

Add the rice and stir for a minute, allowing it to absorb the flavour from the shallots. Add the wine, let it evaporate, then put in a ladleful of hot stock, stirring constantly. As the rice cooks it will absorb the stock.

Continue to add the stock a ladleful at a time. As the stock evaporates and is absorbed by the rice add the next ladleful, continuing to stir, for about 15–17 minutes, until the rice is tender, but al dente (i.e. it still has some bite). About halfway through the cooking of the rice add the celery, so that it softens a little, but retains some crunch.

When the risotto is cooked, take it from the heat and stir in half the cheese.

Serve with the rest of the cheese over the top, along with the chopped walnuts.

Red Wine Spaghetti with Pecorino Cheese

Serves 4

a little olive oil

3 cloves garlic, sliced
  wafer thin

½ chilli, deseeded
  and finely chopped
  (optional)

1 bottle Chianti Classico
  or similar full-bodied
  red wine

400g dried spaghetti

200g pecorino cheese,
  crumbled

6 salted anchovy fillets,
  rinsed and chopped

a handful of flat-leaf
  parsley, roughly
  chopped

Heat a thin layer of olive oil in a large pan. When the oil is hot add the garlic and chilli, if using, and sauté until golden. Pour in the wine, bring to the boil, then turn down the heat to a simmer and let it reduce by half.

Meanwhile, cook the spaghetti in a large pan of rapidly boiling salted water until it is al dente, i.e. just a little firm to the bite.

Strain the pasta, add to the pan containing the red wine reduction and toss together. The spaghetti will absorb the wine and turn burgundy-coloured. Add the pecorino, anchovies and parsley and toss again until everything is thoroughly mixed. Taste and season. You may not need any salt, as the cheese and anchovies may make everything salty enough.

To Go with Cheese

I like cheeseboards to be kept simple, not decorated with fruit and celery or nuts so it looks like you have the makings of a Waldorf salad. But I do like good biscuits with cheese, and I like the idea of preserving fruit in season to make traditional fruit 'cheeses', or pastes, like the Spanish *membrillo* (quince paste), and jellies to eat with a slice of cheese.

Oat Cookies for Cheese

When I was looking for a biscuit for cheese, Eoin came up with this recipe. The slightly digestive biscuity sweet cookies are great with Lancashires and Cheddars especially. They're so good, customers often say, 'Can we have some to take home?'

Serves 4

200g butter
100g Demerara sugar
225g plain flour, sifted
10g baking powder
1 teaspoon salt
6 egg yolks, beaten
100g ground almonds
225g jumbo oats

Preheat the oven to 160°C/Gas 3.

In a bowl, cream the butter and sugar together with the back of a wooden spoon until fluffy. Mix in the flour, baking powder and salt, then the beaten egg yolks. When everything is mixed well, fold in the ground almonds and oats.

Spoon little mounds on to a baking tray and flatten down into cookie shapes, about 1cm thick. Bake in the oven for 25 minutes, until lightly golden. Leave to cool.

Quince
Paste

Peel and quarter the quinces and remove the pith. Put into boiling water and cook for about 30 minutes until really soft. Drain, then push the fruit through a coarse sieve into a bowl. Weigh the pulp and put it into a heavy-based pan with an equal weight of sugar. Cook, stirring, until the quince is reduced to a thick paste and becomes darker in colour. Turn out on to a baking tray and leave to set. When solid, cut up and serve with cheese.

Crab Apple
Jelly

Make this when you have stacks of crab apples. Peel, core and weigh them. Put them into a big pan with half their weight of sugar and enough water to cover. Boil until the apples collapse, then strain the syrup through a fine sieve into a clean pan. Measure the liquid – for every litre you will need 4 leaves of gelatine. (The pectin in the pips gives some natural setting quality, but it needs a bit of help.) Soak the leaves in cold water, squeeze them out, then add them to the pan and stir until dissolved. Take the pan from the heat and, so that you end up with lovely clear jelly, put some muslin over a bowl and strain the syrup through it. Leave to cool, then chill in the fridge. If you want to keep it, pour it into sterilised jars and put into the fridge for the rest of the winter. As well as being beautiful with quite strong cheese, such as Ardrahan, this jelly goes well with smoked mackerel and terrines.

Eggs

My mother used to make eggs in a cup – I suppose what you would call coddled eggs. Such a simple thing: break the egg into a cup or ramekin, sprinkle with a little salt and bake in a slow oven, then pour over a little melted butter or warmed cream and eat the egg with toast and butter. In a modern oven it is best to put the ovenproof cups or ramekins into a bain-marie (a roasting tin filled with enough boiling water to come about two-thirds of the way up the outsides of your cups or ramekins) and bake at about 180°C/Gas 4 for 10 minutes or so, until lightly set.

Often Mum would use the big duck eggs. It was my job to bring in the ducks to guard them from the foxes, and to collect the eggs, and I've always had a fondness for them; for all eggs, in fact. Sometimes we would also make a big family omelette, in a cast-iron pan, which you just cut up and ate with some bread and salad. The eggs were so fresh you didn't need anything else in there, but I also like flat omelettes made with potatoes and onions, Spanish tortilla-style. I like the eggs to be slightly scrambled-egg-runny, though; I hate eggs cooked to solid nothingness.

I love all omelettes: traditional, open frittatas or tortillas, and sweet omelettes, such as the Dutch ones they sell on the streets in October made with apples and a sprinkling of cinnamon and sugar. Sometimes I think as chefs we're all looking for the new, new, new, and we've forgotten about such beautiful things as a well-made omelette. Sometimes you need to stop and think of the happy food you might cook at home, and then just translate it to the restaurant table.

Something that has become a bit of a luxury in London restaurants, around May/June, is gull's eggs. Only licensed climbers are allowed to take the little blue eggs from the nests as part of the culling process. I was a bit reluctant to try them at first, because I've never liked gulls, so to eat their eggs seemed a bit perverse. But I've come to enjoy them a lot. They have a slightly sea/fish flavour in the nicest way. You need to hard-boil them for around 4–5 minutes, then put them into a bowl and let people peel them themselves and sprinkle on some celery salt, or smoked sea salt, which many smokeries are doing these days. Frank Hederman in Cobh smokes mine for me, and it really hits the spot.

Nettle and Sorrel Omelette

This is a rustic variation on the French omelette *aux fines herbes*, and when nettles are out of season, you can substitute something like spinach.

Makes 1 omelette

about 1 dessertspoon butter

½ large onion, finely chopped

1 clove garlic, finely chopped

a small knob of fresh horseradish, grated

a large handful of young nettles, chopped

a small handful of sorrel, chopped

4 eggs

Heat half the butter in a small pan. Put in the onion and garlic and sweat until soft. Add the horseradish, nettles and sorrel, stir and take off the heat.

Meanwhile crack the eggs into a bowl, season and whisk very lightly with a fork.

Heat the rest of the butter in an omelette pan or small frying pan and tilt it so that the butter coats all of the base and sides. When it foams (before it colours), put in the eggs. With your fork, draw the egg continuously from the outside into the centre, tilting and shaking the pan as you do so, so that more liquid egg takes its place. Once it starts to firm up underneath, turn the heat down, spoon the nettle and sorrel mixture on to the left-hand side of the omelette (if you are right-handed), then tilt the pan and slide it on to your plate, folding the top over with your fork as you do so. The omelette should be nice and soft still in the middle. Eat immediately.

Duck Egg Omelette with Crème Fraîche and Chives

Serves 4

150g crème fraîche or
    sour cream
1 tablespoon chopped
    chives
8 eggs (2 per omelette)
butter
slices of gravadlax and
    watercress (optional),
    to serve

This is good with gravadlax, cut into strips and laid over the top, with some watercress on the side.

The omelettes are best made one by one, but they are very quick to make and will be all the better for a little rest before serving.

Combine the crème fraîche and chives, season and spoon into a piping bag.

Beat the eggs 2 by 2 with a fork (not too thoroughly) and season.

Heat a small frying pan and add a little butter.

When it is foaming, but before it colours, add the eggs. With your fork, draw the egg continuously from the outside into the centre, tilting and shaking the pan as you do so, so that more liquid egg takes its place. Once it starts to set on top, carefully roll up the omelette so that it resembles a spring roll shape. Put on a warmed plate and keep warm while you cook the rest of the omelettes.

With the tip of a sharp knife, make a slit along the middle of each omelette roll and gently pipe in the crème fraîche as if you were filling a pastry or cream bun.

Scrambled Eggs, Smoked Eel and Bacon, with Red Wine Sauce

Serves 4

4 thin slices of streaky
  bacon
8 eggs
about 10g butter
a dash of double cream
8–12 slices of smoked eel
a handful of chopped
  chives

Red wine sauce:
¼ bottle red wine
¼ bottle ruby port
1 teaspoon brown sugar

To make the sauce, put the wine and port into a heavy-based pan with the sugar and simmer until reduced and syrupy, almost like a glaze. Watch it for the last 5 minutes or so, in case it catches and burns. Take off the heat.

Grill the bacon.

Beat the eggs with a fork. Melt the butter in a heavy-based saucepan, pour in the eggs and cook over a very gentle heat, moving the egg around all the time with a wooden spoon until it is lightly set. Season and stir in a dash of cream.

Spoon the eggs on to warmed plates and top with the smoked eel and crispy bacon. Spoon a little red wine sauce around and sprinkle with the chives.

Bread

My mother made bread every day of the week: soda bread, white and brown, raisin bread – it was considered embarrassing to have to buy a loaf. Everywhere I've worked I've made bread and encouraged my chefs to get involved in the making of it and value it. Good bread takes its personality from the hands that make it, but Irish soda bread is far easier to make than other styles, since it doesn't involve yeast.

Bentley's Soda Bread

Real soda bread is made with buttermilk. The kind of yellowy buttermilk I drank as a child, which is the liquid left over after cream has been churned into butter and still has buttery bits floating in it, is hard to find these days unless you live near a farm or dairy that can sell you some. Mostly they don't think there is a market for it. Some specialist food shops sell real farm buttermilk, but what you tend to find in supermarkets is branded 'cultured buttermilk', which is made by adding a culture to pasteurised skimmed milk and/or skimmed milk powder to produce something which has that slightly sour flavour of traditional buttermilk, but is thicker. Obviously the real thing is best, but if you can't find it, use the cultured version, and if you can't find that, use milk instead.

The cakey nature of soda bread makes it prone to drying out, so putting a damp cloth over it after it has come out of the oven and while it is cooling down helps to keep as much moisture as possible inside. You can keep a damp cloth over it until it is finished, but in our house that was not for very long. It's the kind of bread you put out on the table with a meal, and by the end of it, the loaf is finished. Soda bread should be eaten the same day, or toasted the next. When we first made this at Lindsay House we added black treacle because it was meant to go with cheese and the richness was terrific with some of the harder cheeses. This is a slightly lighter version which people really love.

Makes 1 large loaf
250g plain flour
10g salt
15g bicarbonate of soda
250g wholemeal flour
150g jumbo oat flakes
1 tablespoon clear honey
1 tablespoon black treacle
500ml buttermilk

Preheat the oven to 200°C/Gas 6. Line a baking sheet with baking parchment.

Mix all the dry ingredients together in a bowl. Make a well in the centre, then mix in the honey, treacle and buttermilk, working everything together lightly with your hands, until you have a loose, wet dough.

With floured hands, shape the dough into a round and lift on to the lined baking sheet. Using a knife, mark a cross in the top. Put into the oven and bake for around 45 minutes, or until the loaf sounds hollow when tapped on the base. Transfer to a wire rack, drape a damp cloth over the top and leave to cool.

Swedish-style Crisp Bread

A great crispy bread, which is gorgeous with things like smoked or marinated fish, such as the home-cured herring on page 42. Maldon salt works really well over the top of this bread, because it is quite hard, and gives an extra crunchiness.

Serves 4
5g dried yeast
5 tablespoons warm water
150g strong flour, sifted
2 teaspoons salt
1 teaspoon chopped dill
2 tablespoons olive oil

Preheat the oven to 200°C/Gas 6.

Mix the yeast with the water and let it foam.

Put the flour, half the salt and the dill into a large bowl. Make a well in the centre, add the yeast mixture and the olive oil and, using your hands, work it into a dough. Cover the bowl with a cloth and leave for about half an hour in a warm, draught-free place, until doubled in size.

Turn the dough out on to a floured work surface and knead for a few seconds, to knock the air out of it. Flour a rolling pin and roll the dough until it is wafer thin. Roll it up around your rolling pin, then unroll on to a large baking sheet. Sprinkle with the remaining salt. Bake in the oven for about 10–15 minutes, until it just colours. It will rise very slightly, just enough to give a lightness to the bread, but as it cools down it will crisp up and you can snap it into pieces.

Chilled Almond and Bread Soup

This is a great soup for using up leftover bread in blisteringly hot weather. It's important to use seedless grapes, because if the seeds go into the blender, there's a chalkiness that comes out of them that isn't nice at all. Warming the almonds in a pan or an oven just briefly brings out all the almondy, nutty oil. How much garlic you put in is up to you, but I'd say more is better, because the coldness will numb the flavour a little otherwise. If you really want it to be extra refreshing you can even hold back a little crushed ice and spoon some into each bowl as you serve it.

Makes 1 loaf
50g crusty bread, 2 days old, crusts removed, soaked in water
50g almonds, lightly toasted
350g green seedless grapes
2–4 cloves garlic, peeled
1 tablespoon sherry vinegar
50ml olive oil
100g crushed ice

Garnish:
extra grapes and toasted almonds, plus some chopped mint
some toasted cubes of bread, and a little extra crushed ice, (optional)
good extra virgin olive oil

Squeeze the soaked bread and put into a blender. Add the toasted almonds, grapes, garlic, sherry vinegar, olive oil and a little salt. Process until smooth. Season to taste.

Add the crushed ice and serve immediately. Garnish with grapes, almonds, mint and toasted bread cubes, if you like, and, most importantly, extra virgin olive oil – no drizzling, a good soupspoonful. An extra spoonful of crushed ice in the centre just before serving would be good.

Butter

When I first opened Lindsay House I was forever asking, 'Where has all the good, local butter gone?' I couldn't find any decent unsalted butter in this country. I had to import butter from France ... there was one I found from the Pyrenees, which was beautiful, with a full, rich, fat flavour, and when you cooked with it there was none of the watery milky residue you often got with British butter once it was melted. But it hurt that I couldn't find good native butter, because I grew up with the butter my mother made. I used to help her shape the pats with the wooden clappers, and then I'd drink the cold buttermilk, which was fantastic for the stomach. That honest-to-God gorgeous taste of my mother's butter haunted me. Over the years local butter has begun to be championed by *Macra na Feirme* (Irish young farmers) at markets all over Ireland. Good stuff, but in tiny quantities, nothing like what I needed for the restaurant.

Then I found a trio of dairies that make wonderful butter: Glenilen, in Drimoleague in County Cork (see page 320), Berkeley Farm, in Wroughton, Wiltshire, and Lincolnshire Poacher. Randolph Hodgson of Neal's Yard Dairy gave me a pack of Berkeley Farm's wonderful, creamy, golden-coloured organic butter to try and the moment I tasted it it said to me 'proper dairy', so I asked them, could they send me ten boxes?

Then one of our chefs, 'Young Chris' as we call him, to distinguish him from Chris McGowan, head chef at Lindsay House, came back with a pat of butter he had bought at one of the London farmers' markets. It's made by Simon and Tim Jones, the guys who make Lincolnshire Poacher cheese in Alford. We tasted it, loved it, and now they supply us directly from the farm.

There are two main styles of butter. The kind we made at home, and which was once made in smallholdings throughout Britain and Ireland, was lactic butter made from raw cream. If you only had a few cows there wouldn't be enough milk to make butter every day, so you'd collect the milk over a few days, even up to a week, during which time it would ripen or sour a bit, and develop lactic acids, which gave each batch a different character before the milk was churned. This is still the style that they tend to favour in Europe though on a modern commercial scale it is made with lactic starter cultures added to pasteurised cream. In Britain, however, once you had big enough dairies, producing enough fresh, pasteurised cream to churn straight away, this 'sweetcream' butter became the norm, as it is in America and New Zealand, too, and in the seventies the big factory butter operations sprang up, with their continuous buttermaking machines. You push cream in one end and a ribbon of butter comes out at the other.

There is a third, 'farmhouse' butter that cheesemakers sometimes make on a small scale, using the whey cream left after cheesemaking, which can sometimes take on quite strong, slightly farmyardy flavours, and you can usually buy it only in small quantities straight from the farm. However, the one made by brothers Simon and Tim Jones, of Lincolnshire Poacher cheese, is lovely: rich, creamy and yellow. Their farm at Alford has been in the family for generations, and they still retain their maternal grandfather's name, Fred W. Read, on their packaging.

They have their own herd of 230 cows, mostly black and white Holsteins, and a handful of Ayrshires, although, says Tim Jones, they are currently crossing some Norwegian and Danish Reds, and brown and white Montbeliards, 'to harden up the Holsteins, which are the racehorses of the milk world'. The nature of their hard cheese is that it needs the relatively low-fat milk that Holsteins produce. 'Rich, fatty Jersey milk, for example, would mean terrible cheese for us,' says Tim. 'We cook our curd quite hard to dry it out; and any change in the fat to protein results in softer curds, which we don't want. Our process is a slightly less extreme version of the hard scalding used by Parmigiano Reggiano producers. There they skim off the cream from the milk before they start, for the same reasons.'

When the cheesemaking is finished they are left with whey, which contains some cream. This is separated off and ripened with a starter culture for about three days to give it its special character (similar to a lactic butter), then churned, balled and patted with traditional wooden 'Scotch hands' and a little salt.

Whatever the style, good butter always comes from good milk, from cows that are well looked after. In countries such as France and Italy, which concentrate more on regional farming, local butter reflects the local grasses and herbs that the cows eat, whereas in Britain the big centralised dairies pool milk from farms all over the country and produce uniform commodified butter designed to always taste the same.

At Berkeley Farm, where the milk all comes from the Goslings' Guernsey herd, which grazes on grasses, clover and herbs, you can taste the individuality and the seasonal differences in the butter. The fresh cream is aged for around two days before being churned into butter that is unsalted or lightly salted with sea salt. Christine reckons it brings out the flavour of the butter, and I'm with her on that one. I like salty butter for eating, as opposed to cooking. The whole idea of unsalted butter with bread does nothing for me. If the butter is unsalted then you need salty bread.

Christine started making their organic butter in a mixer in the farmhouse kitchen, then moved on to a wooden churn, then a stainless steel one. 'I was really worried that the flavour would change, but there was no difference,' she says. In those days she was making about fifty half-pound packs a week, but now she has three boys in the dairy who shape, pat and pack about 1,000 packs, still by hand. 'They work so quickly, whereas it takes me ages,' she says. The important thing is that it leaves her free to be full-time with the cows, looking after their health. She treats them all homeopathically and has Radio 2 playing to keep them relaxed. 'When a cow is happy the milk flows better and the quality is better, too,' says Christine. 'There have been tests done that show that when a cow is stressed, the count of somatic cells, which includes white blood cells and milk-secreting cells, increases. That is a sign that the animal is trying to fight infection, and as a result the milk isn't as tasty and doesn't keep as well. Everything to do with the cows' lifestyle reflects in the milk.'

The Milky
Way

At Glenilen Dairy in Drimoleague in West Cork, Alan and Valerie Kingston produce the most beautiful butter, yoghurt, fromage frais and cream from the farm that has been handed down through generations of Alan's family. The name of the dairy comes from the glen surrounding the river Ilen, which runs through the farm, and they are even looking at using the river to provide hydro-power for the dairy some time in the future.

I have nothing but respect for what these people are doing. Valerie grew up on a farm near Macroom, took a degree in food science and technology and, before she and Alan got married, went off to work as a volunteer on a dairy development project in West Africa, where she learned how to make cheese and butter on an artisan scale.

One day she went out shopping, came back with two fifty-litre saucepans from Roches Stores, and started making yoghurt and fromage frais in their farmhouse kitchen. Then she used the fromage frais, along with farm cream, to make cheesecakes to sell at the local farmers' markets. Alan was sceptical at first. He would have been quite happy with traditional dairy farming, rearing cows and calving, milking in the early morning, with the birds singing. Hard work, but rewarding. It was what his father did and his grandfather before him.

But these days, a small dairy farm with only fifty-five cows isn't a viable option any more. Selling your milk to a cooperative is the only choice for many small farmers. It's a sad thing, but as Alan said to me, 'In Ireland we have some of the best milk in Europe because the cows stay out on the land, grazing on fresh grass for nine to ten months of the year, and then we turn most of it into dried milk powder.' Even then there isn't enough money in just selling your milk, if you are trying to support a young family, and many a local dairy farmer has changed to a different style of farming.

So when people shopping in the markets went mad for the cheesecakes and yoghurt and started bringing along their own jugs to fill up with the fresh farm milk that Valerie also took down there, they both realised they were on to something special. So slowly they have expanded from a small purpose-built dairy to a bigger one, and now they are supplying small shops and delicatessens around the country with everything from butter, cream and yoghurt to farm-made desserts. Everything is still hand-made, 'Scaled up, really, from what we started doing in the kitchen', says Valerie, 'and we're just so thankful to be able to be successful at something we both love doing; even Alan can't imagine going back to traditional dairy farming. It's good to be able to give employment to

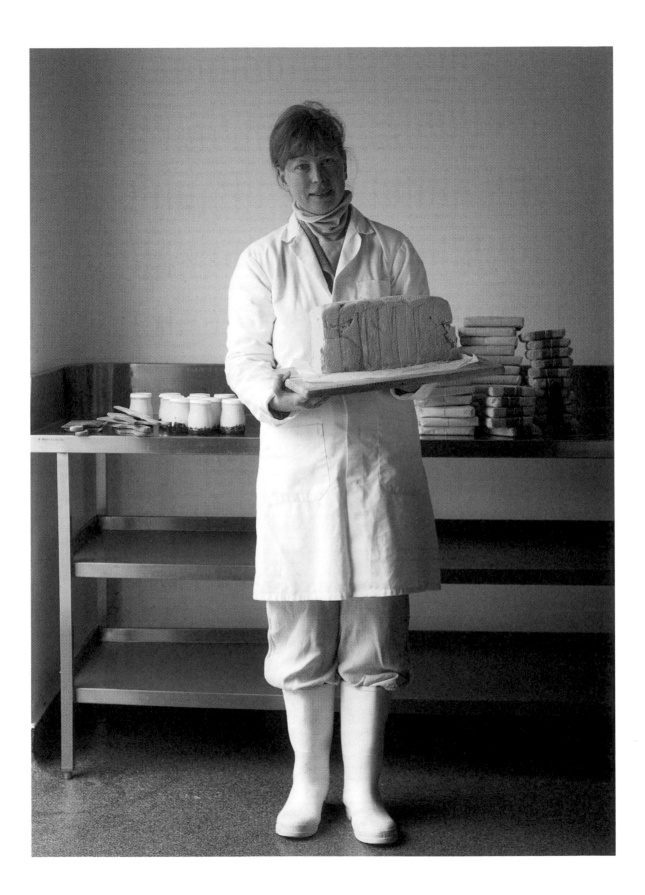

local people to work in the dairy, too, and if we should run short of milk, we have ready access to a neighbour's herd.' What I especially like is the sense of community that means they pay a good price for any milk they have to buy, because farmers should support one another.

The yoghurts are just what you want a yoghurt to be, gorgeous and wholesome; they just feel like they are doing you good as you eat them. No thickeners or stabilisers, no added sugar, sweeteners, flavourings or colours, or any of the things you might see on the label of commercial pots, just milk heated and handled very, very gently, cooled to the correct temperature for adding the live culture, set and decanted into glass jars. For their fruit yoghurts, they make their own compotes with fruit, such as rhubarb and plums bought from a local fruit supplier, and with nothing else but a little bit of sugar. They put a layer into the bottom of the jars, and then gently pour the yoghurt on top, 'so you get a nice clean line between the fruit and the yoghurt'.

In Ireland, if you go into a shop and ask for cream, that is what you get. Cream is cream, more like what in the UK would be thought of as single cream. You wouldn't get the options of double, whipped, extra thick that you see in an English supermarket, all of which have their definitions in law, according to how much butterfat they have in them.

So the Kingstons decided to make their own rich, double cream. 'We gauge the thickness just by the eye, and we say on the pot that the fat content might vary from batch to batch,' says Valerie. They also make a clotted cream, heated to give the slightly cooked, butterscotchy flavour you'd recognise in a Cornish clotted cream, but without the crusty top, and, she says, 'We'd love to do an unhomogenised milk, too, with the cream at the top in the old fashioned way.'

It's their butter that really gets me excited, though: a proper, rich yellow butter, lightly salted, made in a traditional churn, patted by hand and beautifully wrapped in paper, tied with twine, the way their grandparents used to do it. I had a very special day down in Drimoleague making a batch with them. They are lovely people, committed Christians, and of course I swear like a trooper, but we had a great laugh.

The taste of the butter is all about the freshness of the milk, says Valerie. 'It comes straight from the milking, and because the cows are grazing on pasture it is really rich and full of flavour. Of course, it varies according to season, and what stage of lactation the cows are at, whether they have just been calving … It's at its absolute best, soft, very yellow and full of flavour, around May and June. From mid-November to the beginning of February, when we have to bring the cows indoors and their diet is different, the butter will be a little harder and less yellow.'

Most of the butter they produce is a sweet cream one, made with pasteurised milk, but what is really exciting is that they are now making small quantities of traditional lactic butter, made with raw cream that is allowed to ripen naturally and take on an individual flavour in the old-fashioned way before churning. It's the kind of butter that I grew up helping my mother make, and it's the butter their parents made, too, and it's they who have passed on to Alan and Valerie the knowledge and understanding of how to judge when the milk has ripened to exactly the right stage.

'Alan's grandmother used to make butter this way and sell it in the village, long before the days of dedicated, state-of-the-art dairies,' says Valerie. 'There's a story that one day she noticed her wedding ring was missing, and the next day a villager brought it back to her. He'd found it inside the butter! We make the raw cream butter for some of the farmers' markets, and to order, but we'd love to make more of it, because it's a taste that has been lost over the years when people have got used to sweet cream. It was so much a part of our families' lives over the generations, so it's lovely to bring it back.'

Puddings

A bowl of semolina, cold, with some summer fruits; a country apple tart; a beautiful melon or a bowlful of ripe cherries – that's where great puddings start with me. I've never been in love with the idea of pastry chefs. Cooks who understand good puddings, yes. Pastry chefs, no. I've never hired a pastry chef for Lindsay House or Bentley's, because what pastry chefs want to give me is gelatine and sugar, and I would rather eat my sock than overcrafted pastry porn. The only recipes in this book that involve gelatine are ones to make jelly. There's been so much bullshit talked about desserts in chef's circles over the last twenty years, and most of them are just so much eye candy, crafted brilliantly, but often with stabilisers and chemistry sets to keep things looking the way they do.

On the other hand, I love the idea of baking and proper old-fashioned pudding making. I think the British have the best repertoire of puddings; I really do. Kings of the world. You don't have to reinvent the wheel, just revisit the crumbles, the trifles, the country pies. Think of something like cabinet pudding … the old wartime recipe of custard in a dish lined or layered with sponge fingers, baked in a bain-marie and then cut into slices (there are lots of variations), the custard studded with things like angelica and little glacé cherries, which I think are horrible in most things, but when you put them into that pudding they stand out like jewels sparkling. I have a huge soft spot for freshly baked sponge with jam and cream and fresh fruit. I'm a complete sucker for it. Or a good bread pudding … gold leaf and spirals and ten little pastry boxes sitting on a wall, each with a different decoration, don't come close.

When I get to the end of a meal, I'm not looking for a work of art, I'm looking for something deeply satisfying. It could even be just a soft, freshly churned vanilla ice cream that leaves you with that wonderful, happy ending to lunch or dinner.

The English chap who went to Eton or Harrow probably remembers semolina as the worst form of torture, but ask an Irish farmer would he like a bowl of it, or rice pudding or tapioca, and he will say, 'Oh yes, how lovely.' Funny how people can feel so differently about the same thing. Anyone brought up on old-fashioned school meals might feel they were force-fed these puddings, but in our family we ate them out of love. Thomas Keller, at the French Laundry in California, has taken hold of tapioca and turned it into something else entirely with his 'Oysters and Pearls' – caviar and oysters on a bed of tapioca – but I'm talking about old-fashioned tapioca pudding served cold, which I think is one of the most refreshing things you can have in the summer, with a little fruit compote or just some dried Spanish raisins, plumped up in alcohol and a little sugar syrup.

I like a bit of refreshing bitterness and farmyardy sourness in desserts: a yoghurt or a buttermilk sorbet or even blancmange with fresh fruit that still has a natural country tartness. I don't like masking fruit in sugar. Less is more where sugar is concerned; otherwise you're just eating sweet food with no character. Though I quite like that Turkish idea of fruits in syrup with a touch of rosewater and crushed green cardamom, so the fragrance and spice takes the edge off the sweetness.

My mother didn't have that many pudding recipes. Apart from the stewed fruits and pies she made sponge cakes, and there would usually be fruitcake in a tin. Alcohol wasn't big in our house, but any left over from Christmas or a special occasion would end up being poured into the cake. Fruit, though – whatever was growing, and in season – was the main pudding.

As kids on the farm we really looked forward to the harvest from the orchard, when the apple, pear and plum trees would bear fruit. We had cherry trees, too, but I only remember picking the fruit once as a child. One scorching year, I think it was 1976, the branches were laden with cherries in all different colours, so heavy they were falling off. I climbed up into one of the trees and gorged myself on them. We used to layer up the pears with hay in boxes, but we were never that successful at ripening them, which always annoyed us. Apples were always much more dependable, though we never sprayed or treated the apple trees – we hardly used any chemicals on the farm – and some years fungus would get them. But mostly in the autumn the quantity of fruit was staggering. Some of the apples, especially the cookers, would be wrapped up and put away in boxes, a lot would be given away and the rest would be stewed with custard or made into crumbles or tarts. We took those old, traditional apples, full of flavour, for granted. They were just there, along with the salads and the vegetables growing in the gardens. It never occurred to me that thirty-odd years later we would be in danger of losing most of the varieties in favour of the handful of global ones the supermarkets like to sell. Or that it would take a brilliant organisation like Irish Seed Savers (see page 250) to rescue the heritage fruits for future generations.

At other times of the year there would be rhubarb, gooseberries or damsons. There were also fruit bushes in the less shaded areas of the woods that had maybe once been planted on common land and then left alone to grow wild, and we picked everything we could find. In June the bog would be covered in little wild blueberries and we'd spend our Saturday afternoons out with buckets picking them, then later on the brambles in the lanes would be covered in blackberries, so for a limited time you'd have that great combination of apples and blackberries.

We kids ate so many wild fruits we'd almost be sick, and my tongue tingles just thinking about the lovely bitterness of the gooseberries and currants. I still have a fondness and a longing for wild fruit. I even love eating crab apples, tiny sour ones, when they are just at the point of dropping from the tree.

The last fruits of the season would be sloes, which grew on the blackthorn bushes in the hedgerows. You could never eat a raw sloe because they really are way too sour. As kids you'd be daring each other to see who was the bravest and try one. And we didn't move in sloe gin circles, but my mother used to put them in jams because the pectin around the stone made a good gelling agent.

It's the tarts that stay in my mind from those childhood days more than anything else. Fruit tart, Irish country style, was really a pie: two pieces of pastry, never mind how thick, with loads of fresh fruit in the middle, sprinkled with sugar before baking and cooled down on the windowsill, the jam from the fruit oozing down the sides on to the enamel plates that would have been used for hundreds of pies over the years. People talk about tarte tatin, but some things in the culinary world are glorified – yes, it's lovely, but how often are you going to make it at home? I'd rather have a freshly-made, countrywoman's apple, gooseberry or rhubarb tart, the kind that was made in every family's kitchen every week when I was growing up, any day. With a big mug of tea, I equate that with the best of desserts. Gorgeous, just gorgeous.

Quince
Tart

In Victorian times every walled garden would have had a quince tree, and the fruit would have been made into compotes to serve with game, puddings and jams, but so many orchards have been grubbed up over the years that the fruit was beginning to look like a bit of an endangered species. Now, they are right back in favour. When you see a quince, this hard-fleshed thing which, like a sloe, is too bitter to eat raw, you can't quite get your head around the idea that when it is cooked in syrup, especially where honey is involved, it will become gorgeously sweet and aromatic. We poach quinces in Sauternes, slice them up and bake them on little puff pastry circles, spread with almond cream. Don't waste the leftover poaching liquor – you can use it to make a quince granita. Pour it into a freezer tray and freeze for about half an hour, then take it out and agitate it with a fork to break up the crystals, scraping well around the sides and bottom of the container. Keep doing that every half an hour until it is completely frozen.

You won't need all the almond cream either, but it isn't easy to make very small quantities. You can use the rest for the Toffee Apple and Pecan Tart on page 335; or spread it over a layer of jam or marmalade inside a pastry case (baked blind first, as for that recipe) to make a Bakewell-style tart. Or when pears are in season, spread the almond cream quite thickly over the base of your pastry case (again baked blind), peel, halve and core your pears and arrange them on top. When you bake the tart the almond cream will puff up around the pears.

Peel and quarter the quinces and remove the pith. Put them into a pan with the water and add the sugar, honey, lemon juice and zest, the spices and the wine. Bring to the boil, then turn the heat down to a simmer for about 10 minutes until the quinces are cooked and have turned golden, but still retain a little firmness. Leave to cool down.

Meanwhile, make the almond cream. Cream the butter and sugar together until pale. Beat in the eggs a little at a time, then beat in the ground almonds and flour.

Preheat the oven to 200°C/Gas 6. Roll out the puff pastry to the thickness of a £1 coin. Using a saucer as a guide, cut out 4 rounds and spread each with a little almond cream. You only need enough to rub over the surface. The fruit will stick to it and it will soak up the juice, keeping the pastry crisp. Lift

Serves 4
6 large quinces
1 litre water
250g caster sugar
100g honey
juice and zest of
    2 lemons
1 star anise
¼ stick cinnamon
1 vanilla pod
135ml Sauternes or
    other dessert wine
500g puff pastry

Almond cream:
100g butter
100g caster sugar
2 eggs
100g ground almonds
25g plain flour

the quinces out of their poaching liquor (reserve this for later), slice each one lengthways and arrange on top of each tart in concentric circles. Bake in the oven for about 15 minutes, until the pastry is golden.

Meanwhile, pour the poaching liquor from the quinces through a fine sieve into a clean bowl. Put about a cupful into a small pan and bubble up to reduce to a glaze (you can keep the rest to make a granita, see above). When the tarts come out of the oven, brush a little of the glaze over the top of each one, and serve, with vanilla ice cream (see page 347), if you like.

Gooseberry Pie

As a kid I used to love the sensation of popping raw gooseberries in my mouth. They have those funny little hairs and that 'dare you' sourness about them, and when they explode it's like eating capfuls of vinegar with a little bit of sugar.

This whole thing about which chef makes his pastry thinner or crispier or better than the other – does it really matter? I don't think so. We're talking about a good, failsafe pastry here, great fruit and not too much sugar (you want it to be a bit tart, so vary your sugar according to how hard and sour, or slightly more ripe and soft your berries are), all of which adds up to a very simple form of utter deliciousness.

Makes one 20cm pie
Serves 6–8
500g plain flour
a pinch of salt
250g butter, cut into
   cubes, plus a little
   extra for greasing
100g caster sugar
3 eggs, plus 1 egg,
   beaten, for glazing
thick Jersey cream,
   to serve

Filling:
500g gooseberries
100–150g caster sugar,
   depending on the
   sourness of your
   berries

First make the pastry. Put the flour and salt into a bowl and rub in the butter with your fingers until the mixture resembles fine breadcrumbs. Mix in the sugar, then the 3 eggs, a little at a time, mixing well, and bring everything together with your fingers into a dough. Alternatively, put the flour, salt, butter and sugar into a blender and pulse until it resembles fine breadcrumbs. Add the eggs and pulse again until just combined, then turn out into a bowl or on to a clean work surface and mould into a ball. Cover with clingfilm and chill in the fridge for about 20 minutes to make it easier to roll.

Preheat the oven to 200°C/Gas 6. Lightly grease a large ovenproof plate with butter.

On a clean, floured work surface, roll out two-thirds of the pastry into a circle about 5cm bigger than the diameter of the plate. Roll the pastry loosely round the rolling pin then unroll it over the top of the plate, taking care not to stretch the pastry and allowing a little to overhang the edge.

Put in a layer of gooseberries, then sprinkle with sugar, layer up more gooseberries and add more sugar (reserving a heaped tablespoon to sprinkle on top of the pastry before cooking).

Roll out the remaining pastry into a circle big enough to form a lid, and again, using the rolling pin to move it, drape it over the top of the gooseberries. Crimp the edges of the pastry together all round to seal. With a sharp knife, make a couple of incisions in the top of the pie to allow steam to escape. Brush with the beaten egg and sprinkle with the remaining sugar.

Bake in the oven for 20 minutes, then lower the temperature to 160°C/Gas 3 and cook for a further 30–40 minutes until golden. Serve with the cream.

Heritage
Apple Pudding

I love a good old-fashioned crisp apple, with that real burst of individual flavour that you get from traditional varieties. When I was growing up we and all our neighbours had fruit trees, and there were orchards all over Britain and Ireland, planted with local varieties of apple with names most people haven't heard of these days, like Pig's Snout, native to Louth, Green Chisel from Donegal, Irish Molly from Kilkenny, and Ross Nonpareil, from my county of Meath. Since the 1960s, though, orchards have disappeared on a massive scale as small farms have been encouraged to grub them up to grow other crops or the land has been sold off to developers.

In England surveys show that there are only around 20,000 hectares of orchards left out of the 80,000 or so recorded in the 1940s. The majority of apples are grown for cider rather than eating, because we import around 70 per cent of our apples – and only a few varieties at that, from around the world; commodified apples, all the same size and colour and tasting bland. Crazy, when you think that there are around 6,000 varieties of English apples alone listed on the national register, and our climate in these islands is perfect for apple growing.

In Ireland, the Seed Saver Association (see page 250) is doing a great job of finding, propagating and growing over 140 traditional varieties of Irish apple trees, in the same way that the Brogdale Horticultural Trust has done over many years in England, and there are small farms throughout Britain and Ireland growing old-fashioned apples who will pack them up in boxes and send them out to you through the post. And, ironically, having marched on with their aisles of Golden Delicious and Granny Smith and little else for so many years, many of the supermarkets are now making a bit of an effort to flag up seasonal local apples in regional stores.

Preheat the oven to 200°C/Gas 6. Melt 25g of the butter and brush it over the inside of a large earthenware dish, dust with caster sugar, revolving the dish so it is entirely covered, then tap out the excess.

Peel and core the apples and chop into chunky pieces. Put them into a bowl, sprinkle with cinnamon and pour over the Calvados or brandy. Leave to marinate while you make the pudding.

Put the bread into a bowl.

Serves 4

125g butter

6 heritage apples

a pinch of cinnamon

a good splash of
    Calvados or brandy

250g stale bread, torn up

250ml milk

zest of 2 lemons

150g caster sugar, plus
    extra for dusting

125g ground almonds

4 eggs, separated

a pinch of salt

Put the milk into a saucepan with the lemon zest and bring to the boil. Take off the heat and pour over the bread.

In a separate bowl, mix the sugar, ground almonds, egg yolks and salt. Melt the rest of the butter and mix in, then stir in the bread mixture.

Whisk the egg whites until fluffy, then fold into the mixture. Spoon into the buttered and sugared dish and put the apple pieces on top – some will sink in.

Bake for 30 minutes until golden brown and serve immediately.

Custard

This is a great, creamy custard, which you can flavour with orange (for serving with the marmalade puddings on page 357) by just adding the zest of 3 oranges to the saucepan along with the vanilla seeds. When elderflowers are in season, you could put in a handful of petals instead of the orange zest. A little cognac at Christmas, cinnamon … flavour it as you like.

Makes enough for 4
1 vanilla pod
250ml double cream
125ml milk
3 egg yolks
50g caster sugar

Split the vanilla pod in half and scrape the seeds into a saucepan. Add the cream and milk and bring to the boil.

Have ready a shallow bowl of ice big enough to take the base of the saucepan.

Beat the eggs and sugar together in a bowl and pour the hot milk and cream over, mixing well.

Pour back into the saucepan and cook over a low heat, stirring constantly, until the custard thickens. Take the pan off the heat and immediately plunge the base into the bowl of ice to stop the custard cooking any more.

Toffee Apple and Pecan Tart

This is a tart with a crumble topping. Even though there seem to be lots of elements to it, it is really simple, and the toffee, especially, is the easiest thing to make, the way the South Americans do it, by boiling a can of condensed milk. They call it Dulce de Leche.

Serve the tart with custard (see opposite) if you like.

Makes one 25cm tart
250g plain flour
a pinch of salt
125g butter, cut into cubes, plus extra for greasing
50g caster sugar
2 eggs, plus 1 egg, beaten, for eggwash

Filling:
1 tin condensed milk
4 apples, heritage preferably, or a quite sharp, full-flavoured variety
a little caster sugar

Almond cream:
100g butter
100g caster sugar
2 eggs
100g ground almonds
25g plain flour

Crumble:
125g butter
50g plain flour
250g Demerara sugar
100g ground almonds
a good handful of pecan nuts

To make the toffee for the filling, put the unopened tin of condensed milk into a pan of boiling water and let it simmer for about 4 hours (topping up with water when necessary). Lift it out carefully, and when you open the tin you will have a thick, rich toffee.

To make the pastry, put the flour and salt into a bowl and rub in the butter with your fingers until the mixture resembles fine breadcrumbs. Add the sugar and mix well, then mix in the eggs a little at a time, bringing the mixture together with your fingers until you have a dough. Alternatively, put the flour, salt, butter and sugar into a blender and pulse until it resembles fine breadcrumbs. Add the eggs and pulse again until just combined, then turn out into a bowl or on to a clean work surface and mould into a ball. Try not to work the dough any more than you have to in order to bring it together. Cover the pastry with clingfilm and chill in the fridge for about 20 minutes to make it easier to roll.

Preheat the oven to 150°C/Gas 2. Have ready a 25cm, loose-bottomed flan tin, greased with a little butter.

On a floured surface, roll out the pastry into a circle about 5cm bigger than your tart tin. Roll the pastry loosely round your rolling pin, then drape it over the tin and gently press it in. Trim carefully round the edge with a knife.

To bake 'blind', line the pastry with greaseproof paper and scatter over a layer of dried beans (or ceramic baking beans) – this will stop the pastry rising up. Bake in the oven for about 45 minutes until pale golden, then remove and turn the oven up to 180°C/Gas 4.

Immediately after taking the tart tin out of the oven, remove the greaseproof paper and beans and brush the whole of the inside of the pastry case with eggwash. This will seal it and prevent it cracking as it cools – it may still crack a little, but don't worry.

While the tart case is in the oven, make the almond cream. Cream the butter and sugar together until pale. Beat in the eggs a little at a time, then beat in the ground almonds and flour. Keep on one side.

To make the crumble topping rub the butter into the flour and then mix in all the other ingredients. Again, keep on one side.

To make the filling, peel, quarter and core the apples and put them into a pan over a high heat. Sprinkle in a little sugar as they start to soften and stir them around so that they caramelise a little, then mix in around 4 tablespoons of the toffee.

Spread a layer of almond cream over the base of the pastry case, then spread the apple mixture over the top and finish with the crumble topping. Bake in the oven for 30 minutes, keeping an eye on the crumble so that it doesn't burn.

Honey and Stout Tart

I made this for a TV programme with the London Irish rugby team one St Patrick's day in the old Irish pub the O'Conor Don in London – all fifteen of them squashed into the kitchen. It was quite mad, but it's a lovely pudding, similar to treacle tart.

Makes one 25cm tart
Serves 6–8
250g plain flour
a pinch of salt
125g butter, cut into cubes, plus extra for greasing
50g caster sugar
2 eggs, plus 1 egg, beaten, for eggwash
sweetened buttermilk or double cream, to serve

Filling:
4 Bramley apples
1 x 330ml bottle stout, such as Guinness
200g rolled oats
250g golden syrup
250g honey
250g stale breadcrumbs
6 eggs, beaten
4 dessertspoons lemon juice
zest of 1 lemon and 1 orange

First make the pastry. Put the flour and salt into a bowl and rub in the butter with your fingers until the mixture resembles fine breadcrumbs. Add the sugar and mix well, then mix in the eggs a little at a time, bringing the mixture together with your fingers until you have a dough. Alternatively, put the flour, salt, butter and sugar into a blender and pulse until it resembles fine breadcrumbs. Add the eggs and pulse again until just combined, then turn out into a bowl or on to a clean work surface and mould into a ball. Try not to work the dough any more than you have to in order to bring it together. Cover the pastry with clingfilm and chill in the fridge for about 20 minutes to make it easier to roll.

Preheat the oven to 150°C/Gas 2. Have ready a 25cm, loose-bottomed flan tin, greased with a little butter.

On a floured surface, roll out the pastry into a circle about 5cm bigger than your tart tin. Roll the pastry loosely round your rolling pin, then drape it over the tin and gently press it in. Trim carefully round the edge with a knife.

To bake 'blind', line the pastry with greaseproof paper and scatter over a layer of dried beans (or ceramic baking beans) – this will stop the pastry from rising up. Bake in the oven for about 45 minutes until pale golden, then remove and turn the oven up to 180°C/Gas 4.

Immediately after taking the tart tin out of the oven, remove the greaseproof paper and beans and brush the whole of the inside of the pastry case with eggwash. This will seal it and prevent it from cracking as it cools – it may still crack a little, but don't worry.

Peel and grate the apples. Pour the stout into a saucepan, add the apple, bring to the boil, then turn down the heat and let the liquid reduce by about half. The apple will go brown but it's natural. Take off the heat and allow to cool until just warm.

Add the rest of the filling ingredients and mix well.

Pour the mixture into the pastry case and bake in the oven for 20–25 minutes until set. Serve with sweetened buttermilk or double cream.

Summer Pudding

Put all of the ingredients except the gelatine and bread into a saucepan and heat gently until the fruit is just soft. Add the gelatine leaves and stir slowly until they have dissolved.

Makes 1 large
   pudding
2 punnets blueberries
1 punnet redcurrants
1 punnet blackcurrants
1 punnet blackberries
1 punnet raspberries
1 punnet strawberries
200g caster sugar
200ml water
zest of 2 lemons
1 vanilla pod, split open
   lengthways and seeds
   scraped out
3 gelatine leaves,
   softened in water and
   squeezed out
1 loaf good white bread,
   brioche or panettone,
   sliced and crusts
   removed
clotted cream, to serve

Line a large pudding bowl with clingfilm, leaving it overhanging the edges. (This will make the pudding easier to turn out with no risk of sticking.) Dip about two-thirds of the slices of bread into the fruit mixture and then use to line the bowl – you might have to cut the pieces to fit together. Don't worry if it is a bit of a patchwork.

Spoon in some of the berries, then put in a layer of fruit-soaked bread. Repeat until the bowl is full, finishing with a layer of soaked bread. Cover and put into the fridge until completely set.

Turn out, peel off the clingfilm and serve with clotted cream.

Raspberries with Semolina

This is one of the simplest of desserts, but on a summer's day what more could you want?

Serves 4

1 litre milk

100g semolina

125g caster sugar

1 vanilla pod, split open lengthways

200ml mascarpone or custard (see page 334)

400g raspberries

Put the milk, semolina and sugar into a heavy-based saucepan, then scrape the vanilla seeds into the mixture and put in the pods as well. Stir gently, and as the mixture begins to thicken, take out the pods and whisk vigorously until there are no lumps left and the mixture is thick.

Take off the heat and allow to cool, then add the mascarpone or custard to taste.

Divide the semolina between 4 bowls and scatter raspberries over the top. Serve immediately.

Elderflower Fritters with Early Summer Fruit Jam

Elderflowers are in season from May through to June, depending on the weather, so for the jam you can use a mixture of any berries that are around at the same time, or just go for gooseberries, which have a natural affinity with elderflowers: they bring out the best in each other.

Serves 4

vegetable oil, for
  deep-frying
about 12 good sprigs of
  elderflower
100g icing sugar, for
  dipping and dusting

Batter:
500g rice flour
50g cornflour
5g bicarbonate of soda
1 bottle ice-cold
  sparkling water

Summer fruit jam:
500g mixed summer
  berries
150g caster sugar
zest of 1 lemon

First make the jam. Boil the fruits and sugar together in a pan until reduced by half, then stir in the zest. Leave to cool and set.

With your finger, mix the ingredients for the batter together until it is the consistency of double cream, but still lumpy. This batter doesn't hold well for long, so make it just before you are ready to use it.

Preheat the oil to 175°C in a deep-fat fryer or a large saucepan filled no more than one-third full.

Dip the flowers into icing sugar and then into the batter and carefully lower by their stems into the hot oil. Do this in batches so as not to overcrowd the fryer or reduce the temperature of the oil. Cook the flowers, turning once, until pale golden.

Drain on plenty of absorbent paper. Dust with more icing sugar and serve the fritters immediately while they are still piping hot, with the fruit jam.

Damson and Blackberry Soup with Buttermilk Sorbet

Serves 4

250g damsons, stones removed, plus a few extra for garnish

250g blackberries, plus a few extra for garnish

100g caster sugar

100ml water

zest and juice of 2 lemons

Buttermilk sorbet:

200g caster sugar

250ml water

500ml buttermilk

juice of 2 lemons

To make the sorbet, put the sugar and water in a saucepan and bring to the boil. Turn down the heat and simmer until reduced by around three-quarters. Remove from the heat and leave to cool. Add the buttermilk and lemon juice and churn in an ice-cream machine, then transfer to a clean container and put in the freezer.

To make the soup, bring the fruit, sugar and water to the boil in a saucepan. Turn down the heat and allow to simmer for a minute. Remove the pan from the heat and leave to cool for about an hour.

Add the lemon zest and juice and mix well.

Push the fruit mixture through a fine sieve into a bowl, using the back of a spoon to press the fruit. Throw away any pulp left in the sieve. Put the bowl into the fridge to chill.

Serve the soup in individual bowls with the reserved fruit, a scoop of buttermilk sorbet in the centre of each, and some oatmeal crisps (see page 346).

Oatmeal
Crisps

These are wafer thin, tuile-like biscuits, which will snap when you break them and are fantastic with the damson and blackberry soup on page 345 or any fruit and cream or ice cream.

Makes about 25
125g caster sugar
75g butter, melted
75g wholemeal flour
125g egg white (about 3–4 eggs)
50g jumbo oatmeal
10g salt

Preheat the oven to 160°C/Gas 3.

Mix the sugar and butter together and add the flour. Fold in the egg whites (don't whisk them).

Line a baking tray with a sheet of baking paper, then with a palette knife take small quantities of the mixture at a time and spread thinly over the paper (don't worry about neatness; these are rustic little wafers), leaving a reasonable space between them. Sprinkle a little oatmeal and a touch of salt over the top.

Put into the oven and bake for about 10 minutes, until lightly golden.

Lift off with a palette knife on to greaseproof paper and leave to cool.

Rosehip Soup with Vanilla Ice Cream

Serves 4

250g rosehips
200ml water
50g caster sugar
zest and juice of 1 lemon
¼ cinnamon stick
1 star anise
2 cloves
almond biscuits, to serve
(see page 348)

Vanilla ice cream:
300ml milk
600ml double cream
2 vanilla pods, split open
lengthways and seeds
scraped out
4 egg yolks
175g caster sugar

I love thick rosehip soup, partly because I always like the idea of using wild food that is there for the taking – except that in London we have to pay someone to pick the hips and bring them to us. Rosehips are simply the seed-bearing fruits left over when roses have finished blooming, and they deliver one of the highest doses of vitamin C known to man, which is why rosehip syrup was so popular during the war. The ripe red hips are best left on the bushes until after the first frost, which concentrates the sugars, making them quite sweet.

I grew up thinking rosehips were pretty unusable in cooking because of the seeds and tiny hairy bits they have in the centre, but these get sieved out when you make the soup. The idea for the soup came from a Swedish friend, Ulrich, who worked with me at Lindsay House in the early days. He made a version for me with some Nordic spices, which I wasn't too enamoured of, so we substituted our own: cinnamon, star anise and cloves.

We dry the hips out slightly before we use them, just to concentrate the flavours even more – you put them into an airing cupboard, or into the oven when it is barely warm after a roast – and serve the soup with little almond biscuits (see page 348) and vanilla ice cream. I like ice cream made on the day, but of course if you like you can churn it in advance then transfer it to a clean container and freeze it.

There is something deeply baby-food and honest about all those flavours and textures together, which is fantastic.

Before you start to make the vanilla ice cream, have a bowl of ice ready.

Put the milk and cream in a pan, add the vanilla seeds and the pods and bring to a gentle simmer. Take off the heat and leave for 10 minutes to allow the vanilla to infuse.

Put the egg yolks and sugar in a bowl. Whisk until pale and thick. Pour the hot cream mixture over the egg mixture, whisking constantly. Put back into the pan and simmer until it coats the back of a spoon. Make sure it doesn't boil.

Pass the mixture through a sieve into a clean bowl set over the ice, and allow to cool. Churn in an ice-cream machine.

Pick over and wash the rosehips and allow to dry slightly. To make the soup, put the water, sugar, lemon zest and spices into a pan and bring to the boil. Add the rosehips, turn the heat down and simmer for 5 minutes.

Pour the contents of the pan into a blender, blitz and then put through a fine sieve. Cool and add lemon juice to taste.

To serve, pour the rosehip soup into bowls, spoon some vanilla ice cream into the centre and serve with almond biscuits (see below).

Almond Biscuits

These are lovely little biscuits – crunchy on the outside like little rock cakes and gooey in the middle.

Makes 20–25
500g ground almonds
300g caster sugar
seeds from 1 vanilla pod
4 egg whites
50ml Amaretto

Preheat the oven to 160°C/Gas 3.

Mix together the almonds, sugar and vanilla seeds.

Fold the egg whites (don't whisk them) into the mixture along with the Amaretto.

Have ready a baking sheet lined with greaseproof paper. Take small spoonfuls of the mixture and dot over the sheet. Bake for 10–15 minutes until golden.

Transfer to a cooling rack and leave to cool.

Bentley's
Fruit Jelly

When I first suggested we make some of these soft little jellies at Bentley's everyone said, 'Oh no, we don't want jellies.' Then when they tasted them, they all said, 'Oh yes we do!' They are so good, so tasty and so comforting, whether on their own or with ice cream or custard.

Serves 4

2 punnets raspberries
1 punnet strawberries
1 punnet blackberries
2 punnets blueberries
100g caster sugar
200ml water
3 gelatine leaves,
 softened in cold water
 and squeezed out

Put all the fruit, sugar and water into a saucepan. Bring to the boil and simmer for about 5 minutes, until the liquid has reduced a little. The more you reduce the stronger the flavour.

Add the gelatine leaves and stir until dissolved. Take off the heat and leave to cool.

Pour into 4 moulds or glasses (or one big bowl) and put into the fridge to set.

Lemon
Posset

This is lovely served with stem ginger shortbread (see page 350). When they are in season, you could also serve some fresh raspberries on the side. We often serve lemon posset in little pots with raspberries at the bottom.

Serves 4

600ml double cream
140g caster sugar
seeds from ¼ vanilla pod
zest and juice of
 2 lemons

Put the cream, sugar and vanilla seeds into a saucepan and bring to the boil, then add the lemon juice and zest and whisk in. Bring back to the boil for about 30 seconds, stirring constantly.

Take off the heat and pour into 4 glasses. Cool, then put into the fridge for 1–2 hours to chill and set.

Alfonso Mango with Rhubarb, Vanilla Ice Cream and Stem Ginger Shortbread

Alfonso mangoes move away from the British feel of a lot of our ingredients, but they are a real speciality. They come from the Maharashtra state of India and are small and yellow with pink tinges, a brilliant orange flesh and an intense mango flavour that beats the usual kind of mangoes we get, which can be a bit stringy and not wonderful for cooking. The Alfonso mangoes are briefly available at the same time as rhubarb, and the two combined are awesome. Really, I do think these two fruits served with vanilla ice cream add up to one of the most heavenly desserts we've ever come up with.

The mangoes are also delicious sliced and served with rice pudding, made with 250g of short-grain rice and 125g of sugar, put into a pan with 2 litres of milk and a couple of vanilla pods, split and their seeds scraped into the pan. I bring the mixture to the boil, then turn down the heat and simmer gently, stirring occasionally, for about an hour and a half to two hours, until thick and creamy. Sometimes I might also make some lime syrup. To make the syrup I put about 200ml of water into a pan with 100g of sugar and 25g of tapioca and bring to the boil, then turn down to a simmer for 5 minutes to thicken. I put the mixture through a fine sieve, let it cool and then stir in the zest and juice of a lime, together with a little grated ginger, some fine slivers of red chilli and fresh mint. (Tapioca is a great thickening agent because it stays clear and doesn't discolour.)

If you prefer to make plain shortbread for this dessert, just leave out the stem ginger.

To make the shortbread, preheat the oven to 160°C/Gas 3.

Put all the ingredients for the shortbread into a mixer and pulse until combined, or rub together by hand. Form into a ball and then, on a sheet of greaseproof paper, roll out to a rough rectangle about 1cm thick.

Place (still on the greaseproof paper) on a baking tray and bake for 30–40 minutes until evenly risen and lightly golden brown in colour.

Dust lightly with sugar. While still warm, cut into whatever shapes you like, then leave to cool.

Serves 4

vanilla ice cream (see page 347) made with a pinch of freshly grated nutmeg, plus a little extra nutmeg for dusting

300g rhubarb

150g caster sugar

300ml water

a sprig of rosemary

a splash of grenadine

3 Alfonso mangoes

Stem ginger shortbread:

250g plain flour

250g butter, cut into cubes

125g cornflour

125g caster sugar, plus extra for dusting

a knob of stem ginger, chopped

Meanwhile, make the vanilla ice cream according to the method on page 347, but stir in the grated nutmeg just before you churn the mixture.

Cut the rhubarb into batons. To cook the rhubarb, first make a syrup by heating the sugar and water in a pan, stirring to dissolve the sugar. Add the rosemary and cook for 8–10 minutes or until syrupy. Remove the rosemary.

Add the rhubarb and grenadine and cook over a low heat for 5–6 minutes or until the rhubarb is just tender. Remove from the heat and leave to cool.

Peel, stone and slice the mangoes. To serve, arrange the mango and rhubarb in bowls and serve with the shortbread biscuits and ice cream dusted with freshly grated nutmeg.

Lime and Mascarpone Soufflé

This is a stunning soufflé based on the idea of a mascarpone and lime cheesecake. You make a thick, syrupy, marmaladey jam by reducing the lime juice down with sugar (you need masses of limes for this), then pour it into the soufflé at the end, and the aroma and flavour is quite special.

I'm not actually a big fan of soufflés in general, I'll be honest with you, but when you get an interesting one, it can be gorgeous.

I look at a soufflé as a slightly underdone sponge, a little soft on the inside. I don't like a soufflé that is puffed-up nothingness, visually stunning but inside, nothing but air. Yes, of course it should be light, but I still want flavour and texture.

There are a few key points to keep an eye on when you make soufflés. When you whisk your egg whites, make sure your bowl and whisk are spotlessly clean. Any sign of grease will stop them from holding up properly. Then when you fold your whisked egg whites into the pastry cream base do it very gently, so you don't knock out all the air you have painstakingly put in.

And line your moulds carefully. When you brush them with butter, make sure your pastry brush is running upwards always, so if there are any ridges formed by the brush they won't stop the mixture from rising on its upward path – if you criss-cross, then it might snag as it rises. Then rub your finger around the rim to make sure it is absolutely smooth.

With soufflés it really is a case of practice makes perfect. There should be enough of the base mixture (which is really a pastry cream) for you to make 4 or 5 soufflés, with enough left to have a second go if your first batch don't work out – though you'll need another 8 egg whites to mix into it. If all goes well, you can spread the mixture you don't use over a pre-cooked pastry case and cover it with fresh fruit to make a tart. A nice bonus.

To make the syrup, put the lime juice and sugar into a saucepan, bring to the boil, then turn down to a simmer and reduce and thicken to a sticky syrup. Keep warm.

Separate 8 of the eggs into whites and yolks. In a bowl, whisk the 8 egg yolks with 200g of the sugar until thick, then fold in the flour (if you, like you can mix all these ingredients together in a food processor).

Makes 4–5
12 eggs
300g caster sugar
400g plain flour, sifted
1 litre milk
1 vanilla pod
125g mascarpone
zest of 15 limes

Syrup:
juice of 15 limes (see above)
50g caster sugar

To prepare the moulds:
25g butter
icing sugar, for dusting

Bring the milk to the boil with the vanilla pod in a heavy saucepan. Immediately take off the heat and remove the vanilla pod.

Pour the boiling milk on to the egg yolk mixture a little at a time, whisking continuously so that there are no lumps. Return the mixture to the pan and cook gently, stirring, for another 2 minutes, to cook out the taste of the flour, then pour back into the bowl.

Separate the remaining 4 eggs and beat the egg yolks into the mixture, along with the mascarpone and lime zest. The extra egg yolk will lighten the soufflés and help them to rise, as without the addition of any fruit or jam, which soufflés often have, the pastry cream is quite dense. You don't need the separated egg whites, but keep them, just in case you need to make a second batch of soufflés – see introduction to the recipe. Cover the mixture with clingfilm to prevent a skin forming and leave to cool.

To prepare the moulds, melt the butter and, with a brush, paint it over the inside of the soufflé moulds carefully and completely, using upward strokes only. Run your finger around the rim to make sure it is smooth. Dust with sugar, revolving the moulds so that the butter is entirely covered with the sugar, then tap out the excess.

Preheat the oven to 220°C/Gas 7.

Weigh out 400g of the cooled mascarpone mixture.

Whisk the 8 egg whites with the remaining sugar until stiff. Whisk a quarter of this into the mascarpone mixture, then fold in the rest very gently, taking care not to knock out any of the trapped air.

Divide the mixture between your prepared moulds and put into the oven straight away.

Bake for 8 minutes (don't be tempted to open the oven before at least 6 minutes), until risen and golden brown. Take out of the oven and sprinkle with icing sugar. Serve immediately, with the warm syrup in a jug – the idea is to break open your soufflé and pour in a little of the syrup (if you like, you can actually turn the soufflés out and serve them upside down – provided they have risen properly, they won't collapse!).

Pancake
Soufflé

These are another way of using the soufflé mixture above, and are just as good with the same hot lime syrup over them.

Make some pancakes following the recipe on page 380, and preheat the oven to 200°C/Gas 6.

Lay a pancake on a baking tray and spoon some soufflé mix on to one half of it, leaving a border of about 2.5cm around the outside. Fold the other side of the pancake over the top so that it resembles an omelette. Repeat with the remaining pancakes and soufflé mix.

Put into the oven for about 5–6 minutes, during which time the soufflé mix will puff up. Dust with icing sugar, and serve the pancakes immediately with the hot lime syrup.

Steamed Marmalade Pudding

Every January we buy in sackfuls of Seville oranges and make our own marmalade – we've been doing it for about ten years. We use it for these little steamed marmalade puddings that we serve with custard, sometimes flavoured with orange. We also use a layer of the marmalade instead of jam when we make Bakewell tarts.

Serves 4
120g butter, plus extra for greasing
80g Demerara sugar
3 eggs
100g plain flour
1 teaspoon bicarbonate of soda
100g marmalade
icing sugar, for dusting
custard (see page 334), to serve

Preheat the oven to 180°C/Gas 4.

Cream the butter and Demerara sugar together until pale and creamy. When creamy add the eggs one at a time.

Fold in the flour and bicarbonate of soda, and finally the marmalade.

Grease 4 individual moulds (about 150ml) with butter, then tip in a little icing sugar and shake each mould around until the sugar has entirely covered the butter.

Spoon the mixture into the moulds and cover each one with clingfilm. Put into a deep roasting tray and pour in enough hot water to come one-third of the way up the outside of the moulds, to create a bain-marie. Cover the whole thing loosely with foil (this will just protect the puddings from the heat and help them to cook gently) and put in the oven for 15–30 minutes until the puddings are springy to the touch. Serve hot, with custard.

Japanese Knotweed Crumble with Horseradish Ice Cream

The Victorians are responsible for giving us this concrete-choking weed, which originally came from Japan, Taiwan and China, and is a kind of relative of rhubarb. They introduced it to walled gardens as an ornamental plant, but the roots escaped and grew rampant. It's so strong it grows through floors of houses and tarmac roads and is a big headache for farmers around the country. The government spends millions of pounds trying to destroy it and researching how to control it, but it comes back each year. We like it, though. The shoots are what we want. They have a terrific tart flavour, cooked with sugar, and we add horseradish to give it a kick: a bit like adding ginger to rhubarb.

There is very little flour in the crumble mix – just enough to keep it together – because we like to add lots of ground almonds instead. The Demerara sugar is what gives it that lovely crunch.

Serves 4
1kg knotweed shoots
50g caster sugar
zest of 2 lemons

Crumble:
125g butter
50g plain flour
250g Demerara sugar
100g ground almonds
75g oatmeal

Horseradish Ice cream:
150ml milk
300ml double cream
50g freshly grated
  horseradish
100g caster sugar
3 egg yolks

First make the ice cream. Have ready a shallow bowl of ice big enough to take the base of the saucepan. Bring the milk, cream and horseradish to the boil in a saucepan. Whisk the sugar and egg yolks in a bowl until thick. Slowly pour in the hot milk and cream mixture, whisking continuously, then return to the pan and cook gently until the mixture thickens slightly, but don't boil. Take the pan off the heat and immediately plunge the base into the bowl of ice to stop the custard cooking any more.

Put through a fine sieve. Churn in an ice-cream machine.

Meanwhile, preheat the oven to 180°C/Gas 4. Peel the knotweed shoots. Remove the leaves and discard. Cut the shoots into short batons. Put into a saucepan with the sugar and lemon zest and a tablespoon of water and cook gently until the sugar has dissolved and the knotweed begins to soften.

Make the crumble while the knotweed cooks. Rub the butter into the flour and then mix in all the other ingredients.

Transfer the knotweed and its syrup to an ovenproof dish, sprinkle generously with the crumble mixture and bake for 15 minutes. Serve hot with the ice cream.

Chocolate Pots with Hazelnuts and Mascarpone

In the woods around our farm in Ireland, there were hazelnuts galore. We had to cross a few fields to get to them, but we'd come back with baskets and bags full of them, and we'd be cracking and eating them all the time. Hazelnuts and chocolate is a great combination, which is enhanced by a dash of Frangelico, the Italian hazelnut and herb liqueur.

Serves 4

300g good dark chocolate (75 per cent cocoa solids), chopped
350ml milk
350ml double cream
6 egg yolks
100g caster sugar
50ml Frangelico
toasted hazelnuts, finely chopped, to serve

Mascarpone sabayon:
100ml double cream
7 egg yolks
105g caster sugar
250ml rum
125g mascarpone
2 egg whites

Preheat the oven to 150°C/Gas 2.

Put the chocolate in a heatproof bowl. Bring the milk and cream to the boil in a saucepan. Remove from the heat and pour over the chocolate to melt it. Stir until smooth.

Put the egg yolks and sugar in a bowl and whisk until thick. Fold in the chocolate mixture and then stir in the Frangelico. Pour the mixture into 4 ramekins or ovenproof pots (150ml) and put into a deep baking tin. To create a bain-marie, pour hot water into the tin until it comes one-third of the way up the outside of the pots.

Put into the oven for 15–20 minutes until slightly set – there should still be a little wobble. Take out of the oven, cool, then chill in the fridge for about 30–40 minutes.

While the chocolate pots are cooling and chilling, make the sabayon. Whip the cream until stiff and keep to one side.

Have a bowl of ice ready, big enough to take the base of the bowl you are going to make the sabayon in. Put the egg yolks, 80g of sugar and the rum in a heatproof bowl over a pan of simmering water and whisk until the mixture becomes very thick and reaches ribbon stage: that is, if you drop a little of the mixture from the whisk into the bowl it will make a ribbon-like trail and briefly hold its shape. Take off the heat and immediately plunge the base of the bowl into the ice to stop the mixture cooking further.

Fold the mascarpone into the whipped cream. Whisk the egg whites until they form soft peaks and slowly add the rest of the sugar, carrying on whisking until the mixture resembles meringue. Fold the mascarpone and cream into the cooled egg yolk mixture, then fold in the egg whites. Chill in the fridge.

To serve, spoon some of the mixture on to the top of each chocolate pot and sprinkle with chopped toasted hazelnuts.

Chocolate
Iceberg

In Ireland, we have an ice cream called Iceberger, which is a little block of ice cream, sandwiched in between two chocolate biscuits – so that's what this dessert is named after. The similarity ends there, really, because we make a poppy seed, pine nut and honey parfait, which we sandwich between two slices of chocolate shortbread. You need to set the parfait in the freezer first overnight, but once you have assembled it, you can put it back in the freezer and then slice it when you are ready, so it's perfect if you have people round to dinner.

Serves 4
10g pine nuts
25g honey
50g poppy seeds
3 egg yolks
30g caster sugar
30ml rum
seeds from ½ vanilla pod
200ml double cream

Chocolate shortbread:
230g plain flour
50g cocoa
100g cornflour
80g caster sugar
250g butter, cut into
  cubes

First make the parfait. Lightly toast the pine nuts in a dry pan until just coloured, then chop. Heat the honey in a pan and stir in the poppy seeds and pine nuts. Set aside to cool.

Have ready a shallow bowl of ice.

Put the egg yolks, sugar, rum and vanilla seeds into another, heatproof bowl over a pan of simmering water and whisk until it thickens and reaches ribbon stage: that is, if you drop a little of the mixture from the whisk into the bowl it will make a ribbon-like trail and briefly hold its shape.

Take off the heat and immediately set the bowl into the ice to stop it cooking any more. When egg yolk mixture is cold, whip the cream quite softly and fold it in, then fold in the honey, seed and nut mixture.

Line an oblong terrine with clingfilm so that it overhangs the sides. Spoon in the mixture and put in the freezer to set overnight.

Meanwhile, make the chocolate shortbread. Preheat the oven to 160°C/Gas 3.

Put all the ingredients for the shortbread into a blender and pulse until just combined. Turn out on to a sheet of greaseproof paper and roll out into a rough square, 1cm thick, and twice the size of your terrine (you are going to cut the shortbread in half once it's baked).

Lift the greaseproof paper on to a baking sheet and put in the oven for about 25 minutes. Take out of the oven and, while still hot, cut out your two oblongs, each the size of the terrine mould. Leave to get cold.

Once the parfait is firm, turn it out of the mould on to one of the oblongs of shortbread. Carefully put the other one on top, so that you have a parfait 'sandwich'. Put back into the freezer until ready to serve and then, with a sharp knife, cut into slices.

Lavender and White Chocolate Ice Cream with Summer Strawberries

When you have fresh strawberries at the height of the summer, full of juice and natural sugars, you don't really want to do anything to them except serve them with some great ice cream.

Serves 4

300ml milk

600ml double cream

1 teaspoon fresh or dried lavender flowers

4 egg yolks

150g caster sugar

50g white chocolate, chopped

a punnet or two of strawberries, to serve

Before you start to make the ice cream, have a bowl of ice ready.

Put the milk and cream in the pan, add the lavender and bring to a gentle simmer. Take off heat and leave for 10 minutes to allow the lavender to infuse.

Put the egg yolks and sugar into a bowl. Whisk until pale and thick. Pour the hot cream mixture over the egg mixture, whisking constantly. Put back into the pan and simmer until it coats the back of a spoon. Make sure it doesn't boil.

Pass the mixture through a sieve into a clean bowl set over the ice. Stir in the chopped chocolate so that it melts, and allow to cool.

Churn in an ice-cream machine.

If you have been storing your strawberries in the fridge, bring them out and let them come to room temperature, so that their flavour isn't dulled by the cold, and serve them with the ice cream.

Christmas

Christmas was a huge feast in our house when I was growing up. The feast of all feasts (so I've made all recipes for 8 people). Christmas can be a very sad or a very happy time, and most of ours were about huge happiness. Carol-singing on the radio, a kind of opulence and a sense of plenty and the best cuts of everything. In the run up to Christmas all the houses around were filled with that cinnamon-spicy, Guinnessy aroma of fruit being soaked in alcohol to make the cakes and puddings. Our neighbours, the McKeons, would give us a leg of ham and a turkey as a present, and we'd give them the Christmas pudding.

Sitting down as a little boy in the kitchen, grating the old white loaves to help make the stuffing, that's how I became a cook, really. The smells of melting butter and onion and so much parsley you'd think the whole stuffing would turn green, the bread absorbing the flavours so you could just pick pieces up and put them in your mouth … I still hanker after those tastes and smells of childhood Christmas preparation now, and whenever I make a spice cake, or a Christmas lunch, they come back to me.

Christmas to me is about ham and fowl. You have to have a ham, I'm sorry. We'd have a big rib of beef, too, and we always had turkey rather than goose when I was a kid. My dad did shoot a goose once, but it was tough as a whore's heart: shocking, not like the beautiful farm geese you can buy now. There were nine of us, so there wasn't much of the turkey left after dinner and none of that feeling of the bird lasting the week, and what should we do with it next. Afterwards there would be the pudding and cream, then in the evening, sandwiches and cake. Dad might have a bottle of stout, and we kids often nicked a bottle and drank it between us, then my dad's brothers might come round later and have a glass, or a whiskey.

Next day, Boxing Day, which we call St Stephen's Day in Ireland, if we were lucky, there would be my favourite breakfast: a piece of wild salmon fried up in the pan, with brown bread.

Traditional as Christmas is, I often think it's a time of year when you want to reach for a cookbook, just to get a few ideas for some variations on a favourite theme. I would steam a ham in a bottle of wine, over a trivet of vegetables, following the recipe on page 173 but substituting a whole ham for the hocks (for 4 hours), to have alongside either the goose on page 370 or a turkey. Pork and sage stuffing, cranberry sauce with grated fresh horseradish in it, great roast potatoes, Brussels sprouts, creamed or sautéed with chestnuts and bacon – and pancakes to make with leftover Christmas pudding the next day: great stuff. I've also included a recipe for an old-fashioned tipsy trifle to have over the holiday.

Scallops with Clementine, Ham, Almond and Oloroso Salad

If you want to serve a starter, this is a really refreshing, slightly Spanish-style salad which has a great Christmas feel to it, because it uses clementines, nuts, the outer leaves of the Brussels sprouts, and oloroso sherry in the dressing, and it looks very festive: the white of the scallops against the orange, pink and green of the other ingredients. You can use either Parma ham, or some slices of your Christmas ham.

Serves 8

8 clementines
200g outer leaves of
  Brussels sprouts (kept
  back from preparing
  them for dinner)
16 slices of Parma ham
  or Christmas ham
a little olive oil
16 scallops
200g salted almonds

Dressing:
juice from 2 clementines
2 tablespoons caster
  sugar
2 tablespoons sherry
  vinegar
4 tablespoons oloroso or
  other dry sherry
12 tablespoons extra
  virgin olive oil
a good pinch of sea salt

Mix all the dressing ingredients.

Peel the clementines, removing as much of the white pith as possible, and break into segments.

Have a bowl of iced water ready. Blanch the Brussels sprout leaves in boiling salted water for 30 seconds, then refresh in the iced water to stop them cooking further and to keep their bright green colour. Drain and pat dry.

Tear the ham into bite-sized pieces.

Heat a large frying pan with a film of olive oil. Season the scallops, and when the oil is really hot, sear for about 2 minutes without disturbing, until golden brown and caramelised on the underside. Then turn them over and cook for another 2 minutes to colour and caramelise the other side.

Serve the scallops on warmed plates. Scatter the clementine segments, sprout leaves, ham and almonds around. Drizzle with a generous amount of the dressing and serve immediately.

Marmalade Goose
with Gravy

Serve this with stuffing balls – use the stuffing recipe on page 372. Roll into balls, wrap each one in a piece of pancetta and put into the oven (in a roasting tray with a little hot goose fat) 30 minutes before the end of the cooking time for the goose.

Serves 8

1 x 5kg goose, giblets and neck reserved for the gravy

50g marmalade

Gravy:

goose giblets and neck (reserved from above), washed

goose wings (reserved from above), washed

1 large onion, halved

2 sticks celery, halved

1 large carrot, halved

a sprig of thyme

1 bay leaf

4 peppercorns

1.2 litres water

3 tablespoons Calvados

1 tablespoon marmalade

Preheat the oven to 200°C/Gas 6.

With a pair of scissors, remove the goose wings and keep them for the gravy. Tie the legs together with a piece of string. Lightly pierce the goose all over with a fork (this will allow the fat to run out when cooking), then pour boiling water all over the skin, which will help to crisp it up. Sit the goose on a trivet set in a roasting tin. Season generously and cover with foil.

Roast the goose for 30 minutes, then turn the oven down to 180°C/Gas 4 for a further 2½–3 hours, basting it with its own fat every so often. Ladle out any excess fat and keep for roasting stuffing balls and potatoes.

While the goose is cooking, make the stock for the gravy. Put the giblets, neck and wings in a large pan with the onion, celery, carrot, thyme, bay leaf, peppercorns and water. Bring to the boil and skim away any scum that rises to the surface. Loosely cover with a lid, reduce the heat and leave to simmer for 1½ hours.

Put the 50g marmalade into a pan and warm until it melts to a syrup. Remove the foil from the goose for the last half hour of cooking and brush with the melted marmalade. When the goose is ready, take it out of the oven and leave it to rest in a warm place for 20 minutes before carving (this will allow the meat to relax).

While the goose is resting, pour away any excess fat from its roasting tin. Put the tin on the hob over a high heat and pour the stock through a fine sieve into the pan. Add the Calvados, the 1 tablespoon of marmalade and seasoning and bring to the boil, scraping any caramelised pieces of meat from the bottom of the tin. Turn the heat down and simmer for 3–4 minutes, then strain again through a fine sieve into a serving jug.

Butter Poached and Roasted Bronze Turkey

The beauty of this is that the meat only has to be cooked for around half an hour! Sometimes I add a tablespoon of mustard fruits to the stuffing mix.

Serves 8

Crown (both breasts on the bone) and legs from a 4kg bronze turkey (ask your butcher to prepare it for you and, if possible, bone out the legs; or do this yourself, see method)

a little butter, for greasing

Turkey leg stuffing:

4–6 slices of bread

100ml double cream

1 clove garlic

2 sprigs of thyme

25g butter

2 small onions, chopped

300g good sausage meat

2 eggs

1 teaspoon ground mace

1 teaspoon chopped sage

Turkey breast poaching liquor:

2 litres chicken stock

750g butter

a small bunch of tarragon, leaves picked

Preheat the oven to 200°C/Gas 6.

To make the stuffing, put the bread, cream, garlic and thyme into a pan and warm over a very gentle heat until the bread has absorbed the cream. Allow to cool.

In a frying pan, melt the butter and sweat the onions until soft. Turn into a bowl and add the sausage meat together with the reserved bread mixture, the eggs, mace and sage. Season well.

If you are boning out the turkey legs yourself, take a small sharp knife (preferably a slightly bendy boning one) and make an incision from the top of the thigh to the middle joint (the knuckle), cutting all the way through to the bone, then turn the knife at a right angle and cut crossways. Make a similar cut crossways on the other side of the bone. Now you should be able to work the meat away from the bone, then slide your knife underneath and work it around the knuckle. Remove the bone and open out each leg. Lay between two sheets of clingfilm. Bat with a meat mallet or rolling pin to tenderize the meat a little, then season. Lay each batted-out turkey leg on a double layer of buttered foil. Divide the stuffing mixture between them and roll them up tightly, like a sausage, in the foil. Seal tightly at each end.

Now prepare the poaching liquor for the turkey breasts. In a large pan, heat the chicken stock, butter and tarragon and season. Bring to a simmer, then either blitz with a hand blender or pour into a blender, blitz and pour back into the pan. Bring back to a simmer, then put in the turkey breasts and poach for around 30 minutes, until the juices run clear. Remove and leave to rest in a warm place.

While the turkey breasts are poaching, roast the boned and stuffed legs in the oven for 45 minutes. Remove and allow to rest in a warm place, then slice. Carve the turkey breast and serve.

Creamed
Sprouts

Serves 8

1kg Brussels sprouts

8 rashers unsmoked
bacon, cut into lardons

250ml double cream

2 cloves garlic, crushed

Peel the sprouts (you can keep the outer leaves to make the scallop salad on page 368).

Cook in boiling salted water for 8–10 minutes, then drain.

Heat a non-stick pan, put in the bacon lardons and fry until crisp.

Put the cream and garlic into a small saucepan and bring to the boil. Add the sprouts to the bacon in the frying pan, stir in the cream and season to taste.

Brussels Sprouts
with Chestnuts
and Bacon

There's something very Christmassy about roasting or steaming your own chestnuts, but on Christmas Day I'd let someone else do the work – you can buy great-tasting whole chestnuts that have been vacuum-packed immediately after roasting and peeling.

Serves 8

a little sunflower oil

75g good unsmoked
streaky bacon, cut into
lardons

600g small Brussels
sprouts, trimmed

400g vacuum-packed
cooked chestnuts

Heat a little sunflower oil in a pan and sauté the bacon lardons until crisp.

Meanwhile, blanch the sprouts in a pan of boiling salted water for 2 minutes, or until just tender. Tip into a colander and run cold water over them, to stop them cooking further, and drain well.

Heat a film of oil in a frying pan, add the chestnuts and cook gently to heat and colour on all sides. Add the sprouts and bacon. Heat through, stirring all the time, season to taste, and serve.

Cranberry Sauce with Grated Fresh Horseradish

Serves 8

250g fresh cranberries
100g sugar
100ml port
juice and zest of 1 orange
25g fresh horseradish, grated

Wash the cranberries and put into a large saucepan with the rest of the ingredients.

Bring to the boil, then turn down the heat to a simmer and cook until the cranberries pop and turn mushy.

Take off the heat and leave to cool. As the sauce gets cold it will turn more jammy.

Rosemary Roast Potatoes

Choose a roasting potato that veers towards the fluffy, rather than the waxy. It's best to buy big ones and halve them, as if you cut them any smaller they will crisp up without absorbing the flavours of the goose fat.

Serves 8

12 large roasting potatoes
about 100g goose fat
100g butter, at room temperature
2 tablespoons rosemary or thyme leaves

Preheat the oven to 220°C/Gas 7.

Cut the potatoes in half, bring to the boil in plenty of salted water, then turn down the heat and simmer for about 10 minutes, until the insides are still firm if you test with a knife.

Drain the potatoes well in a colander, shaking gently, to roughen the outsides a little. This will give you those nice crunchy edges, but don't scuff them too much or you'll end up with potato purée.

Put enough goose fat into a roasting tin to form a thin layer and heat it on top of the stove. When it is good and hot, add the potatoes and cook, tossing well until they turn a light golden brown. Transfer the tin to the oven and cook the potatoes for about 15 minutes, turning as necessary, then add the butter and the rosemary or thyme and cook for another 15 minutes or so, turning a couple more times until the potatoes are golden and crunchy and caramelised on the outside, and soft, light and fluffy inside.

Tipsy Trifle

Serves 8
1 home-made or bought
    sponge for the base '
about 200ml sherry
50ml whiskey
6 fresh figs
a small jar of maraschino
    cherries
chopped toasted almonds
chopped pistachios

Jelly:
500ml wine
500ml port
350g caster sugar
3–4 pears, peeled, but
    left whole
7 thin sheets of gelatine,
    soaked in water and
    squeezed out

Custard:
1 vanilla pod
125ml milk
250ml double cream
3 egg yolks
50g caster sugar

Creamy topping:
100g mascarpone
400ml double cream
1 tablespoon icing sugar

To make the jelly, pour the wine, port and sugar into a pan and bring to a rolling boil for a couple of minutes. Add the pears, boil gently for a few more minutes, then take off the heat. Leave the pears to cool down a little in the liquid and take on the colour of the wine and port.

Remove the pears, keep to one side, then add the gelatine to the warm port and wine, and stir well to dissolve. Leave to cool.

Cut the sponge into evenly sized pieces and lay them in the bottom of your bowl. Pour over enough sherry and whiskey to ensure that each piece of sponge is soaked.

Slice the poached pears and the figs into even-sized pieces and arrange them on top of the sherry-soaked sponge. Pour the jelly mixture over so it covers the fruit. Put it into the fridge and leave to set.

To make the custard, split the vanilla pod in half and scrape out the seeds into a saucepan. Put the vanilla pod in, too. Pour the milk and cream into the pan and bring to just under the boil. Remove the pod.

Have ready a bowl of ice.

Beat the egg yolks and sugar together in a large bowl. Pour the hot milk and cream mixture slowly over the egg mixture, stirring continually. Pour the mixture back into the saucepan and cook over a low heat, stirring continually, so the eggs don't scramble, until it thickens.

Take off the heat and immediately plunge the base of the pan into the bowl of ice to stop it cooking any further. Leave to cool, then spoon the custard over the set jelly.

To make the topping, whisk the mascarpone and cream in a bowl until it has nearly doubled and has a light but firm consistency. Sieve in the icing sugar and give a gentle whisk.

Spoon the creamy mixture over the custard and top with maraschino cherries, chopped toasted almonds and pistachios.

Crozier Blue Soaked in Banyuls

This is a Christmas and special occasion recipe that is based on the old idea of port and Stilton. Soaking cheese in wine is also traditional in some parts of Europe, and the cheese really takes to the Banyuls, a deep purple, fortified dessert wine from Roussillon in southern France, so near the Spanish border that many people there speak Catalan. The particular one we use is from Les Clos de Paulilles.

Crozier Blue is a creamy sheep's milk cheese made by Jane and Louis Grubb of Cashel Blue using milk from their nephew Henry Clifton Browne's herd of 350 sheep. It is still creamy like Cashel Blue (which is made from cow's milk) but more seasonal, and can often be a little firmer and tangier.

Serves 4
1 whole Crozier Blue cheese
½ bottle (350ml) Banyuls

Pierce the cheese several times with a skewer. Put it into a container that allows a space of about 1.5cm around the edge of the cheese and pour the Banyuls over the top. The space should be big enough to allow you to get your fingers in and lift out the cheese, but narrow enough to concentrate the wine around the cheese.

Leave to soak for 3–4 days, turning the cheese over after 2 days.

Lift out and eat with oat cookies (see page 304).

Christmas Pudding Pancakes

This is a great way to use up leftover Christmas pudding. Serve the pancakes with ice cream or leftover brandy custard, butter or cream.

Serves 8

350g plain flour

a pinch of salt

1 teaspoon mixed spice

225ml milk

3 eggs, beaten

100g caster sugar

40g butter, melted, plus a little extra butter for cooking the pancakes

leftover Christmas pudding

icing sugar, for dusting

Preheat the oven to 180°/Gas 4.

Sieve the flour and salt into a bowl and add the mixed spice. Add the milk, eggs, sugar and melted butter and whisk well to make a smooth batter.

Cook the pancakes one at a time. Heat a non-stick pan with a little butter. Add a ladleful of the batter and tilt the pan to coat the base. Crumble some Christmas pudding on to one half, and fold the rest of the pancake, which should be golden underneath by now, over the top. Lift on to a baking tray and repeat until you have used all the batter. Put the tray in the oven for 3–4 minutes, or until heated through.

Put the pancakes on a big platter, dust with icing sugar and serve with a big bowl of brandy cream.

Continued...

There is a plot of land, twenty-five acres, with a cottage, somewhere outside Dublin, that has my name on it. It won't be the best land, a bit boggy and peaty, but it will be just right for growing vegetables and salads and raising a few chickens and pigs.

Life comes full circle, sometimes, doesn't it? It's extraordinary to think that my parents, like so many other smallholders, left the land for the towns in the seventies, for what they thought was a better life. And now, like so many other people who have felt the pace of city life, I have a hankering to go back.

You might be a success, but how do you measure success? You can break your neck at this restaurant game and, don't get me wrong, I love it, but you can end up a crazy individual ready for an early grave.

When I come back to London after a week in Ireland, having eaten gorgeous, simple local food at Ballymaloe House, or having had the stress massaged out of me on the lawn at Seed Savers, or listened to the gentle wisdom of Bill Hogan, talking politics and cheese, sometimes I think, am I just running to stand still?

I get a deep satisfaction from being out in the open fields, or feeling that I can walk through the vegetable garden and pick my food for dinner. So I think, why not have the best of both worlds? Finish what my parents began, and have a little farm, supplying my restaurants? I think I'd be a very efficient farmer, and I like to think I'd be able to work with other local farmers and producers, and put something back into the community.

A big larder and maybe a little smokehouse, a bit of an orchard with native varieties of fruit, drills of heritage potatoes. Bring the ducks and chickens in at night for fear of the foxes, and when the crab apples fall, pick them up as a treat for the pigs. It would feel like coming home.

Acknowledgements

To Sheila Keating, without whom the words wouldn't be on paper; Tom Doorley for his initial inspiration; Louise Haines of Fourth Estate for having the vision and flair to make everything happen; Mark Wogan who convinced me to do the book; and of course Cyril, Chris, Brendan and Eoin who help me every day.

To Kristin Perers and Joby Barnard who made everything look so beautiful, including me (ha-ha!) and the long suffering Gary Simpson and Sarah Clay who put up with all the last minute changes.

To Elizabeth Woabank of Fourth Estate for keeping a sane eye on everything, Sue Lewis for logging all our recipes, and Valerie and Anna for making sure I was there… sometimes.

Producers
and Suppliers

Butter:

Berkeley Farm Butter
from Abel & Cole
+44 (0)845 2626262
www.abelandcole.co.uk

Glenilen Farm
Drimoleague
Co. Cork
Ireland
+353 (0)28 31179
glenilen@eircom.net
www.glenilen.com

Lincolnshire Poacher
FW Read & Sons Ltd
Ulceby Grange
Alford
Lincolnshire LN13 0HE
+44 (0)1507 466987
www.lincolnshirepoachercheese.com

Neal's Yard Dairy, shops at:
17 Shorts Gardens
Covent Garden
London WC2H 9UP
+44 (0)20 7240 5700

6 Park Street
Borough Market
London SE1 9AB
+44 (0)20 7367 0799
www.nealsyarddairy.co.uk
Butter includes Berkeley Farm Dairy

Cheese:

Bellingham Blue Cheese
Glyde Farm Produce
Mansfield
Castlebellingham
Co. Louth
Ireland
+353 (0)42 9372343
glydefarm@eircom.net

Bill Hogan and Sean Ferry's West Cork
    Natural Cheese Company
Dereenatra
Schull
Co. Cork
Ireland
+353 (0)28 28593
bh@wcnc.ie
www.wcnc.ie

Crozier Blue Cheese
Cashel Blue Irish Farmhouse Cheese
Beechmount
Fethard
Co. Tipperary
Ireland
+353 (0)52 31151
info@cashelblue.com
www.cashelblue.com

Neal's Yard Dairy
(see details opposite)
Good selection of British and Irish cheeses

Fish and Shellfish:

Matthew Stevens & Son Ltd
Back Road East
St Ives
Cornwall TR26 3AR
+44 (0)1736 799392
shop@mstevensandson.co.uk
www.mstevensandson.co.uk/shop

Forced Rhubarb:

E. Oldroyd & Sons Ltd
Hopefield Farm
The Shutts
Leadwell Lane
Rothwell
Leeds
West Yorkshire LS26 0ST
+44 (0)113 282 2245
www.yorkshirerhubarb.co.uk

Fruit, Vegetables and Herbs:

Secretts
Hurst Farm
Chapel Lane
Milford
Godalming
Surrey GU8 5HU
+44 (0)1483 520500
www.secretts.co.uk

Game:

Yorkshire Game Ltd
Station Road, Industrial Park
Brompton on Swale
Richmond
North Yorkshire DL10 7SN
+44 (0)1748 810212
www.yorkshiregame.co.uk
www.blackface.co.uk (online orders)

Lamb:

Elwy Valley Welsh Lamb & Mutton
Daphne & David Tilley
Rose Hill Cottage
Henllan
Denbigh
+44 (0)1745 813552
tilley@elwyvalleywelshlamb.co.uk
www.elwyvalleylamb.co.uk

Meat, especially beef:

Jack O'Shea
11 Montpelier St.
London SW7 1EX
+44 (0)20 7581 7771

30 Rue le Titien
1000 Brussels
+32 (0)2732 5351
www.jackoshea.com

Oils, Hams, Chorizo, Anchovies, Olives, etc.

Brindisa, shops at:
The Floral Hall
Stoney Street
Borough Market
London SE1 9AA
+44 (0)20 7407 1036

32 Exmouth Market
Clerkenwell
London EC1R 4QE
+44 (0)20 7713 1666

7–9 Exhibition Road
Kensington
London SW7 2HQ
retail@brindisa.com
www.brindisa.com

Oysters:

Colchester Oyster Fishery
Pyefleet Quay
Mersea Island
Colchester
Essex CO5 8UN
+44 (0)1206 384141
info@colchesteroysterfishery.com
www.colchesteroysterfishery.com

Pork:

Caherbeg Free Range Pork Ltd
Caherbeg
Rosscarbery
West Cork
Ireland
+353 (0)23 48474
caher@caherbegfreerangepork.ie
www.caherbegfreerangepork.ie

Crowe's Farm
Gurtussa
Dundrum
Co. Tipperary
Ireland
+353 (0)87 8247394
info@crowefarm.ie
www.crowefarm.ie

Frank Krawczyk's West Cork Salamis
Dereenatra
Schull
Co. Cork
Ireland
+353 (0)28 28579
westcorksalamis@gmail.com

O'Doherty's Fine Meats (Black Bacon)
Belmore Street
Enniskillen
Co. Fermanagh
Ireland
+353 (0) 28 66 322152
sales@blackbacon.com
www.blackbacon.com

Poultry:

Goosnargh Duckling and Cornfed Chicken
Johnson & Swarbrick
Swainson House Farm
Goosnargh
Preston
Lancashire PR3 2JU
+44 (0)1772 865251
johnsonandswarbrick@tiscali.co.uk
myweb.tiscali.co.uk/jandsgoosnargh/
   contact.htm

Smoked Fish:

Frank Hederman
Belvelly Smoke House
Cobh
Co. Cork
Ireland
+353 (0)21 481 1089
www.frankhederman.com

Sally Barnes
Woodcock Smokery
Gortbrack
Castletownsend
Skibbereen
West Cork
Ireland
+353 (0)28 36232
sally@woodcocksmokery.com
www.woodcocksmokery.com

Index